ENDORSEMENTS

As Saint Paul says, we must expose the works of darkness. With Kermit Gosnell as one example of a tragic pattern, my colleague Cheryl Sullenger has once again done what she does best, and has exposed abortion!

-Fr. Frank Pavone, National Director, Priests for Life

Kermit Gosnell is not the only abortionist to break the law, as Sullenger's book explains. It illustrates the need for prosecutors and courts to set aside politics and enforce abortion laws in the interest of justice.

-Phill Kline, Former Kansas Attorney General, District Attorney and State Legislator

In *The Trial of Kermit Gosnell*, Cheryl Sullenger debunks the Planned Parenthood myth of "safe, legal and rare abortions." While the Gosnell saga is the proverbial "tip of the iceberg," readers will understand the need to expose legal abortion's underbelly and to join the movement to end the scourge.

-Evangelist Alveda King, civilrightsfortheunborn.com

There is no person who better understands the horrors occurring behind the closed doors of abortion facilities than Cheryl Sullenger, who has spent years documenting and exposing abortion abuses. In *The Trial of Kermit Gosnell*, Sullenger reveals the full story of the courtroom drama that shocked and outraged America. This page-turning narrative of murder, abortion, political cover-ups, and regulatory failure shatters the facade of "choice," and demonstrates that Gosnell isn't the only abortionist committing barbaric crimes in America. Once you read this book, you will never view abortion the same way again.

David Bereit, Former CEO of 40 Days for Life

Shocking! Revealing! *The Trial of Kermit Gosnell* is the roadmap to ending abortion and sending abortionists to jail.

-Mark Harrington, National Director, Created Equal

If it's just about the truth, if you believe facts don't cease to exist because they're ignored, then *The Trail Of Kermit Gosnell* by Cheryl Sullenger is a book on your mind and in your library.

-Walter B. Hoye II, Issues4Life Foundation

Cheryl Sullenger gives an impressive, factual account of the trial of late term abortionist Kermit Gosnell who for thirty years murdered black children in a black neighborhood, perpetuating the epidemic of black-on-black crime. *The Trial of Kermit Gosnell* is a must read because Gosnell was not an anomaly. There are more Gosnells out there, we must strive to end the killing.

-Dr. Day Gardner, President, National Black Pro-Life Union

The Trial of Kermit Gosnell is a captivating account of abortion crimes that reveals the corruption that enables them. It is a must-read for everyone!

-Fr. Terry Gensemer, Director, CEC For Life (Charismatic Episcopal Church)

Without the hard work of Cheryl Sullenger, the public might never have heard of Kermit Gosnell. Cheryl hounded the district attorney, pored over documents late at night, and traveled to Philadelphia to attend the trial when there was only a couple of local news reporters in the courtroom. As you read her book, you will feel like you are sitting in the courtroom with her, experiencing all the emotions of one of the most important abortion-related trials in history.

-Troy Newman, President, Operation Rescue

THE TRIAL OF
KERMIT GOSNELL

THE TRIAL OF KERMIT GOSNELL

The Shocking Details And What It Revealed About
The Abortion Industry In America

By
CHERYL SULLENGER

THE TRIAL OF KERMIT GOSNELL

World Ahead Press is a division of WND Books. The views and opinions expressed in this book are those of the author and do not necessarily reflect the official policy or position or WND Books.

Paperback ISBN: 978-1-944212-84-1
eBook ISBN: 978-1-944212-85-8

Printed in the United States of America
16 17 18 19 20 21 LSI 9 8 7 6 5 4 3 2 1

DEDICATION

To my daughters, Brenna and Rayna, who have given me nine
beautiful grandchildren that brilliantly demonstrate each day just
how precious life really is.

CONTENTS

FOREWORD
BY JILL STANEK

The Midwest, normally considered one of the saner regions of America, inexplicably became a hotbed for serial killers the latter half of the twentieth century.

The horrific details of the tortures and murders by Richard Speck in 1966, John Wayne Gacy in 1978, and Jeffrey Dahmer in 1991 certainly made national and international news. But Chicago media covered the atrocities nonstop, since the first two were committed in the Windy City and the latter in nearby Milwaukee. I know this because I'm a Midwesterner.

Three takeaways from my traumatized mind being steeped in those experiences:

1. Law enforcement investigated every clue and lead;
2. journalists relished relaying all the gory details; and
3. the public was grossly fascinated in all those details.

There have been many frightening serial killers throughout history. And the response is always the same: intense manhunts, sensational reporting, and macabre public hunger for the story.

Until Kermit Gosnell.

In Gosnell's case, public officials ignored decades of warnings, up to and including suspicious deaths. Then, once Gosnell's monstrosities were discovered, the press expressed zero interest. And to this day, most people don't know Gosnell's name, never mind shudder when hearing it.

Why did multiple state and local agencies repeatedly overlook clues that would have stopped Gosnell long before victims of his rampage were accidentally discovered during a drug raid?

Why, after Gosnell's ghastly crimes were finally exposed, did not hordes of press park their trucks in front of his house of horrors and report every last detail ad nauseum?

Why didn't the public care?

In a word, abortion. The reason Gosnell got away with so much for so long was because his cover was as an abortionist, and his victims were preborn babies labeled "products of conception," or newborn babies no one wants to label, or aborting mothers who, worst case, deserved whatever they got in the minds of many (abortion) or best case, were collateral damage for the "freedom of choice."

Even though a dangerous serial killer was clearly in their midst, public health officials protected Gosnell, the press ignored him, and the public just wasn't interested.

It was all just too uncomfortable.

Kermit Gosnell displayed a sadistic fixation on babies and women as early as 1972, when he collaborated with a convicted felon named Harvey Karman to test a new method of abortion that involved inserting razor balls coated with hardened gel into the uteri of fifteen ignorant pregnant mothers. When the gel warmed and melted, the ball sprung the razors so as to slice the preborn babies to death.

Who doesn't think this is barbaric?

Well, the *Los Angeles Times*, for starters, who prefaced its glowing story on the "Karman Coil," as the ball of razors was known, by claiming it had "gained wide acceptance internationally." In other words, you are the crazy one if you think this is crazy.

And now we enter the twisted world of abortion support, where rules of human decency don't apply, where those rules are even turned inside out legally, mentally, and emotionally, and where right is wrong and wrong is right.

Which means Gosnell's three decades of terror escalated unfettered under the unwatchful eye of law enforcement, the media, and even the public, which let him to maintain his filthy and suspicious chop shop in their neighborhood and even gave him their business.

All told, Speck was convicted of murdering eight people, Gacy thirty-three, and Dahmer seventeen.

When Gosnell's clinic was finally searched, agents discovered a total of forty-seven murder victims. Forty seven.

As if that number isn't horrific enough, it is no exaggeration to say there were thousands more victims. But they will never be found, disposed of in a variety of ways, authorities believe, such as down the clinic's garbage disposal or toilets if tiny enough, or, if larger, eaten by fish and crustaceans after being dumped in the oddly present crab pots that were discovered (by then empty) at the end of the boat dock at Gosnell's New Jersey home.

Speck stabbed his victims to death. Gacy buried his victims in the crawl space under his home. Dahmer dismembered his victims and kept body parts in a freezer and scattered around his apartment.

Gosnell was a composite of all three. He murdered many of his newborn victims by severing their spinal cords at the nape of the neck with scissors. He stored some of the tiny corpses in the clinic basement, some in various freezers. And he kept body parts. Investigators found several jars containing baby feet preserved in formaldehyde.

In this book, my friend Cheryl Sullenger chronicles the ghastly saga of America's most prolific serial killer, Kermit Gosnell, whose name should be on the tip of every tongue, and I hope will be after this.

Cheryl will detail how the Pennsylvania Department of Health, Pennsylvania Department of State, Pennsylvania State Board of Medicine, and Philadelphia Department of Public Health were repeatedly made aware over the course of thirty years about Gosnell's negligence, malpractice, and ghastly clinic conditions, and yet repeatedly turned a blind eye, much of that time at the behest of pro-abortion Republican Governor Tom Ridge.

And even though the National Abortion Federation refused to credential Gosnell by what its inspector saw, it, too, said nothing. Neither did the staff of a Philadelphia Planned Parenthood, who later said they had received complaints about Gosnell from wary patients who left his clinic to come to theirs.

Cheryl is one of the few people who attended the entirety of Gosnell's trial.

In fact, Cheryl has sat for countless hours in significant trials of aberrant abortionists, of which there have been many, around the country.

This is actually the heart of Cheryl's work. She and Troy Newman, the two-person team at Operation Rescue, focus on exposing the underbelly of the abortion trade and holding bad actors responsible.

Exposure is sometimes not hard. What becomes hard is ensuring criminals are prosecuted and convicted, and nefarious chop shops are shut down.

And exposure sometimes *is* hard, in which case Cheryl doggedly files Freedom of Information Act requests for police reports, autopsy reports, and 911 tapes, and searches public records for lawsuits and settlements. Operation Rescue keeps an exhaustive compendium of its finds at AbortionDocs.org.

Whatever the scenario, Cheryl will, if necessary, prod law enforcement, public health, legal, and legislative officials until they *do something*.

Cheryl will then attend trials to provide a first-person account to the public. Because along with all the other hats she wears, Cheryl is also a journalist, posting stories on Operation Rescue's website and releasing press statements.

Operation Rescue produces more work than an organization ten times its size. Operation Rescue is responsible for scores of clinic shutdowns and criminal prosecutions of abortionists and clinic owners. And Troy will freely admit Cheryl is the gumshoe detective behind it all.

I've known Cheryl for almost two decades, meeting her after my own foray into pro-life activism, when as a registered nurse I held an abortion survivor for forty-five minutes until he died. Unbeknownst to me, the hospital where I worked committed late-term abortions that sometimes resulted in babies being aborted alive, in which case they were shelved to die in the soiled utility room, one of which I intercepted so he wouldn't die alone.

Operation Rescue helped publicize my story, adding information from their own exhaustive body of work to corroborate what I was saying. Mine wasn't an isolated experience. (Of course, Gosnell has now proved beyond a shadow of a doubt that babies survive abortions.)

I launched a second career writing a blog on the abortion issue, which is when my relationship with Cheryl took a collegial turn. Cheryl was my go-to person for details, corroboration, and connecting dots between one abortionist or mill and another. I was always amazed that no matter the question, Cheryl had the answer or knew exactly where to get it. You've heard the term, "mind like a steel trap"? That would be Cheryl's.

In this book, Cheryl weaves firsthand accounts from her years of experience investigating and exposing abortionists and the abortion industry into the sordid details of Gosnell's own decades of crime.

Nowhere else will you read a detailed description of Gosnell's trial, as if you were there. As I said, Cheryl was.

This book is a must read—tragic, maddening, compelling—a page-turning condemnation on Gosnell, the abortion industry, and our society.

Some day our collective conscience will be awakened. Cheryl's book will hurry that day.

CHAPTER 1

PROBLEMS

Philadelphia had a problem, but it wasn't the one law enforcement officials thought they had.

In the waning months of 2009, the Philadelphia District Attorney's Dangerous Drug Offender Unit had become increasingly aware of illegal drug scripts for Oxycontin that had flooded the streets of Philadelphia and other Pennsylvania cities. Their investigation into the shadowy world of prescription drug trafficking, conducted in conjunction with the Federal Drug Enforcement Agency and the Philadelphia Police Department, began to focus on the largest source of those illegal prescriptions – a medical office euphemistically called the Women's Medical Society, located at 3801 Lancaster in a rundown brick building in the poor urban West Philadelphia neighborhood of Mantua.

Adding to the urgency of this investigation was disturbing information gathered by a detective with the District Attorney's office, James Wood, who had conducted an interview with an employee of the Women's Medical Society in early January, 2010. She described squalid conditions and unqualified workers who essentially were engaged in the unlicensed practice of medicine in Gosnell's absence. Of particular interest was her account of untrained workers administering dangerous controlled substances and sedation without supervision, and that a woman had died as a result just a couple of months before.

As Detective Wood began to look further, he discovered that there had been no police report filed on the woman's death. A visit to the Medical Examiner's office was more productive. There, Wood learned that a Woman's Medical Society patient named Karnamaya Mongar died from an overdose of Demerol, a cheap narcotic that had fallen out of favor in the medical community due to its numerous dangerous side effects.

The owner of the facility was Dr. Kermit Gosnell.

At the time, that name did not mean much to investigators, but perhaps it should have.

***

Kermit Barron Gosnell had a promising future as a young man, despite his humble beginnings. He was born in Philadelphia in February 9, 1941, to a father who worked as an attendant at a gas station and a mother who held down a job as a government worker.

Kermit was a bright boy who excelled in school. In 1959, he graduated among the top students in his class at Philadelphia's Central High School. Later, he earned a bachelor's degree from Dickinson College in Carlisle, Pennsylvania and in 1966, he earned his medical degree from the Jefferson Medical College in Philadelphia.

Wanting to give back the poor urban community where he was raised, as a new doctor Gosnell opened a practice in West Philadelphia, where he offered medical care to the impoverished. He also worked at a substance abuse rehabilitation clinic in the blighted neighborhood of Mantua, and for a teen aid program.

But somewhere along the line early in his career, Gosnell's altruistic work with the poor took a turn, and he became interested in what was then the illegal practice of abortion, and the big money that could be made doing them.

In the early 1970s Gosnell became acquainted with Harvey Karmen, a psychologist with a dark history that included his own ghoulish fascination with abortion. While working on his doctorate at UCLA in the 1950s, Karmen started an "underground railroad" for women seeking illegal abortions. Soon, despite being completely unqualified, Karmen began doing abortions on women himself—that is, until 1955, when he checked a young pregnant woman into a seedy California motel and used a speculum and a nutcracker to abort her unborn baby. Tragically, the woman died from complications to Karmen's butchery. As a result, Karmen was convicted of committing illegal abortions and spent 2 1/2 years in a California State Prison.

Apparently, his incarceration did little to convince this back-alley abortionist to amend his ways. After his release, Karmen continued his experimentation with abortion techniques on vulnerable women he that used as human "guinea pigs," according to an article written by James Taranto that appeared in the *Wall Street Journal* on April 18, 2013. Taranto describes

Karmen's invention of a grisly abortion device known as the "Super Coil," which Karmen had earlier used experimentally on rape victims in Bangladesh, thanks to a sponsorship provided by International Planned Parenthood.

Complication rates were high, and little wonder. A colleague of Karman's Philadelphia collaborator described the contraption as "basically plastic razors that were formed into a ball. . . They were coated into a gel, so that they would remain closed. These would be inserted into the woman's uterus. And after several hours of body temperature. . . the gel would melt and these. . . things would spring open, supposedly cutting up the fetus."[1]

Karmen's "Philadelphia collaborator" was none other than Kermit Gosnell, who was already involved (and apparently well-known in the Philadelphia area) for conducting illegal abortions at his West Philadelphia medical office that served double-duty as a back-alley abortion mill.

Karmen would team up with Gosnell for what became known as the "Mother's Day Massacre." To make a statement about abortion, Karman assembled 15 low-income women in their second trimester of pregnancy and put them on a bus from Chicago to Philadelphia on Mother's Day weekend in 1972. Their destination? Gosnell's Women's Medical Society, where Gosnell would conduct experimental "super coil" abortions on them. Gosnell inserted plastic coils invented by Karman into the uteri of the pregnant women.

As one might expect, the experiment went awry, and nine of the fifteen women suffered serious complications, including hemorrhage, infections, retained fetal body parts, a perforated uterus, and one hysterectomy.

Instead of revolutionizing second-trimester abortions, the botched experiment on the naïve women led to a federal investigation that changed the protocols for testing future abortion devices. However, the investigation did not adequately remove Gosnell as a threat to women, and the reforms that were implemented were shallow.

Yet in the end, while one would think that he should have landed in jail for the super coil fiasco, nothing much happened to Gosnell. When the US Supreme Court issued its landmark *Roe v. Wade* decision that decriminalized abortion, it appeared that Gosnell was in the clear.

Yet it seems that Gosnell was always a bit lax in following the rules. In 1990, Gosnell admitted that he had engaged in the "aiding and assisting in the unlicensed practice of medicine" by allowing a physician's assistant who worked for him to see patients and prescribe drugs as if he was a licensed physician. Gosnell was issued a reprimand and ordered to pay a fine of $1,000 in Pennsylvania.

Four months later, the New York State Board of Professional Conduct also reprimanded and censured Gosnell for his unprofessional conduct in Pennsylvania and fined him another thousand dollars. Gosnell eventually stopped practicing in New York and allowed his license there to lapse.

This disciplinary episode, along with the super coil fiasco, should have raised red flags and prompted authorities to monitor him closely. Instead, the warning signs were ignored, and Gosnell was left to conduct his affairs as he saw fit without much worry of regulatory oversight.

By all accounts, Gosnell continued to practice as a likeable and surprisingly well-respected doctor and community member. He maintained the appearance of an intelligent, soft-spoken and well-educated physician whose friendly manner made him an unthinkable candidate for the title of "Philadelphia's Biggest Drug Pusher," much less its most prolific serial killer.

As the years went by, Gosnell married and divorced twice before wedding his third wife, Pearl. He fathered two children and settled down to an outwardly unremarkable, though respectable life.

After 43 years of practice, it appeared that Gosnell settled into a mundane daily routine, fading from any media spotlight. Even the local pro-life activists who were nominally aware that abortions were being done at the Women's Medical Society mostly ignored his clinic, except for a small group of Catholics who prayed the rosary outside every Saturday morning.

But that was soon to change forever.

CHAPTER 2

RAID

As the Dangerous Drug Offender Unit prepared to raid Gosnell's clinic on February 18, 2010, their main focus was on shutting down what was thought to be a "pill mill." Because there had been a patient drug overdose death and allegations of squalid conditions, DEA Special Agent Stephen Doughtery notified the Pennsylvania Department of State and the Department of Health of the impending raid and invited them to send representatives to accompany law enforcement personnel as they executed the search warrant.

The Pennsylvania State Board of Medicine, which operates under the authority of the Department of State, oversees the licenses and professional practices of physicians in the state. It was the Department of Health's responsibility to oversee medical facilities. Later, the District Attorney detectives were surprised to learn that the Department of Health had not visited the Women's Medical Society for inspection in at least fifteen years.

The team of law enforcement officers and state regulators waited until Gosnell arrived at the clinic before attempting to execute their search warrant. At about 8:30 pm, Gosnell entered his business for what he thought would be just another routine evening at the clinic.

There was a reason that Gosnell arrived at his clinic in the evening and often worked into the wee hours of the morning, but law enforcement officers who soon entered the Women's Medical Society did not know it until they stepped inside the clinic for the first time.

At about 9:00 pm, investigators with the FBI, DEA, and the Philadelphia Police Department raided the Women's Medical Society. What they found that February evening shocked them, and frankly should have shamed them.

Immediately, investigators understood that Gosnell's clinic was unlike any pill mill they had ever seen or hoped to ever see again. District Attorney Seth Williams described it like this:

There was blood on the floor. A stench of urine filled the air. A flea-infested cat was wandering through the facility, and there were cat feces on the stairs. Semi-conscious women scheduled for abortions were moaning in the waiting room or the recovery room, where they sat on dirty recliners covered with blood-stained blankets.

All the women had been sedated by unlicensed staff—long before Gosnell arrived at the clinic—and staff members could not accurately state what medications or dosages they had administered to the waiting patients. Many of the medications in the inventory were past their expiration dates.

Investigators found the clinic grossly unsuitable as a surgical facility. The two surgical procedure rooms were filthy and unsanitary—Agent Doughtery described them as resembling "a bad gas station rest room." Instruments were not sterile. Equipment was rusty and outdated. Oxygen equipment was covered with dust, and had not been inspected. The same corroded suction tubing used for abortions was the only tubing available for oral airways if assistance for breathing was needed. There was no functioning resuscitation or even monitoring equipment, except for a single blood pressure cuff in the recovery room.[1]

Ambulances were called for pregnant women drugged into various states of stupor who were found languishing throughout the clinic.

As the investigators looked further, they made a grisly discovery. Severed body parts of what appeared to be late-term aborted babies were displayed in jars over a filthy sink inside the clinic as if they were trophies. This was the behavior of a sick serial killer or a deranged maniac, not a drug pusher. What had been going on here?

Then they discovered the babies. Lots of them. In all, the remains of forty-seven aborted babies were packed into a freezer and shoved into boxes in the basement. All of them bore suspicious wounds on the backs of their necks. Later, we would learn why.

Investigators separated the employees and began to interview them one by one.

Lynda Gale Williams was a tired-looking woman in her early 40s with vacant eyes and dirty-blonde hair that fell to her shoulders in unkempt tresses. She had been working for Gosnell at his Philadelphia clinic for about three years, despite the fact that her only "qualifications" included an eighth-grade education and a certificate as a phlebotomist.

Williams admitted under questioning that she conducted several medical tasks for which she was completely unqualified. She told investigators that she had administered diazepam, temazepam, and Cytotec orally and vaginally to the women that filled the clinic that day. She also said she routinely conducted vaginal exams on patients. These things were all done under orders from Gosnell, according to Williams, but while he was absent from the clinic.

Williams also admitted to investigators that she was working at the clinic November 20, 2009, when a tiny immigrant women named Karnamaya Mongar received her fatal abortion.

Williams said she gave Mongar 10 mg of Demerol and 12.5 mgs of promethazine. When Mongar began to experience painful cramping, Williams said that Mongar asked for more pain relief. However, Mongar had only recently emigrated to the US from a Bhutanese refugee camp in Nepal, and could only speak a few words of English. It was clear that Williams was lying about Mongar asking for anything.

Williams told investigators that she contacted Gosnell by phone and was instructed by him to give her additional medication. Williams stated that she had given Mongar an additional 75 mg of Demerol, 12.5 mg of promethazine, and 10 mg of diazepam, and after Gosnell arrived at the clinic, Mongar was given additional drugs "for anesthetic purposes."

According to Williams, Gosnell then performed the second-trimester abortion on Mongar, during which she experienced irregular heartbeats, a condition known as arrhythmia, and eventually suffered a heart attack.

The Department of Health issued an order shut down Gosnell's office three days after the initial raid. Soon, investigators were back with a new search warrant collecting evidence, including those jars of severed fetal limbs that had so stunned investigators during the initial raid. Crime Scene Investigators swarmed Gosnell's home. They began impounding evidence and building their case, but what they suspected, no one exactly knew.

***

Local Philadelphia news reports concerning the raid began showing up in my email inbox in one of the many Google News Alerts that I get every day. It especially caught my attention. The more I read, the more excited I became. It wasn't every day that an abortion clinic is raided by police. Early reports indicated that conditions at Gosnell's clinic were worse than anything anyone had ever seen. I knew this was going to be huge story with national implications.

In my job as senior vice president of Operation Rescue, I research and investigate abortion clinics and seek out information that might shine daylight on the dirty underbelly of the abortion industry that I had come to know so well over three decades of pro-life activism. I am constantly on the lookout for information about abortion providers and their clinics, especially if it is related to a clinic closure, disciplinary action, or criminal conduct. Hence, I have subscribed to numerous Google News Alerts that keep me as up to the-minute on breaking developments as possible related to what those of us at Operation Rescue refer to as the "abortion cartel."

I write extensively, exposing the abortion cartel's abuses almost daily on Operation Rescue's primary website, OperationRescue.org. Raw documentation and story links are posted to our secondary website, AbortionDocs.org, which is a repository of documents, photos, videos, and news story links on every abortion clinic and known abortionist in America. My reports are usually picked up by pro-life news sites and occasionally generate interviews for me and my colleague, Troy Newman, who serves as president of an ever-evolving Operation Rescue, which has morphed from a group focused on street protest to one that is now the most effective abortion industry watchdog organizations in the nation.

The minute I read the first local news report out of Philadelphia, one might say that my "Spidey senses" were tingling like never before. There was no telling what kind of revelations about abortion clinic abuses were going to be laid bare.

My first article about the raid on Gosnell's Women's Medical Society appeared on February 23, 2010, five days after the initial raid on Gosnell's clinic. It included a link to documents filed by the Commonwealth of Pennsylvania Bureau of Professional and Occupational Affairs on February 22, 2010, temporarily suspending Gosnell's medical license.

The Petition of Immediate Temporary Suspension described in cold, clinical terms the situation discovered at 3810 Lancaster.

"Respondent has unlicensed individuals working in the clinic," it read. "The conditions are deplorable and unsanitary . . . . There was blood on the floor and parts of aborted babies were displayed in jars."[2]

The narrative went on to describe how unlicensed, unqualified workers conducted pelvic exams and administered dangerous drugs all without Gosnell, the only licensed physician, being present and how that practice caused the death of a patient in 2009.

"Based upon the foregoing factual allegations, the Respondent's continued practice of medicine within the Commonwealth of Pennsylvania makes Respondent an immediate and clear danger to the public health and safety," the petition concluded.[3]

"Shop of Horrors: Abortion Death Prompts Raid, Grisly Discovery," my headline screamed. It was salacious and sensational, as the best headlines usually are. However, in my reporting of a story, I always tried to maintain a level-headed tone, sticking to known facts and leaving the amped-up rhetoric for the quotes that I always attributed to Troy, with his consent. This was the press released we issued in reaction to the raid:

Philadelphia, PA – Authorities investigating an abortion death raided a West Philadelphia abortion clinic for the second time in two days and made a grisly discovery. Dozens of apparently late-term fetuses were found frozen, some dating back 30 years.

Investigators are now examining the remains to determine if illegal late-term abortions were done.

Police and Federal authorities raided the abortion clinic run by Kermit Gosnell after an abortion patient died last November. Massive amounts of drugs found in the victim's system led authorities to suspect that Gosnell was illegally prescribing pain-killers. There were indications that the victim had been treated by unlicensed personnel.

Gosnell's medical license has been suspended. The suspension order described "deplorable and unsanitary" conditions at the clinic, indicating that "there was blood on the floor, and parts of aborted fetuses were displayed in jars."

The order declared Gosnell to be "an immediate and clear danger to the public health and safety."

The clinic is temporarily closed. No charges have yet been filed.

"Here is yet another filthy abortion mill with another unlicensed abortion worker causing another abortion death in another shop of horrors. This is not the exception to the rule in our nation's abortion clinics. It is standard operating procedure," said Operation Rescue President Troy Newman. "This clinic is no better than a back-alley abortion mill, and in fact may be worse. Collecting the remains of dead babies over a 30-year time frame is reminiscent of the actions of deranged serial killers who keep body parts as trophies. It doesn't get much sicker than that."[4]

We also immediately began calling for a criminal investigation in light of the Gosnell scandal and another case involving New Jersey abortionist Steven Chase Brigham.

When I wrote the "deranged serial killers" quote for Troy, I believed that I was perhaps overstating our case for the purpose of raising eyebrows and public awareness that abortion facilities are not the happy clean medical offices with doctors channeling the skill and compassion of Albert Schweitzer, as the abortion industry wants us all to believe. Once more of the facts came out, I realized the phrase "deranged serial killers" was hitting the nail on the head.

On March 12, the Pennsylvania Department of Health stepped in and permanently shut down the clinic due to the appalling and dangerous conditions that existed at the clinic that would soon become known as Gosnell's "House of Horrors."

CHAPTER 3

CRIME SCENE

To Officer John Taggart, it began as just another day on the job. As a seventeen-year veteran of the Philadelphia Police Department Crime Scene Unit, he had seen a lot. Because of his experience, and strong stomach, he was sent to New York City after the September 11, 2001, terror attacks to help recover bodies from the demolished Twin Towers.

But as he arrived at his new assignment, gathering evidence in the Kermit Gosnell case, what he was about to see, much like those unforgettable memories from Ground Zero, would be burned in his memory forever.

Gosnell's clinic was a patchwork maze of four buildings that had been haphazardly combined to form one rambling three-floor office space. At the front was a waiting area featuring grimy white paint, grungy flooring, and security bars on the door and windows. To the left of the front door was a murky turtle and fish tank. A narrow hallway leading to the only "handicapped" entrance was blocked with a clutter that included a wheelchair, office equipment, boxes and plants.

In fact, the entire clinic was filled with plants that were now in a wilted state of neglect. Taggart noticed that some of the pots contained feces from a cat that had lived on the premises.

Other hallways that snaked throughout the office space were crowded with chairs, empty water jugs, and more plants.

"The smells were just unbearable," Taggart later told a reporter from the local NBC News affiliate. "You could tell there was death somewhere."[1]

Soon, Taggart came across a sink station where abortion instruments were apparently washed, but doubtfully sanitized. On a shelf in the cabinet above the dirty sink, he found five specimen jars. Inside four of the clear plastic containers capped with a green lid floated small severed feet of various lengths. One appeared to have been severed at the thigh. The fifth container held a mesh-like substance that Taggart couldn't identify. These were the severed feet that those raiding the clinic first discovered that appeared to be displayed like trophies.

"Opening up that cabinet and seeing all the feet that were still in there, that was—I'll remember that for a long time," Taggart stated during the news interview.[2]

He described one of the garbage disposals that was later removed from the clinic and presented in court as evidence. "They were shoving body parts down this garbage disposal that, we found out later that it jammed up quite a few times to the point where they plunged it one day and an arm popped out on Lancaster Avenue."[3]

Taggart moved on to a room with a stained floor he referred to as the "dentist office" because it contained an old tan dentist chair. He didn't know what that chair could have been used for, but it immediately spun up mental images of an apparatus of torture.

To the left were narrow stairs that led to the basement where medical supplies were stored and where boxes and bags of refuse were tossed. Inside those boxes and bags that littered the floor or were crammed in a freezer were the remains of forty-seven aborted babies.

Taggart came across two rooms that were in fact the abortion procedure rooms. There was the Monet Room and the smaller O'Keefe Room, which were named after the cheap painting reproductions that hung in each room.

The procedure rooms were as foul as the rest of the facility appeared.

The O'Keefe Room was furnished with a torn brown vinyl procedure bed with stirrups, the large copy of a Georgia O'Keefe painting, an outdated ultrasound machine, and a rusty suction machine caked in dried blood with brownish-yellow tubing attached. The cabinet area was junky and cluttered with supplies while the sink appeared, like the rest of the facility, not to have been cleaned for some time.

The Monet Room was only slightly better. Along with the featured copy of a Monet painting and the procedure table, there was a slightly newer-looking ultrasound machine, a defibrillator, and an oxygen tank. A space-saving pocket door was used for privacy. This room, it was learned, was reserved for Gosnell's suburban white patients. When one of his employees, Tina Baldwin, questioned why his white patients were given better treatment, Gosnell brushed it off saying, "That's the way of the world."[4]

The recovery area of Gosnell's clinic was a cramped space with chairs blocking the two bathrooms to the extent that a woman would have to squeeze by to gain access to the restroom facilities. Five gray-and-black cloth recliners and other chairs lined the walls of the recovery room. Under the chairs was a trap door that led to the basement storage area.

On the second floor, there was another waiting and bathroom area that was slightly more spacious. The toys that littered the floor appeared as macabre, out-of-place artifacts.

There was also a "lab" area that was about the size of a closet. The "junky" lab contained a microscope and refrigerator. A sign on the wall reminded workers, "Please do not dispose of speculums." Gosnell was referring to the disposable clear plastic instruments used by doctors to open the vagina for examination or procedures.

In fact, speculums were not the only disposable instruments that were reused. Taggart noted a plastic "shoe box" container that held a collection of warped, brownish-yellow cannulas that had originally been sterile and clear. Properly sanitizing the disposable plastic instruments, which were used during early abortions to suction out the contents of the uterus, was impossible.

On the third floor, metal poles held up the leaky, decaying roof that Taggart thought would soon collapse. There, more small offices and hallways were cluttered with junk and lined with empty milk jugs, more fish tanks, and dying plants. Curiously, among the maze of clutter, there was also a small, unkempt bedroom with a television.

Perhaps less curiously, Taggart found safes were everywhere, crammed into the offices already jammed with boxes and other junk. These safes were presumably used to hold the large amounts of cash that was the clinic's primary form of payment.

Taggart dutifully photographed nearly every detail of the squalid, ramshackle office as evidence that would later be used in court and collected the human remains for inspection by the coroner.

Taggart and other members of the crime scene unit were then sent to Gosnell's two homes. His primary residence in Mantua was a red brick multi-level Victorian row house that was connected on one side to another home. It appeared that Gosnell had a taste for high-end appointments. His home featured expensive appliances, a flat-screened television, and other expensive items. But the inside of the home looked like it belonged to a hoarder. The main bedroom was painted a gaudy dark purple color and was littered with boxes, files, trash, and plates with half-eaten food.

"He just lived in squalor. I mean, he would leave plates of food on the floor. There was stuff everywhere in the bedroom. You couldn't see the bed," Taggart remembered.[5]

But then it came time to search the basement.

Calmly, Gosnell sat down at his piano and began to entertain investigators with a Chopin selection while pausing only to warn police that his basement, which they were about to search, was infested with fleas. Indeed, Crime Scene Unit officer Bobby Flade donned a Tyvek hazmat suit and descended into the cellar where fleas immediately attacked, "roiling in piles over his shins" according to an account by journalist Steve Volk, who later corresponded with Gosnell and interviewed him from his prison cell.

"As soon as they went down into the basement, they were covered in fleas," Taggart told reporters. "He actually gave us a bottle of flea repellent and said, 'See what a nice guy I am? I told you there were fleas in the basement.' He said 'I didn't have to tell ya's'."[6]

While the bodies of aborted babies were plentiful at Gosnell's clinic, there were no tiny bodies in Gosnell's basement or anywhere else at his Mantua home. Yet, there were many aborted baby remains for which there was no accounting.

The search moved to his upscale shore home in Brigantine, New Jersey.

"We went down there because we thought maybe some of the babies were thrown into the bay. There's a lot of babies that are still unaccounted for that we don't know where they're at," Taggart explained.[7]

The Brigantine house was in much better condition that his primary Mantua residence, and the property itself was beautiful. Gosnell's land ran along the bay and featured four boat slips. Gosnell's own large and very expensive boat, of which he was so proud, sat on a trailer on the property.

Again, the search for bodies continued. The investigators pulled up several crab pots, but found nothing. Divers were even brought in to explore the bay behind Gosnell's shore home. Still nothing.

"I believe they are either buried out there or I don't know where they are. We've looked, we've looked for three years," Taggart told reporters.[8]

Wherever Gosnell hid them, they were never found.

CHAPTER 4

DELAWARE & LOUISIANA CONNECTIONS

After discovering the horrific conditions and practices at what has now become known as Gosnell's "House of Horrors," the Pennsylvania State Board of Medicine took immediate action to prevent Gosnell from practicing. As mentioned, a February 22, 2010, Order of Temporary Suspension noted that "the resumption of practice by [Gosnell] presents an immediate danger to the public health and safety."[1]

But Pennsylvania was not the only state where Gosnell had been practicing.

While Gosnell's West Philadelphia abortion clinic was his primary office, he moonlighted one day per week in nearby Delaware for his friend and associate, Leroy Brinkley, who owned the Atlantic Women's Services abortion facility in Wilmington and a second one in Dover. Brinkley also owned a notorious Delta Clinic of Baton Rouge in Louisiana where horrific abortion abuses have been documented.

Like Gosnell, Brinkley used unlicensed workers at Delta to perform medical tasks for which they were not qualified. Eileen O'Neill was one such worker. O'Neill was an unlicensed medical school graduate who began work in the abortion industry in 1998 when she hired on at Brinkley's troubled Delta Clinic for what would become a two-year stint.

For O'Neill, her work at the Delta Clinic was a "side job" while she was living in Texas. She had relinquished a medical training license she held in Louisiana due to what she called "post-traumatic stress," which speaks volumes about her time at the high-volume Delta abortion business.

Brinkley later recommended the unemployed O'Neill to Gosnell, who, in spite of her compromised mental state (or maybe because of it) hired her on to his Women's Medical Society staff in West Philadelphia to perform duties as a physician, knowing full well that she did not hold a valid medical license.

Records I have reviewed in the way of health department inspection reports and witness affidavits indicates that hiring unlicensed and untrained workers is a common practice in abortion clinics across America. Why hire the unqualified? Licensed professionals require higher salaries than unqualified workers. Hiring those with negligible or non-existent training is a way of cutting corners on costs, but it comes at the expense of women's lives and health.[2]

Shelia Hebert, 27, was one woman who paid for the corners-cutting at Delta with her life. In 1984, she went to Delta for an abortion, after which she began to complain of chest pain and labored breathing. Soon, Sheila suffered cardiac arrest and respiratory failure due to an acute asthma attack, according to a lawsuit later filed against the clinic and abortionist Richardson Glidden on behalf of Sheila's ten-year old son. Clinic staff gave her a shot of adrenaline, but failed to restart her heart. Paramedics responding to a 911 call that was eventually placed by a clinic worker found Shelia cold, blue, and lifeless. Efforts to resuscitate her failed and she was pronounced dead at a local hospital. After an autopsy, the medical examiner concluded that Shelia died from "cardio respiratory arrest due to acute asthmatic bronchitis" after "surgical termination of pregnancy."[3]

The Hebert family suit alleged that the clinic had failed to properly monitor Shelia while she was in recovery, failed to react properly when her condition was discovered, and failed to promptly call 911 for emergency assistance. In addition, the clinic failed to maintain adequate emergency equipment, which may have saved Shelia's life.

Another fatality at Delta was Ingar Lee Whittington Weber, who died of acute kidney failure after an abortion in January, 1990.[4]

While those are the only two known fatalities, abortion facilities are notorious under-reporters. In my work researching abortion abuses, I have seen evidence of other abortion clinics going to great lengths to hide any involvement in patient deaths. There was just no way to know for sure how many women actually died from abortion complications at Brinkley's Delta Clinic of Baton Rouge.

What is known is that Delta has botched one abortion after another over the years. I learned from reading law suits, medical board disciplinary records, and news reports that one woman suffered a lacerated uterus and a retained fetal leg that caused a massive infection. Another woman was so badly mangled internally from her Delta abortion that she required a hysterectomy to save her life.

One Delta patient called me at my office and related her horrific experiences. She went to Delta for a medication abortion that failed. Suffering and in pain the woman returned to Delta for help. According to the patient's affidavit, which I submitted to the Louisiana State Board of Medical Examiners with a complaint on her behalf, abortionist Mary Frances Gardner was responsible for her pain and suffering. Gardner was rude to her and angry that she required additional treatment for which Gardner would receive no additional payment. The patient alleged that Gardner was infuriated that she had a cell phone in the facility, and physically and verbally abused her in an attempt to get the phone from her. Gardner called her a "crybaby" and told her, "I can't wait to do this and get you out of my hair."[5]

Finally, Gardner performed the surgical procedure without giving the patient anesthesia, causing pain the patient could barely tolerate, according to the patient's affidavit. Later, the suffering woman went to her family physician, who determined that she had abnormal tissue in the uterus and "a lot of old scarring." The abortion was the only surgical procedure she ever had. So extensive was the damage that she was later given a hysterectomy.

"The [Delta] Doctor butchered me to say the least," the woman wrote in her affidavit. "That is my opinion." She now expresses great remorse for her abortion.

After reviewing my complaint over the course of several months, the Louisiana State Board of Medical Examiners and Department of Health sent me a letter indicating they were unable to substantiate the patient's claims. However, after my personal conversations with the woman, I am convinced she was traumatically mistreated at Delta, but the Board had made the decision to turn a blind eye.

When it came to regulatory boards giving abortion providers a pass, it seemed that Brinkley and Gosnell were peas in a pod.

***

One day per week, Gosnell would drive the 45-minute commute from Philadelphia to Wilmington, Delaware, to do abortions at Brinkley's Atlantic Women's Services. While there, Gosnell would often see women in the late stages of pregnancy and begin their abortions by inserting laminaria into their cervixes. In order for their abortions to be completed, Gosnell would tell them to report to his Women's Medical Society in West Philadelphia. The most likely reasons for sending those women across state lines was first, that this arrangement was most convenient for Gosnell. He also may have wished to avoid abortion laws in Delaware that restricted abortion after viability and control the number of witnesses to his unorthodox abortion methods.

When Pennsylvania suspended Gosnell's license in February, 2010, it notified the Delaware Board of Medical Practice of its actions. In turn, the Delaware Board gathered for an emergency hearing on March 2, 2010, and voted to suspend Gosnell's license to practice in that state as well. Members of the Delaware Board based their decision to suspend Gosnell's license on action taken against him in Pennsylvania.

Information about Gosnell's practices caused Delaware regulators to take a closer look at Brinkley's abortion operation. As a result, the medical licenses of two more of Brinkley's Delaware abortionists, Albert Dworkin and Arturo Apolinario, were also temporarily suspended at the request of then-Attorney General Beau Biden for not reporting Gosnell's illegal activities and allowing him to improperly take or destroy patient medical records that contained evidence of his crimes.

Perhaps not surprisingly, Apolinario was also accused of prescribing and dispensing controlled substances without proper licensing or authorization.

Raymond L. Moore Sr., the president of the Board of Medical Practice, issued the following statement upon the suspension of Gosnell's Delaware medical license:

> *Based upon the severity of the violations alleged in the complaint, and based upon the suspension of Dr. Gosnell's license in the state of Pennsylvania, we have concluded that the suspension of Dr. Gosnell's license to practice medicine in Delaware is necessary to protect the public until we can fully hear the matter.*[6]

Meanwhile, Brinkley transferred total ownership in his two Delaware abortion offices to a woman named Panzy Myrie. Soon, Attorney General Biden sought a cease and desist order against her for posing as a licensed physician and gynecologist, even though she had never been licensed in Delaware. In April 2011, Myrie reached an agreement, with the Delaware

Board of Medical Licensure and Discipline to permanently close the two Atlantic Women's Services abortion businesses in Delaware.

For the time being, Gosnell and his disreputable Delaware associates were out of business.

CHAPTER 5

PATIENTS SPEAK

In the wake of news reports of the clinic raid in Philadelphia, local news organizations scrambled for their own unique sensational angles on the Gosnell story. They began publishing the salacious details concerning additional abortion nightmare stories from patients and others who had come forward to tell of their own experiences at the Women's Medical Society.

Karnamaya Mongar's close family friend, Dambher Ghalley, who often identified himself as Mongar's brother, told reporters that Gosnell's abortion clinic was "dirty and bloody" and that Mongar died after being rushed to the hospital by ambulance. Mr. Ghalley would have a lot more to say when he finally testified at Gosnell's trial three years later.[1]

But Mongar's death wasn't the first maternal death for Gosnell and company. Reports began circulating of a young African-American woman named Semika Shirelle Shaw, 22, who died from an abortion done by Gosnell in March 2000. Gosnell had torn a hole in her uterus during the abortion, but neglected to tell her about it or repair it.

This kind of injury is called a uterine perforation. It is a life-threatening condition that most abortion clinics simply are not equipped to handle. Usually, women suffering uterine perforations are rushed to nearby hospitals where the hemorrhaging can be stopped and the tear repaired. Sometimes, the injuries can be so severe that emergency hysterectomies are required to save the women's lives.

But in Semika's case, Gosnell called no ambulance. In fact, according to civil court records, he sent Semika home as if nothing had gone wrong. Semika called Gosnell's office the following day complaining of pain and heavy bleeding, but no one told her to get checked either at Gosnell's clinic or the hospital.

One can hardly imagine the pain and suffering she endured during the final hours of her life as a raging infection known as sepsis coursed through her body. Two days after Gosnell perforated her uterus, Semika was dead. She left two children motherless.

A lawsuit filed by her surviving family was settled two years later. Professional Underwriters Liability Insurance Company paid a $400,000 to Semika's surviving family. The settlement amount was reported to the medical board, but a decision was made not to investigate, even though they were made aware of details concerning dirty conditions and substandard practices at Gosnell's facility. It was easier to turn a blind eye, when it came to reports – even well-substantiated ones – of abortion abuses.[2]

Later, Semika's cousin, Pennsylvania State Rep. Margo Davidson, stood in support of 2011's HB 574, legislation that would require abortion clinics to meet the same safety standards as ambulatory surgical facilities. In addressing her support for the bill, an emotional Davidson noted that she believed she was the only member of the Pennsylvania House that had been personally touched by Gosnell. Choking back tears, Davidson eulogized Semika on the State House Floor:

> *Today, I honor her memory by voting yes on this legislation, that seeks to safeguard the health of women, that is long overdue, so that never again will a woman walk into a licensed health care facility in the State of Pennsylvania and be butchered as she was—with her uterus perforated and her death of sepsis and infection, permeating in her body, till she writhed in pain on the floor of her home, to her ultimate death.*[3]

Sadly, Rep. Davidson was the only African American to vote in favor that bill that could have saved her young cousin's life, as well as the life of Karnamaya Mongar. With Davidson's help the bill was approved, and sent on to the Senate, where it also passed. In a fitting Christmas present to women and babies, it was signed into law on December 22, 2011.

***

As news coverage continued, some of Gosnell's former patients came forward to share their own nightmarish experiences at 3801 Lancaster.

Marie Smith is lucky to be alive after having had a botched abortion by Gosnell in 1999. She developed a high fever and slipped into unconsciousness a week after her abortion. She was rushed to the hospital where the source of her condition was confirmed.

"They showed me X-rays and said he [Gosnell] left an arm and a leg inside me," Smith told a reporter. "I almost died. I thought he knew what he was doing, but I guess I was wrong."[4]

In fact, Gosnell was named in over fifty lawsuits over the preceding twenty years. One of those suits involved Dana Haynes, who had an abortion by Gosnell in November, 2006. Haynes alleges that Gosnell lacerated her cervix, ruptured her uterus, and seriously damaged her small bowel during the abortion.

Davida Clark was a young African-American teen who, like so many in her neighborhood, succumbed to the temptation to run with the wrong crowd. One night, she was raped. That rape resulted in a pregnancy. Davida's friends told her of a clinic at 3801 Lancaster.

She said in an interview for the well-made short movie, *3801 Lancaster*, that she remembered her experience at Gosnell's clinic as if it was yesterday. She remembered the fish tank and the receptionist that seemed only to care about taking money. As her name was called and she was moved into the abortion room, she said she saw drugged women who looked "half dead" languishing about the clinic. She noticed there was blood all over the chairs and on the floor.

"But I just kept going," she said.[5]

Davida was hooked up to an IV and her midsection strapped with a fetal heart monitor. That's when she saw Gosnell for the first time. But by then Davida had had enough. She told Gosnell that she had changed her mind, but Gosnell would have none of that.

Davida recalled, "He's like, 'Stop being a little baby,' and he's pounding on my legs. 'Stop being a little baby! Stop being a little baby!' And now, I'm outnumbered. All these women came in and I'm like tied to the bed, and the next thing I know, I was out of it."[6]

When she came to, Davida was groggy from the drugs, but she knew she wasn't pregnant any more. She began to repeatedly sob, "I want my baby!" but the women who worked in the clinic simply ignored her.

Today, Davida is unable to bear any more children and thinks with grief of the baby she should have had, but didn't.

Then there was the illegal abortion of 13-year old Malina Williams, who says she obtained an abortion by Gosnell without the required parental consent. Williams, who was thirty-two when she came forward after the raid on Gosnell's clinic. She told reporters that she could see bottles of jars filled with the remains of "little babies" and that after her abortion "she saw Gosnell cradling a bottle that contained the dead body of her fetus."[7]

To combat the obvious "creep factor" and outrage produced by such revelations, Gosnell hurled himself into a bizarre media campaign to declare his innocence and attempt to rehabilitate his reputation. This was done in disregard to urgings by his attorney that he keep quiet.

Gosnell phoned Channel 29 Fox News reporter *Thomas* Drayton and said he wanted to talk. Drayton wasted little time getting a camera crew to Gosnell for his first interview after the clinic raid.[8]

Gosnell appeared on camera to be a polite, genteel man who was not easily ruffled by the hard questions.

"I expect to be vindicated," Gosnell told Drayton in a voice barely above a whisper.

"I didn't realize how hard I'd been working until I had a couple of days off," laughed Gosnell, then added somberly, "But it's been a very difficult time."

Gosnell continued, "But I know that I have done my very best to provide the very best of responsive care for my patients."

Then Drayton asked Gosnell about Dayna Hanes, who had come forward to tell her story of the botched, incomplete abortion she suffered that led to her filing an unsuccessful lawsuit suit against Gosnell. (Her case was dropped on a technicality after she missed a filing deadline.) Hanes told the reporter that Gosnell could not finish the abortion and left her waiting hours before finally calling an ambulance.

"I really felt like he was just going to let me die," Hanes said.[9]

Gosnell insisted he knew nothing about it.

"I haven't seen a negative comment that a patient has been dissatisfied with the services that I have provided," Gosnell said.

Pointing to a large stack of over forty law suits, the reporter confronted Gosnell's lack of forthrightness.

"If you're not making mistakes, you are not really attempting to do something," Gosnell responded. "So I think my patients are aware that I do my very best by them."

Gosnell dodged a question about the fetal remains found at his clinic that were stored in jars on display, answering instead, "I provide the same care that I would want my daughter to receive."

As a postscript to the news story, Drayton remarked, "I truly believe, sitting down with him tonight, that he believes he has done nothing wrong."

It's hard to imagine how a man who had been sued so many times for malpractice could claim that he had never heard a negative comment from a patient about the care she received, especially in light of the squalid conditions discovered by investigators at his clinic just a few days before that interview.

This was the public's first look at Gosnell and the self-delusion in which he was cocooned. In Gosnell's self-made universe, he was a heroically selfless provider of excellent medical care for poor women who desperately needed him.

Maybe, in the end, that was the only way he could live with himself. Or maybe he was just a manipulative con man, trying to sweet-talk his way out of another mess in his life. In any case, District Attorney Seth Williams was getting ready to smash Gosnell's fantasy world to smithereens.

For those of us at Operation Rescue, that moment couldn't come soon enough.

Meanwhile, the flurry of mostly local media coverage that followed the police raid quickly died out. The District Attorney's office went silent, and the long wait began for a decision on whether Gosnell would ever be brought to justice.

***

We were impatient to see criminal charges brought against Gosnell, but we knew that the District Attorney Seth Williams had requested that the case be reviewed by a grand jury. I had some experience with grand juries, having been involved in citizen-called efforts for investigations of other abortion providers, so I was aware that once a case goes to a grand jury, public comments from prosecutors pretty much dry up.

The grand jury process is very secretive. Evidence in a case is usually presented by a district attorney to a panel of twelve to fifteen citizen jurors picked from voter registration rolls at random in much the way citizens are selected for regular jury duty in civil and criminal cases. Members of the grand jury are seated for a period of weeks or months, which under certain circumstances can be extended, if necessary. Jurors are sworn to confidentiality concerning the proceedings. Grand juries have the authority subpoena documents and witnesses to testify before it as part of its fact-finding function, which can take months. After the evidence is presented, the grand jurors will vote on a "true bill," which means there is enough evidence to file criminal charges. A majority of the jurors must agree on the charges before a true bill can be brought.

As the Gosnell grand jury investigation quietly dragged on, the case ceased to generate even local news stories. Soon, those few that had ever heard of Kermit Gosnell had forgot about him.

Except me.

I continued to search for any inkling into what was happening with the case, but there was simply no news. I began to worry that pro-abortion politics were in play, which aggressively protect abortion businesses, and that the murder of Karnamaya Monger and forty-seven babies had already quietly faded into oblivion.

I have seen it before. The abortion cartel wields a lot of political power and they have never been afraid to use it.

A notable example was a long and complex case in Kansas, where Phill Kline, a former State Attorney General who later served as Johnson County District Attorney, filed 107 criminal charges against Planned Parenthood in Overland Park. The media and the Democratic administration of then-Gov. Kathleen Sebelius worked overtime to vilify Kline to the point that everyone forgot about Planned Parenthood's alleged crimes that were related to the commission of illegal late-term abortions and falsifying evidence to cover their crimes. To protect the abortion business, the media and abortion-supporting politicians ginned up a false narrative to distract from any wrongdoing that may have been committed by Planned Parenthood. The story became all about Kline and his "crusade" to access women's "private medical records" so he could "shame" them. That false narrative cost him two re-election bids in Kansas.

It was ludicrous, but the intensive media campaign was so coordinated and aggressive that it worked spectacularly. All charges against the abortion facility were dropped.

But it couldn't be left at that. His political enemies, including the majority of Kansas news outlets, believed Kline had to pay for his audacious attempt to prosecute Planned Parenthood, so no one would ever dare attempt such a foolish thing again.

An abortion clinic attorney filed an ethics case against Kline that resulted unjustly in his law license suspension. Kline was literally run out of Kansas and remains in exile in Virginia where he teaches law to Liberty University students, waiting for the truth to vindicate him. The "abortion distortion" won out over truth.

I did not want to see the Gosnell case end up like that. Just to let the Philadelphia District Attorney Seth Williams know that people were in fact watching, I would occasionally ask Operation Rescue's supporters to email him demanding criminal charges be filed.

Then, on January 14, 2011, about a year after the grand jury was empanelled, its long silence was finally broken.

CHAPTER 6

GRAND JURY PRESENTMENT

When the news finally came, it was in a flurry of fast-paced developments. On the night of January 18, 2011, police raided the Mantua home of Kermit Gosnell and took him into custody after a grand jury issued hundreds of indictments against him and nine of his employees.

Their mug shots, which were available to the public the next morning, made it look like they were rousted out of bed and taken into custody. Some of the women's much shots, which are never flattering, depicted the red, swollen eyes of a person that had been crying.

But not Gosnell's. His mug shot showed a serene smile, almost a smirk, that gave the impression he was not concerned in the least.

District Attorney R. Seth Williams released the stunning 281-page grand jury report illustrated with color photos taken by law enforcement. It was accompanied by a 63-page presentment, which summarized the grand jury's reasoning behind the extensive list of recommended charges.

I could hardly believe the vast and powerful case that had just revealed. Nothing even close to this scale of a prosecution had ever taken place against an abortionist and his staff in America before.

The presentment stated, in part:

Gosnell and his staff operated the clinic in a reckless and criminal manner. Karnamaya Mongar died as a result. She was overdosed with a narcotic illegally dispensed by Gosnell's unlicensed, untrained, and unsupervised employees, at his direction, in his absence. This dangerous and criminal practice was routine at Gosnell's clinic.

Our investigation revealed that the criminal conduct of Gosnell and his workers extended beyond the drug violations to nearly every aspect of the clinic's operations. Gosnell routinely and deliberately killed babies born alive by severing their spinal cords with surgical scissors, and encouraged his employees to do the same. He performed illegal abortions after the 24th week of pregnancy, often falsifying gestational ages to disguise his criminal conduct. He employed unlicensed and unskilled workers, including bogus doctors, to treat unsuspecting patients.[1]

Even that statement was just a foreshadowing of the grisly details that were to come.

The full list of charges brought by the grand jury was impressive.

Kermit Gosnell, who was 69 at the time of his arrest, was considered the man in charge with the most culpability. Upon his arrest, another search of his residence uncovered $240,000 in cash stashed in a closet in his daughter's bedroom. This made Gosnell a flight risk. Because of this, he was denied bail.

In all, Gosnell was charged with having committed 39 different crimes, often multiple times, for a total of 395 counts, including eight counts of murder. The following is a complete list:

Murder (Karnamaya Mongar), 3rd degree, 18 Pa.C.S. § 2502(c)
Murder, drug delivery resulting in death (K. Mongar), 18 Pa.C.S. § 2506
Controlled Substances Act, 35 P.S. 780-§113(f)(30), F-1
Controlled Substances Act, 35 P.S. 780-§113(f)(14), F-1
Conspiracy (Controlled Substances Act), 18 Pa.C.S. § 903, F-1
Solicitation (Controlled Substances Act), 18 Pa.C.S. § 902, 2 counts, F-1
Hindering Apprehension or Prosecution, 18 Pa.C.S. § 5105(a), F-3
Obstructing Administration of Law, 18 Pa.C.S. § 5101, M-2
Murder (Baby Boy A), 18 Pa.C.S. § 2502
Murder (Baby Boy B), 18 Pa.C.S. § 2502
Murder (Baby C), 18 Pa.C.S. § 2502
Conspiracy (Murder of Baby C), 18 Pa.C.S. § 903, F-1
Solicitation (Murder, Baby C), 18 Pa.C.S. § 902, F-1
Murder (Baby D), 18 Pa.C.S. § 2502
Conspiracy (Murder of Baby D), 18 Pa.C.S. § 903, F-1
Solicitation (Murder, Baby D), 18 Pa.C.S. § 902, F-1
Murder (Baby E) 18 Pa.C.S. § 2502
Murder (Baby F), 18 Pa.C.S. § 2502
Conspiracy (Murder of Baby F), 18 Pa.C.S. § 903, F-1
Murder (Baby G), 18 Pa.C.S. § 2501

Conspiracy (Murder of Baby G), 18 Pa.C.S. § 903, F-1
Solicitation (Murder of Baby G), 18 Pa.C.S. § 902, F-1
Conspiracy (murder, generally), 18 Pa.C.S. § 903, F-1
Infanticide (Baby Boy B), 18 Pa.C.S. § 3212, F-3
Infanticide (Baby Girl A), 18 Pa.C.S. § 3212, F-3
Abortion at 24 or more weeks (33 counts), 18 Pa.C.S. § 3211, F-3
Conspiracy (Abortion, 24 or more weeks), 18 Pa.C.S. § 903, F-3
Informed consent violations (310 counts), 18 Pa.C.S. § 3205, M-3
Abuse of Corpse (5 counts), 18 Pa.C.S. § 5510, M-2
Theft by deception (10 counts), 18 Pa.C.S. § 3922, M-1
Conspiracy (Theft by deception), 18 Pa.C.S. § 903, M-160
Controlled Substances Act (Massof), 35 P.S. 780-(§113(f)(30), F-1
Controlled Substances Act (Massof), 35 P.S. 780-(§113(f)(14), F-1
Conspiracy (Controlled Substances Act), 18 Pa.C.S. § 903, F-1
Corrupt Organizations, Racketeering, 18 Pa.C.S. § 911(b), F-1
Corrupt Organization, Conspiracy, 18 Pa.C.S. § 911(b)(4), F-1
Corruption of Minors (3 counts), 18 Pa.C.S. § 6301, M-1
Obstructing Administration of Law, 18 Pa.C.S. § 5101, M-2
Tampering with or Fabricating Evidence, 18 Pa.C.S. § 4910, M

***

Lynda Williams, 42, was charged with murder in the first degree for killing at least one born-alive infant and murder in the third degree for her part in the death of patient Karnamaya Mongar and was held without bail. In all she was charged with 12 crimes with a total of 24 counts. Here is a full listing of her charges:

Murder (Karnamaya Mongar), 3rd degree, 18 Pa.C.S. § 2502(c)
Murder, drug delivery resulting in death (K. Mongar), 18 Pa.C.S. § 2506
Controlled Substances Act, 35 P.S. 780-§113(f)(30), F-1
Controlled Substances Act, 35 P.S. 780-§113(f)(14), F-1
Conspiracy (Controlled Substances Act), 18 Pa.C.S. § 903, F-1
Murder (Baby C), 18 Pa.C.S. § 2502
Conspiracy (Murder of Baby C), 18 Pa.C.S. § 903, F-1
Conspiracy (murder, generally), 18 Pa.C.S. § 903, F-1
Abortion at 24 or more weeks (13 counts), 18 Pa.C.S. § 3211, F-3
Conspiracy (Abortion, 24 or more weeks), 18 Pa.C.S. § 903, F-3
Corrupt Organizations, Racketeering, 18 Pa.C.S. § 911(b), F-1

Corrupt Organization, Conspiracy, 18 Pa.C.S. § 911(b)(4), F-1

***

Sherry West, 51, was charged with one count of murder in the 3rd degree for her part in the overdose death of Karnamaya Mongar. Her bail was originally set at $2 million. Her charges included:

Murder (Karnamaya Mongar), 3rd degree, 18 Pa.C.S. § 2502(c)
Murder, drug delivery resulting in death (K. Mongar), 18 Pa.C.S. § 2506
Controlled Substances Act, 35 P.S. 780-§113(f)(30), F-1
Controlled Substances Act, 35 P.S. 780-§113(f)(14), F-1
Conspiracy (Controlled Substances Act), 18 Pa.C.S. § 903, F-1
Tampering with or Fabricating Evidence, 18 Pa.C.S. § 4910, M-2
Tampering with records, 18 Pa.C.S. § 4104, M-1
Hindering Apprehension or Prosecution, 18 Pa.C.S. § 5105(a), F-3
Obstructing Administration of Law, 18 Pa.C.S. § 5101, M-2
Conspiracy (murder generally), 18 Pa.C.S. § 903, F-1
Abortion at 24 or more weeks (1 counts), 18 Pa.C.S. § 3211, F-3
Conspiracy (Abortion, 24 or more weeks), 18 Pa.C.S. § 903, F-3
Corrupt Organizations, Racketeering, 18 Pa.C.S. § 911(b), F-1
Corrupt Organization, Conspiracy, 18 Pa.C.S. § 911(b)(4), F-1

***

Adrienne Moton, 33, was charged with one count of murder for one of the larger babies born alive during abortions done at Gosnell's "House of Horrors" and was held without bail. She was charged on five counts:

Murder (Baby D), 18 Pa.C.S. § 2502
Conspiracy (Murder of Baby D), 18 Pa.C.S. § 903, F-1
Conspiracy (Murder generally), 18 Pa.C.S. § 903, F-1
Corrupt Organizations, Racketeering, 18 Pa.C.S. § 911(b), F-1
Corrupt Organization, Conspiracy, 18 Pa.C.S. § 911(b)(4), F-1

***

Steven Massof, 48, a foreign medical school graduate that never received a medical license in the US, was charged with twelve counts, including two murder charges related to snipping the necks of two babies who were born alive during late-term abortions. He also caught federal drug charges for selling a large number of prescriptions. He was, thankfully, held without bail on the following charges:

Murder (Baby F), 18 Pa.C.S. § 2502
Conspiracy (Murder of Baby F), 18 Pa.C.S. § 903, F-1
Murder (Baby G), 18 Pa.C.S. § 2502
Conspiracy (Murder, of Baby G), 18 Pa.C.S. § 903, F-1
Conspiracy (Murder generally), 18 Pa.C.S. § 903, F-1
Controlled Substances Act, 35 P.S. § 780-113(f)(30), F-1
Controlled Substances Act, 35 P.S. § 780-113(f)(14), F-1
Conspiracy (Controlled Substances Act), 18 Pa.C.S. § 903, F-1
Theft by deception, 18 Pa.C.S. § 3922 , M-1
Conspiracy (Theft by deception), 18 Pa.C.S. § 903, M-1
Corrupt Organizations, Racketeering, 18 Pa.C.S. § 911(b), F-1
Corrupt Organization, Conspiracy, 18 Pa.C.S. § 911(b)(4), F-1

***

Elizabeth Hampton, 51, received four charges related to lying to law enforcement agents and the grand jury. Her bail was set at $250,000.

Obstructing Administration of Law, 18 Pa.C.S. § 5101, M-2
Hindering Apprehension or Prosecution, 18 Pa.C.S. § 5105(a), F-3
Perjury, 18 Pa.C.S. § 4902, F-3
False Swearing, 18 Pa.C.S. § 4903, M-2

***

Eileen O'Neill, 54, another unlicensed medical school graduate, was charged with six crimes for a total of 14 criminal counts. Her bail was set at $1 million.

Theft by Deception (9 counts), 18 Pa.C.S. § 3922, M-1
Conspiracy (Theft by Deception), 18 Pa.C.S. § 903, M-1
Corrupt Organizations, Racketeering, 18 Pa.C.S. § 911(b), F-1
Corrupt Organization, Conspiracy, 18 Pa.C.S. § 911(b)(4), F-1
Perjury, 18 Pa.C.S. §, 4902, F-3
False Swearing, 18 Pa.C.S. § 4903, M-2

***

Tina Baldwin, 45, was charged with three criminal counts, one related to allowing her 15-year old daughter, Ashley, to work long hours into the night administering sedation and assisting in abortions. Baldwin was held on $150,000 bail.

Corrupt Organization, Racketeering, 18 Pa.C.S. § 911(b), F-1
Corrupt Organization, Conspiracy, 18 Pa.C.S. § 911(b)(4), F-1
Corruption of Minor, 18 Pa.C.S. § 6301, M-1

***

Pearl Gosnell, 49, was Gosnell's wife at the time of her arrest. Taking full advantage of spousal immunity, she never testified at her husband's trial.

Abortion, 24 or more weeks, 18 Pa.C.S. § 3211, F-3
Conspiracy (Abortion, 24 or more weeks), 18 Pa.C.S. § 903, F-3
Corrupt Organization, Conspiracy, 18 Pa.C.S. § 911(b)(4), F-1

***

Maddline Joe, 53, was charged with one criminal count that was later dismissed. Joe never made an appearance during Gosnell's trial and her name was not even mentioned. She was held on $250,000 bail for the following charge:

Corrupt Organization, Conspiracy, 18 Pa.C.S. § 911(b)(4), F-1

***

On the morning after the arrests, District Attorney Williams held a press conference where he detailed the horrifying case against Gosnell and his accomplices.

"I am aware that abortion is a hot-button topic," he said. "But as district attorney, my job is to carry out the law. A doctor who knowingly and systematically mistreats female patients, to the point that one of them dies in his so-called care, commits murder under the law. A doctor who cuts into the necks severing the spinal cords of living, breathing babies, who would survive with proper medical attention, is committing murder under the law."[2]

These were tough words, but words that were backed up by a voluminous grand jury report, which told us more than we could have asked.

CHAPTER 7

GRAND JURY REPORT

"**N**ow, this next story comes with a strong word of caution. The details are gruesome. You won't want young children to watch," warned CBS news anchor Katie Couric as she introduced a story about the grand jury report.[1]

Of the case, conservative news commentator Glenn Beck said, "It is filled with details that make Hannibal Lecter look like Mother Theresa."[2]

The grand jury report was published online in a full-color PDF file that anyone could download and read. Since it was released on a Friday, I downloaded and printed my copy and spent the weekend pouring over the pages.

"This is a case about a doctor who killed babies and endangered women," it began.[3]

Then there was this caveat:

Let us say right up front that we realize this case will be used by those on both sides of the abortion debate. We ourselves cover a spectrum of personal beliefs about the morality of abortion. For us as a criminal grand jury, however, the case is not about that controversy; it is about disregard of the law and disdain for the lives and health of mothers and infants. We find common ground in exposing what happened here, and in recommending measures to prevent anything like that from happening again.[4]

The report went on to describe in detail the Gosnell's Women's Medical Society, a filthy office that "reeked of animal urine, courtesy of the cats that were allowed to roam (and defecate) freely."

There was filth, blood, and trash everywhere. Medical equipment was broken or unused. The emergency exit was cluttered with debris and padlocked, despite the part it played in a woman's death, as will be discussed later. Fetal remains were scattered about in cabinets, in freezers, in the basement.

"It was a baby charnel house," the report stated.

Throughout the pages of the grand jury report there were pictures, published in color, depicting the conditions. There was the rusty, torn abortion table that eventually made a starring appearance at Gosnell's trial. Other photos showed boxes and black trash bags full of biohazardous material stored in the basement and red bags of baby remains packed into a freezer. A dust-covered oxygen tank with corroded tubing looked like it was a refugee from a decade long past.

Then there was the color-coded sedation chart belonging to 15-year old Ashley Baldwin, made to help her remember the drug dosages she was ordered to give laboring women so she didn't overdose or kill someone.

The employees' competency levels were no better than the condition of the facility. There were unlicensed medical school grads posing as doctors. There were unlicensed and unqualified workers dispensing sedation and other drugs. And it was all done for profit. Because his staff was unqualified, he could pay them well below the going rate for competent medical staff.

One of Gosnell's employees explained how it was that Gosnell gathered together such a collection of motley souls to run his abortion clinic. Tina Baldwin testified that certification did not matter to Gosnell. He told his workers that there was a "grandfather clause where if you–since he's a doctor and he taught you, you could be automatically whatever it is he taught you to be. You could be certified because he taught you to do that."[5]

The grand jury report went on to describe how things were done at what they referred to as Gosnell's "criminal enterprise."

During the day, Gosnell's clinic served as a "pill mill." Folks would come in, pay cash, and walk out with prescriptions for Oxycontin or some other controlled substance that was abused by the "patient," shared with friends, or sold on the streets.

Of course, Gosnell never engaged in this behavior himself. He left that for his hapless minions who, for a fee, liberally dished out the pre-signed prescription forms that Gosnell left at his clinic. It's no wonder the police thought Gosnell's clinic was a front for the sale and distribution of illegal drugs that flooded the streets of Philadelphia.

But the drug side of Gosnell's business was not the focus of the grand jury. That was left for the federal authorities. This grand jury had a grislier task; investigating the abortion side of Gosnell's criminal enterprise.

Their investigation found that Gosnell was all about doing the abortions that others wouldn't touch, primarily because they didn't want to risk engaging in illegal conduct. But for Gosnell, laws regarding parental consent, waiting periods, and fetal age limits were no hurdle. For a price, anyone could get an abortion at the Women's Medical Society.

If a woman was too far advanced into her pregnancy, the ultrasound results were simply falsified. Curiously, Gosnell routinely recorded the standard age of 24.5 weeks in medical records for the babies that were too big to be aborted legally. He did not seem aware that his favored gestational age, no matter how big the babies were, was still over the legal limit.

Cutting corners and spending a minimum of time and effort on each risky late-term abortion was a way for Gosnell to maximize profits.

The grand jury report described his approach to late-term abortions this way:

> But the illegal abortion business also posed an additional dilemma. Babies that big are hard to get out. Gosnell's approach, whenever possible, was to force full labor and delivery of premature infants on ill-informed women. The women would check in during the day, make payment, and take labor-inducing drugs. The doctor wouldn't appear until evening, often 8:00, 9:00, or 10:00 p.m., and only then deal with any of the women who were ready to deliver. Many of them gave birth before he even got there. By maximizing the pain and danger for his patients, he minimized the work, and cost, for himself and his staff. The policy, in effect, was labor without labor.[6]

There remained, however, a final difficulty. When you perform late-term abortions by inducing labor, you get babies. Live, breathing, squirming babies. By twenty-four weeks, most babies born prematurely will survive if they receive appropriate medical care, but that was not what the Women's Medical Society was about. Gosnell had a simple solution for the unwanted babies he delivered: he killed them. He didn't call it that. He called it "ensuring fetal demise." The way he ensured fetal demise was by sticking scissors into the back of the baby's neck and cutting the spinal cord. He called that "snipping."[7]

When Gosnell wasn't available, his staff snipped the necks. He trained them how and told them that was how these things were done. Over the years, hundreds of snippings occurred. However, Gosnell knew full well that this practice was illegal, so he destroyed most of the files, leaving no way to prosecute those cases.

While Gosnell otherwise took few measures to conceal the majority of his illegal conduct, he knew there were some things would raise suspicion even among his gullible and poorly educated staff. For the really big abortions, Gosnell would do them on Sundays with the assistance of only his wife, Pearl. While six- and seven-month abortions were common at clinic, the Sunday abortions exceeded that age.

Amazingly, the grand jury report included photos of Gosnell's snipping victims. With all the public backlash we hear about how horrible pro-life activists are to show photos of disfigured or dismembered abortion victims, it was surprising to see the photos of Gosnell's victims in full color published in such an official document. But there was more than surprise. There was heartbreak.

Baby Boy A looked no different in size to any other newborn. He had opaque skin, brown hair, and feet that appeared larger than those of my own daughters when they were born. He laid with his legs tucked under his chin on a bloody blue chux pad in a plastic shoe-box container into which he barely fit. It was estimated that he was at least thirty-two-weeks' gestation, maybe later. This was the child that Gosnell joked was large enough to "walk me to the bus stop."

Another photo depicted a baby girl with a full head of dark brown hair and beautiful, soft features. For size perspective, her body was stretched out, with a seamstress' measuring tape entangling her limbs. There were no visible signs of trauma, and if I had not known any better, I might have thought that she was napping.

But the last baby photo showed only the little boy's upper back and neck area. There was a gaping wet slit in the back of his neck where scissors had pierced his skin and muscles and sliced his spinal cord. I couldn't help but gasp when I first saw the remarkably bloodless wound, but what I saw next was even more horrific. It was the feet. Floating in a clear liquid in three plastic containers that resembled urine specimen cups were severed feet from very large aborted babies. They were lined up like trophies on a shelf.

Who could do such a thing and why? It was inconceivable to me what would prompt this mutilation. Just the thought made me shudder. There was no medical reason severed feet to be kept. None whatsoever. It was an act reminiscent of the behavior of serial killers who commonly take trophies from their victims, but I doubted if many were as grisly as these tiny, perfectly formed feet.

That was only the beginning of the evidence against Gosnell and his misfit co-defendants. The grand jury report also detailed case after case of harm his shoddy abortion practice inflicted on women unfortunate enough to become his patients. Those incidents Gosnell took aggressive measures to cover up.

One woman, for example, was left lying in place for hours after Gosnell tore her cervix and colon while trying, unsuccessfully, to extract the fetus. Relatives who came to pick her up were refused entry into the building; they had to threaten to call the police. The family members eventually found her inside, bleeding and incoherent, and transported her to the hospital, where doctors had to remove almost half a foot of her intestines, damaged by Gosnell's sloppy abortion procedure, in order to save her life.

There were times Gosnell would fail to remove all of the fetal parts, but would send women home thinking everything was fine. Some nearly died. Others received emergency hysterectomies to prevent them from dying.

One time a woman suffered convulsions and fell off the abortion table. Her head took a hard blow as she hit the floor. Not only did Gosnell refuse to call an ambulance, but he kept the person that accompanied the woman from leaving the clinic or calling 911 for help.

Assistants who had no idea what they were doing were tasked with administering sedation. They often dangerously drugged women into senseless stupors.

Disposable surgical equipment was used and reused. Instruments that could be sterilized weren't. So unsanitary were the surgical implements at the Women's Medical Society that by using them, the staff unwittingly spread venereal diseases from one woman to the next.

If there was one thing the grand jury report made clear, it was that Gosnell's shoddy practices were illegal and extremely unsafe, especially for the poor women of color who were particularly targeted by his carelessly deficient abortion business.

Only white women were treated better, which seemed strange since Gosnell himself was a Black man. When his predominately black clinic workers questioned why the white women got preferential treatment, he told them simply, that it was "the way of the world."

***

One woman who found out firsthand the dangers of Gosnell's illegal cut-rate abortion operation was 41-year old Karnamaya Mongar, who died of a drug overdose during her late-term abortion, which was done amid squalor and without working emergency equipment. The only exit that could accommodate a gurney was blocked with junk and chained shut, as a photo from the grand jury report illustrated. More details about her tragic death were to come out later in heart-wrenching testimony during the trial.

The report also contained of list of Gosnell's primary employees and how they fit into the day-to-day operations of the facility after 2000. This was helpful in understanding the grand jury's narrative, even though some of them were never arrested or charged when Gosnell and nine others were taken into custody in 2011.

Latosha Lewis was employed by Gosnell for eight years. She attended a vocational training institution for eight months, but received no certification that qualified her to perform the tasks that Gosnell assigned her. Those tasks, which were primarily done outside Gosnell's presence or supervision, included ultrasound exams, drawing blood, administering Cytotec (a drug that causes strong uterine contractions) and intravenous medications, and even delivering babies. She assisted in abortion procedures and took care of women in the recovery room. She also collected money from patients.

For these duties, Lewis was paid $7.00 per hour, time and a half for overtime hours, and $20 bonuses for each second-trimester abortion she assisted. She later got a raise to $12.00 per hour, but Gosnell, being the cheap bastard he was, cut corners where ever he could, certainly without regard for such inconveniences as labor laws. Therefore, Lewis' raise disqualified her from receiving overtime pay, even though she frequently worked long hours.

Lewis stopped assisting with abortions in 2008 and quit working the late-night to early morning shift. However she was the one who conducted the pre-exam on Karnamaya Mongar. Lewis was still working for Gosnell during the February 18, 2010 police raid on Women's Medical Society.

Tina Baldwin was employed by Gosnell for nine years, but was uncertified as a medical assistant until the last year of her work at the Women's Medical Society. She essentially performed all the same duties as Lewis until 2005 when she moved to the receptionist desk and began overseeing the medical workers and "making sure everybody else did what they were supposed to do" —that is, until the police raid shut the clinic down.

Baldwin understood that she was not qualified to perform many of the tasks that Gosnell assigned her, including administering Cytotec and Restoril to second trimester patients, as well as ultrasounds, administering IV drugs, and conducting ultrasounds. However, she not only continued to do them but also supervised others she knew were also unqualified.

Baldwin is perhaps best known for allowing her 15-year old daughter, Ashley, to work long hours after school and on school nights (sometimes to as late as 1:00 or 2:00 am), medicating and otherwise assisting with abortion patients.

Kareema Cross was employed by Gosnell for three and a half years, but stopped working for Gosnell in 2008. She essentially performed the same tasks as Lewis and Baldwin. As Lewis and Baldwin moved away from involvement in the surgical abortions, the responsibility for that unpleasant task fell more and more to Cross. She had a stormy relationship with Gosnell and photographed the frightfully appalling conditions that existed at the clinic prior to Karnamaya Mongar's death, which had motivated Gosnell's first attempt at making the clinic more presentable, if not clean.

Ashley Baldwin was Tina Baldwin's teenaged daughter who started working for Gosnell in 2006. Ashley was an apparently intelligent girl who learned quickly to administer sedation and assist with abortion procedures, conduct ultrasounds, and deliver babies who arrived before Gosnell began his late-night shift. Ashley often worked 50-hour weeks in addition to attending high school full time. She was present at the clinic the night Karnamaya Mongar died.

Sherry West worked for Gosnell from 2008–2010 when the police raid shut down Gosnell's "House of Horrors." She was completely unqualified to conduct medical duties and was perhaps one of the most dangerous of Gosnell's workers. She worked essentially as a medical aid, conducting ultrasounds and administering drugs, including IV sedation, to women. She was allowed to administer drugs pretty much at will, without necessarily consulting Gosnell. She was also supposed to monitor women during recovery. She was paid about $8–$10 per hour in cash "under the table" and off the books. She was also working the night Karnamaya Mongar died from a drug overdose during an abortion.

Lynda Williams worked for Gosnell from 2008 until the clinic was closed. She previously knew Gosnell from having worked with him at LeRoy Brinkley's abortion clinic, the Atlantic Women's Medical Services, in Delaware. Williams was hired at first just to clean instruments, to the extent they were ever cleaned, but before long, she was conducting ultrasounds, sedating patients, administering vaginal doses of Cytotec, and assisting in the birth of babies, all in Gosnell's absence.

Williams teamed with Sherry West and, together at the clinic, the pair ran amok over patients, whom they essentially terrorized when Gosnell was not present. It was Williams that administered the lethal drugs that took Karnamaya Mongar's life. Williams continued to work for Gosnell until the Women's Medical Society was, mercifully, shut down by authorities

Elizabeth Hampton worked for Gosnell on and off. She was Pearl Gosnell's foster sister. She was also the common-law wife of the clinic's handyman, James Johnson. Hampton generally answered phones and did cleaning around the clinic. Exactly what she cleaned and how well she cleaned it was a matter of some debate at Gosnell's trial, since there was little evidence that anyone cleaned anything. Hampton was present when Karnamaya Mongar came to Gosnell's clinic for her fatal abortion and was still in Gosnell's employment at the time the clinic closed down.

Adrienne Moton was a young lady acquainted with Gosnell through his niece. She once lived briefly with the Gosnell family. Like everyone else hired by Gosnell, she was completely untrained and unqualified to conduct medical duties. Nevertheless, she worked the late-night shift, assisting with abortions and sometimes even snipping the necks of babies that were born alive, as Gosnell had taught her to do.

Randy Hutchins was the only licensed worker at the Women's Medical Society. He worked for Gosnell for a time in the 1980s, but was terminated after he stole from his boss to pay for a cocaine habit. He returned to work for Gosnell in July 2009, in order to work off his debt. He told the grand jury, "I really didn't get paid." Hutchins conducted "pain management" on Gosnell's patients, and his name appeared on Karnamaya Mongar's chart as the one who inserted laminaria dilators into her cervix the day before her death.

Maddline Joe was a seventeen-year employee of Gosnell's who worked primarily as the office manager. Her duties appeared to be mostly administrative and included payroll, handling insurance forms, and filing reports on abortions that were required under the Abortion Control Act.

Anna Keith was Kermit Gosnell's aunt. She worked for him until her retirement in 2007 and served as his office manager.

Jennifer Leach, 28, had an unusual relationship with Gosnell. At age 17, Leach was a patient of Gosnell's and later was supposed to provide "psychosocial counseling" for patients one day per week. Despite having a time card at the clinic, her employment situation was sketchy, and she admitted that she often did not report for work. Leach also raised eyebrows after she admitted to having an "on and off" affair with Gosnell that ended only the week before Leach testified before the grand jury.

Pearl Gosnell, Kermit's third wife, was licensed in cosmetology. She had been raised in the same foster family as Elizabeth Hampton and considered her a sister. Pearl told the grand jury that she came to the clinic about "every other day" with supplies such as "paper towels, toilet paper, cleaning supplies, soap." But Pearl had another duty. She assisted Gosnell with the abortions on women far advanced into their pregnancies, primarily on Sundays when the rest of the staff was off. While Pearl told the grand jury that she was certified to "take temperatures and blood pressure," she could not produce any evidence of such certification.

Two others employed by Gosnell were passed off as licensed physicians. They were Eileen O'Neill and Steven Massof.

O'Neill told the grand jury that she held a "graduate medical training license" in Louisiana during the late 1990s when she worked a "side job" at an abortion clinic owned by Gosnell's friend and associate, Leroy Brinkley.

O'Neill's testimony was somewhat contradictory and tended to minimize her work hours and duties at the Women's Medical Society. She said she was more of a "volunteer" who was paid "gas money" in cash, sometimes as little as $200 per month. She testified that she never "treated" patients and only saw them under Gosnell's supervision. She indicated that her primary duties were doing paperwork. However, the grand jury described this as a "sham" and noted the testimony of Kareema Cross and Steven Massof, who both confirmed that O'Neill saw patients every day before Gosnell arrived at the clinic, and that she routinely diagnosed their conditions and prescribed medications on her own.

Steve Massof was a 1998 graduate of St. George's University Medical School on the Caribbean island of Grenada. He was certified to work within the constraints of a residency program, but could find no US program that would accept his suspicious degree.

He was employed by Gosnell from July 2003 to June 2008, and performed the duties of a licensed physician for which he received $300 per week. At first, Massof treated non-abortion patients, diagnosing their conditions and prescribing drugs. But soon, he became involved in the abortion side of Gosnell's business, where he conducted abortions as late as the third trimester.

Massof was paid a bonus of $30 for each second- or third-trimester abortion he performed.

Massof did abortions the way Gosnell trained him. He falsified the ultrasound reports for babies over twenty-four weeks, administered sedation, delivered babies, cut umbilical cords, and delivered placentas, then snipped the spinal cords of the babies that were born alive.

In the report, the grand jury noted that several agencies and groups became aware of Gosnell's frightening practices at the Women's Medical Society, but did nothing due to a political climate that discouraged investigations of abortion-related businesses.

Just the day after the death of Karnamaya Mongar, Gosnell had applied for membership to the National Abortion Federation, probably in an attempt to make his chop shop appear safe in the event anyone ever questioned Mongar's death.

Gosnell ordered the clinic cleaned up. Latosha Lewis and Gosnell's wife, Pearl, rushed to clean the clinic, to the extent they could. New lounge chairs replaced the bloody ones in the recovery area and the walls were freshly painted.

Gosnell even re-hired one of his former employees, a registered nurse named Della Mann. But Mann's employment was a sham and was only for the purpose of convincing an NAF evaluator that a legitimate registered nurse was overseeing patient care. Mann worked for only four days, which coincided with the NAF facility review.

The NAF boasts of its high facility standards, and insists its members need no other oversight. However, in my own experience investigating and researching NAF facilities, I have found their "standards" to be among the worst, some of which I witnessed firsthand.

I was working with Operation Rescue when it purchased an NAF-approved abortion facility in Wichita, Kansas, in 2006 and evicted the abortion business. When Troy took possession of the building, he and I, along with a couple of our friends, went in to take our first eager look around. The clinic was filthy. From the carpet to the walls to the ceiling, everything was worn, outdated, and dirty. Plumbing leaked. Mold grew in the ceiling where the roof chronically dripped. The electrical system was hazardously out of code. The junction box could not be closed due to the obstruction of a water pipe that extended from the water heater, which had been dangerously installed under it.

The entire office was permeated with a putrid odor. Under a dirty sink was an industrial garbage disposal that was clogged with rotting material, possibly human in origin. That sink was the source of the stench.

In the twenty-three years that the abortion business had occupied that building, never had a representative from the Kansas Department of Health and Environment ever darkened the doorway of that clinic, and it showed. However, on the window separating the receptionist from the patient waiting area, there was a proudly-displayed sticker indicating that the facility had met NAF's so-called "standards" that same year.

So when I read that the NAF evaluator rejected Gosnell's application for membership, I was surprised. I knew that if Gosnell could not meet the NAF's abysmal standards, even with a spring cleaning and the hiring of a nurse for appearances sake, it meant things there must have been worse that even I imagined. And I could imagine a lot.

The grand jury report explained that when the NAF evaluator arrived at Gosnell's Women's Medical Society, she found the place so cluttered that she could find no place to set her bag. The layout was so convoluted and confusing that she worried that patients would not be able to find their way around or out of the ramshackle building.

She also told the grand jury that she was concerned about a bedroom where Gosnell told her he allowed out-of-state patients to stay overnight without supervision. She doubted anyone could find their way to the bathroom facilities through the maze of narrow, junk-filled hallways.

She was also concerned about the level of sedation that patients were given and the fact that at least one patient appeared to have been sedated by unqualified staff. As she observed several first-trimester abortions, she noticed that patients were not properly monitored. For example, she learned that oxygen levels were not monitored because the only pulse oximeter in the facility was broken.

The NAF representative also noted the clinic engaged in shoddy record keeping, violated state's twenty-four-hour waiting period, failed to meet consent standards, and "flagrantly" ignored patient confidentiality.

"The deaths of women and the countless viable babies were the direct and foreseeable consequence of the reckless and illegal manner in which Gosnell operated his clinic," stated the grand jury report.[8]

Nevertheless, despite the egregious and hazardous violations discovered by the NAF evaluator, she never bothered to report him to the proper authorities. She knew full well that women were being subjected to his dangerous practices on a daily basis, and apparently, she didn't seem to care, as long as the NAF wasn't involved.

However, the NAF certainly was not alone in ignoring and enabling Gosnell's grisly crimes. There was plenty of culpability to go around. The NAF shared it with state oversight agencies who were essentially asleep at the wheel.

So exactly where were the regulators who were tasked with overseeing Gosnell's abortion clinic? They were turning a blind eye.

CHAPTER 8

REGULATORY FAILURE

"The State Department of Health neglected its duty to ensure the health and safety of patients in Pennsylvania's abortion clinic," the grand jury concluded. In fact, those words were printed in bold capital letters at the beginning of the report's section entitled, "How Did This Go On So Long?"[1]

The report issued a scathing assessment of several regulatory failures that enabled Kermit Gosnell to murder women and their living newborns.

We discovered that Pennsylvania's Department of Health has deliberately chosen not to enforce laws that should afford patients at abortion clinics the same safeguards and assurances of qualify health care as patients of other medical service providers. Even nail salons in Pennsylvania are monitored more closely for client safety.[2]

But the report didn't stop there. The grand jury was just getting warmed up!

The grand jurors were surprised more than anything by oversight neglect as regulators stood by and enabled the deterioration of Gosnell's practice to the detriment of women and their babies. They discovered through their investigation that the Department of Health (DOH) conducted "sporadic, inadequate inspections" of Gosnell's clinic for thirteen years, then stopped inspecting it altogether in 1993.

The grand jury report took on a cynical tone when referring to the DOH officials who appeared before them for questioning:

State officials knew that Gosnell and his clinic were offering unacceptable medical care to women and girls, yet DOH failed to take any action to

stop the atrocities documented by this Grand jury. These officials were far
more protective of themselves when they testified before the Grand jury.
Even DOH lawyers, including the chief counsel, brought private attorneys
with them – presumably at government expense.[3]

The Women's Medical Society was first inspected in 1979. Inspectors checked on things like cleaning procedures, emergency preparedness, and whether women were made aware of alternatives. The DOH even noted that there was adequate room for stretchers to access the clinic, a suspicious finding that did not escape the grand jury, which remarked, "that proved not to be the case when EMTs needed to transport Karnamaya Mongar from the facility in November, 2009."[4]

Over and over, despite untrained staff, no nurse on duty, dangerously incomplete record keeping, Gosnell's lack of Board Certification, and a host of other violations, Gosnell's abortion clinic continued to qualify for the DOH's stamp of approval. DOH representatives testified before the grand jury that sometime in 1993, the abortion clinic inspection policy was changed so that facility inspections would only take place in the event of a complaint. However, when complaints were made, they were simply ignored.

An attorney representing the family of Semika Shaw requested inspection reports from Gosnell's clinic and was told there were none because there had been no complaints. That also turned out not to be true.

Another attorney representing a different patient submitted a complaint to the DOH in 1996. As a result of Gosnell's negligence, his client had endured a perforated uterus that resulted in the need for a complete hysterectomy.

Yet another complaint had been submitted by Dr. Donald Schwartz sometime in 1996 or 1997. He sometimes referred patients to Gosnell's Women's Medical Society until he began seeing them returning to him with infections of Trichomoniasis, a sexually transmitted parasite. Dr. Schwartz hand-delivered his complaint against Gosnell to the DOH, but he later told the grand jury he never heard back from them.

No facility inspection was ever conducted at Gosnell's clinic in response to any of the complaints.

"If Dr. Schwartz's complaint did not trigger an inspection, we are convinced that none would," the grand jury wrote.[5]

Another case that the DOH refused to investigate was one related to the stillbirth of a thirty-week fetus born to a fourteen-year old girl at Crozier-Chester Medical Center. Dr. Frederick Hellman, the Delaware County medical examiner who conducted an autopsy on the baby determined that the delivery had been induced during an abortion conducted by Gosnell. But according to Pennsylvania's Abortion Control Act, thirty weeks was far too late to conduct an abortion legally. He notified the DOH.

However, DOH representative Kenneth Brody told Hellman that neither the DOH nor the state medical board had any authority to act on this patently illegal late-term abortion. Brody referred Dr. Hellman to the district attorney's office, which ultimately took no action. Yet, Brody was incorrect in saying that the DOH had no authority. The information should have been treated as a complaint and a facility inspection should have been initiated along with a thorough investigation.

The grand jury report went into detail concerning the death of Karnamaya Monger during an abortion conducted by Gosnell on November 18, 2009. As I read through their narrative, I found it interesting that Gosnell reported her death to the DOH via fax on November 24, 2009, especially since I have observed that abortion businesses usually go to great efforts to conceal patient deaths from the public. The registered nurse serving as the health quality administrator received the fax and promptly reported the incident to her immediate supervisor. After some passing the buck up the ladder and a number of discussions, the DOH determined that it had no authority to investigate Mrs. Mongar's death. The matter was dropped.

I wondered what in the world the DOH *did* have the authority to investigate.

During the grand jury proceedings, several DOH representatives appeared, and of course, all of them denied culpability. One had the idea of charging Gosnell with failing to report the death in a timely manner, but the grand jury viewed that as both "absurd" and "preposterous."

It became clear that the grand jury considered Janet Staloski to be the most responsible for abortion facility oversight and the main roadblock for abortion clinic inspections at the DOH. Over and over, as she testified before the grand jury, she attempted to justify her inaction (and in some cases her overt efforts to block investigators from investigating) by wrongly claiming that the DOH had no authority.

But Staloski couldn't have stonewalled investigations without help. DOH chief counsel Christine Dutton actually had the nerve to defend Staloski's obstructions of an investigation of Mongar's death to the grand jury. Pushed as to whether the death of a woman following an abortion should have prompted more action, perhaps an investigation or a report to law enforcement, Dutton argued there was no reason to think the death was suspicious. "People die," she said.

"Even after the initial raid on Gosnell's clinic, where investigators discovered ample evidence to shut him down, Staloski balked. When DOH inspectors finally entered Gosnell's clinic in February 2010, not at Staloski's direction, but at the urging of law enforcement, Staloski seemed more annoyed than appalled or embarrassed," noted the grand jury.

There was testimony that members of the District Attorney's office badgered DOH investigators who were called to the clinic to shut him down. Staloski said in an email to one of the investigators, "I'd say we were used."

With great reluctance, the DOH shut down the Women's Medical Society in February 2010, after it could no longer justify doing otherwise. But if Staloski had her way, Kermit Gosnell would still be in business.

The grand jury also determined that "Pennsylvania's abortion regulations, written by the Department of Health, are totally inadequate to protect the health and safety of women at abortion clinics."

After the Gosnell raid, the DOH was finally forced to change their policy and began once again to inspect abortion clinics in Pennsylvania.

The grand jury's additional findings related to DOH negligence and other oversight agencies follow:

Assuring the safety at abortion clinics has been a low priority for Pennsylvania's DOH for decades.

State Department of Health inspectors refused to share information with law enforcement.

Pennsylvania's Department of State neglected its duty to discipline a doctor engaged in unprofessional conduct.

Pennsylvania Department of State attorneys failed to investigate the death of 22-year old Semika Shaw whose death was caused by Gosnell's recklessness even after having been told of Gosnell's illegal practices.

In 2009, another Department of State prosecutor closed – without any investigation – a complaint that Gosnell acted recklessly in perforating another woman's uterus, cervix, and bowel.

The Department of State only pursued allegations aggressively when the case was very public, or when the complainant knew somebody.

The Departments of Health and State did not work together to protect the public.

Anyone trying to file a complaint found it hard to file a complaint with the state.

The Department of State complained of inadequate police powers, but failed to use the ones they had.

The Philadelphia Department of Public Health also ignored alarming warnings about Gosnell's practice, including ignoring two nurses' complaints.

The Philadelphia Health Department's Environmental Engineering Section failed to follow through after receiving a complaint in 2003 about aborted fetuses stored in an employee refrigerator.

Fellow doctors who observed the results of Gosnell's reckless and criminal practices failed to report him to authorities.[6]

The report concluded that state and local agencies bore culpability for the death and mayhem at Gosnell's clinic. They knew of problems, and if they had acted within their authority, they could have prevented it all from continuing.

"Had state and local officials performed their duties properly, Gosnell's clinic would have been shut down decades ago," the grand jury stated. "Gosnell would have lost the medical license that he used to inflict irreparable harm on women; to illegally abort viable, late-term fetuses; and to kill innumerable babies outside the womb."

I knew that regulatory failure was not something confined to Pennsylvania. Over the decades of researching and documenting abortion abuses, first with my own organization, the California Life Coalition, and later with Operation Rescue, I discovered the most difficult in a host of challenging tasks required to bring an abortionist to justice was the matter of enforcement.

Over and over again, abortionists we knew *for a fact* were breaking the law or committing some other egregious act, were either allowed by oversight agencies to get away scot-free or were given just a slap on the wrist, even when complaints were filed that contained complete, credible documentation.

That is known as the "abortion distortion." If the same conditions existed involving a non-abortion provider, there would be hell to pay, but when an abortion provider was involved, agencies all over the country were more than likely to look the other way.

The Gosnell case, along with the grand jury's indictment of state agency corruption, finally began to change all that. A tectonic shift was coming. This was the pivotal first moment when Americans were forced to look at what the pro-abortion chant, "abortion on demand without apology," really looked like.

It looked like Kermit Gosnell.

The grand jury made extensive recommendations to correct the lapses and negligent practices of state agencies, noting that it was a political climate created by those at the top that allowed Gosnell's practice to degrade into what could accurately be described as a murder mill.

But the grand jury stopped short of holding those criminally accountable for turning a blind eye to abortion abuses.

It is not our job to say who should be fired or demoted. We believe, however, that anyone responsible for permitting Gosnell to operate as he did should face strong disciplinary action, up to and including termination. This includes not only the people who failed to do the inspection, the prosecuting, and the protecting, but also those at the top who obviously tolerated, or even encouraged the inaction.

The Department of State literally licensed Gosnell's criminally dangerous behavior. DOH gave its stamp of approval to his facility. These agencies do not deserve the public's trust. The fate of Karnamaya Mongar and countless babies with severed spinal cords is proof that people at those departments were not doing their jobs. Those charged with protecting the public must do better.

Whatever else R. Seth Williams does in this life, he stands tall as a courageous hero for taking on a crooked bureaucracy and for overcoming the corrupt political climate that rewarded state workers that looked the other way and frowned down any attempt to prosecute an abortionist that was breaking the law. He stood tall for Karnamaya Mongar and her family. He stood strong for the babies whose necks were callously snipped and whose dismembered feet were kept by a deranged serial killer as trophies. But ultimately, he stood for justice.

All this new information from the grand jury report emphasized something we had been saying for years: the abortion cartel was running amok over the lives and health of women without sufficient oversight.

This prompted us to join with our friend, Rev. Patrick J. Mahoney, Director of the Washington, DC-based Christian Defense Coalition to issue a press release calling for a federal investigation and Congressional hearings to get to the bottom of a number of abortion scandals that we knew to have plagued the US in recent months.

"The illegal and dangerous practices discovered at Gosnell's 'house of horrors' are not isolated incidents," said Operation Rescue President Troy Newman. "We know for a fact that many of the violations discovered at Gosnell's mill exist at abortion mills nationwide. There is a health care crisis in this country that must be immediately addressed to bring an end to the epidemic of abortion abuses inflicted on women and their babies."[7]

In addition to the Gosnell case, we asked for investigations into the following:

- New Jersey abortionist Steven Chase Brigham illegal bi-state late-term abortion scheme. An investigation into a botched abortion in September 2010, uncovered that Brigham was operating an illegal late-term abortion ring that spanned two states. Police raided his Maryland clinic and discovered the bodies of thirty-five late-term babies that were illegally aborted.[8]

- Utah abortionist Nicola Riley, Brigham's associate, was an accomplice in his criminal abortion scheme, which was exposed when Riley seriously botched an abortion on one young patient at Brigham's illegal late-term abortion mill in Elkton, Maryland. Her suspicious behavior at the emergency room, where the woman was transported in the back seat of Brigham's rental car, led to their illegal operation being uncovered. Operation Rescue discovered she lied about a previous felony conviction and incarceration in order to fraudulently obtain a medical license.[9]

- Massachusetts abortionist Rapin Osathanondh was convicted and jailed in September 2010 for manslaughter in the abortion death of Laura Hope Smith. Osathanondh lacked trained staff and emergency equipment to save Laura's life after she suffered a reaction to anesthesia. Operation Rescue worked closely with Laura's mother, Eileen Smith, to bring Osathanondh to justice.[10]

- California abortionist Andrew Rutland was what only could be described as an abortion quack who had previously had his medical license revoked for incompetence, then restored under dubious circumstances. He was accused by the state medical board of homicide in the botched abortion death of Ying Chen, who died after an abortion in the back room of a dirty acupuncture clinic in San Gabriel Valley. Rutland surrendered his medical license February, 11, 2011, in order to avoid murder charges.[11]

- Kentucky abortionist Hamid Sheikh, whose medical license was revoked amid revelations that he was running a "hellish abortion operation," was scheduled to go to trial February 8, 2011 on four counts of fraud for bilking Medicaid out of fees for services he did not render. Sheikh avoided trial by taking a plea bargain in that case.[12]

- Nebraska late-term abortionist LeRoy Carhart was supposedly under criminal investigation by the Nebraska Attorney General's office at the time after former employees who came to Operation Rescue to blow the whistle on his illegal and shoddy abortion practices in 2009. That investigation was dropped for political reasons. Based on one of my complaints, Carhart was issued an admonishment after we caught him lying on his Maryland medical license application about the true nature of his practice order to gain licensure in that state.[13,14]

This was only a brief, partial listing of the abuses we had uncovered that required further investigation and merited national headlines; however, the mainstream media mostly ignored these horrific abortion abuses, with the exception of a few limited local news reports. Due to the Gosnell case, the mainstream media's conspiracy to cover up the truth about what really happens behind the closed doors of abortion clinics was soon to be exposed.

CHAPTER 9

PLEA BARGAIN

As Gosnell's trial date approached, a very important determination was made by prosecutors. It was decided that Gosnell's case would in fact qualify him for the death penalty if convicted. This made his case take on somber new overtones.

On March 16, 2013, Judge Benjamin Learner ruled that Gosnell's workers would not be granted separate trials and that all nine of those charged with Gosnell would stand trial with him. While he agreed that testimony against Gosnell would indeed be emotional, he ruled that the family of Karnamaya Mongar should not be forced to testify more than once. This ruling was a win for the prosecution and gave them leverage to offer plea bargains to Gosnell's staff.

And it worked. One by one attorneys for Gosnell's co-defendants began accepting plea bargains. The first to plead out were Adrienne Moton and Sherry West. The others soon followed suit.

A plea bargain deal is offered by prosecutors as a means of avoiding the expense of a trial. Often prosecutors are willing to drop a less serious charge or reduce a more serious charge in order to get a defendant to agree to plead guilty. Plea bargains usually offer reduced sentences in return for cooperation.

Such was the case with Gosnell's co-defendants. District Attorney R. Seth Williams chose his prosecutors well. Joanne Pescatore was appointed the lead prosecutor to be assisted by the crusty and experienced Ed Cameron, a thirty-two-year veteran prosecutor and deputy chief of the District Attorney's homicide division.

Early on, Pescatore and Cameron offered the Gosnell co-defendants leniency at the time of sentencing in exchange for guilty pleas on selected charges and their testimony against Gosnell at the time of his trial. Lesser charges would then be dismissed.

While Pescatore and Cameron could not guarantee that the defendant would receive a lesser sentence, they promised to argue for leniency at the time of their sentencing, which would take place only after the defendant fulfilled his or her promise to testify against their former employer.

Only Pearl Gosnell was exempt from testifying as Gosnell's wife. In exchange for the hope of lenience, Pearl Gosnell pled guilty to performing an illegal abortion on a baby over twenty-four weeks and two counts of conspiracy and participating in a corrupt organization. The charges qualified her for up to fifty-four years in prison, but Judge Benjamin Learner told her she was likely to receive much less time when she was sentenced due to her cooperation with the prosecution. Pearl's defense attorneys confirmed that she would not be required to testify against her husband.

The case against Lynda Williams is a good example of how the plea deals worked. Williams, who had only a ninth-grade education, entered a plea in court on November 9, 2011, after having nearly ten months behind bars to think about it. She pled guilty to two counts of murder in the third degree. One was related to the death of abortion patient Karnamaya Mongar and the other for the death of an infant born alive during a shoddy abortion at Kermit Gosnell's now-closed Women's Medical Society.

In addition to the two counts of third-degree murder, Williams also pled guilty to conspiracy to commit murder, conspiracy to participate in a corrupt organization, and illegally administering drugs to women undergoing late-term abortions.

Williams' crimes could have netted her 200 years in prison, but her plea bargain agreement allowed for a reduced sentence in exchange for providing testimony against Gosnell. Her sentencing was delayed until after the Gosnell trial, which was still months away. Williams remained incarcerated while she awaited Gosnell's trial and her eventual sentencing.

Once Gosnell's co-defendants began to plead, I knew that this was the opportunity of a lifetime to hear first-hand testimony under oath of abortion abuses similar to those I have been complaining to authorities for years.

At that moment, I was determined to attend the trial for at least some of the witness testimony. I just knew that there these people would sing like canaries to save their own hides, and there was no telling what kind of revelations the jury was about to hear. I expected there to be sworn testimony that could be used to point out some of the horrifying practices I knew were common at abortion clinics across the country.

Meanwhile, the rest of Gosnell's co-defendants entered agreements similar to Lynda Williams', including the following:

- Adrienne Moton pled guilty to one count of third-degree murder related to killing a newborn infant and several related charges. She remained incarcerated while awaiting Gosnell's trial and her eventual sentencing.

- Sherry West pled guilty to one count of third-degree murder in the death of Karnamaya Mongar and several related charges. She agreed to testify against Gosnell. She remained incarcerated.

- Elizabeth Hamilton pled guilty to perjury. She was released on bail pending the trial.

- Steven Massof pled guilty to two counts of third-degree murder related to the stabbing deaths of two newborn infants after failed abortions. He confessed that he killed hundreds of babies in this way. He also pled guilty to numerous related charges and promised to testify against Gosnell. He also remained incarcerated while awaiting a resolution to his case.

Eileen O'Neill, however, refused to accept a plea bargain, but her charges were such that she was released on bail pending her trial's outcome. She thought the prosecution's case against her was weak, and that she would be exonerated if she took her case to trial. However, O'Neill was set to be tried alongside Gosnell after the judge denied her request for a separate trial.

If it was me, and that was my only choice, I would have taken the plea bargain like the others and cooperated with the prosecution, rather than sit next to that man at the defense table and allow his appalling acts to prejudice my case.

But O'Neill made her choice, and in the end, she may have wished she had made another.

CHAPTER 10

JURY SELECTION

Jury selection finally began on Monday, March 3, 2013, and was expected to last a week and a half. Yet already before the trial even began, the case had made an impressive impact on the abortion cartel, as my colleague and friend Troy Newman likes to call it.

This was a watershed moment for the issue of abortion. The discovery of Gosnell's horrific practices helped shed light on an abortion industry that has run amok without oversight or accountability for decades, and had already prompted significant changes in abortion laws and attitudes toward enforcement in several states.

The grand jury report had prompted changes in abortion policies, not just in Pennsylvania, but several other states as well. It exposed in no uncertain terms the political climate that created conditions where abortionists were never investigated and clinics were never inspected, no matter how egregious the allegations. It had forced resignations of those who looked the other way, even in the face of complaints related to patient deaths.

But most importantly, the case had prompted a before-unseen willingness to enforce abortion laws, not only in Pennsylvania, but also in Maryland, Delaware, and elsewhere.

Clinic inspections that followed in Pennsylvania revealed massive violations at clinics across the state. At least two abortion clinics closed rather than clean up. In Delaware, two additional abortion clinics closed that had associations with Gosnell, who was using the clinics to begin late-term abortion processes that would be finished across state lines at his Philadelphia abortion clinic.

In Maryland, the Gosnell case, along with the discovery of a similar illegal bi-state abortion operation run by the notorious Steven Chase Brigham, helped enact new clinic licensing regulations and accountability in a state where essentially no meaningful abortion laws existed.

I was looking forward to the court testimony of Gosnell's co-defendants whom I knew would have much more to tell us about this horrific case.

"The frightening thing about all this is that we know Gosnell is not unique," Troy told me. "We know other shoddy abortionists are out there running filthy operations that endanger the lives and health of women, such as the filthy abortion mill that was recently discovered and closed in Muskegon, Michigan. We know that abortionists are landing women in hospital emergency rooms at an alarming rate, and have the frantic 911 recordings to prove it. We also know that many times, babies are born alive after failed late-term abortions, then secretly murdered. We have heard many reports of this dirty little secret – and worse."

As jury selection continued without much fanfare, news broke of a significant development in the case.

On Thursday, March 5, Gosnell was brought into court from the jail cell where he had been held since his arrest in January, 2011. There, he was to engage in plea negotiations with prosecutors. Gosnell was offered a deal that would have taken the death penalty off the table in exchange for his guilty pleas.

Those plea negotiations failed. Gosnell continued to maintain his innocence and his firm belief that he would be exonerated by a jury of his peers. As he had so many times before with the lives of his patients, Gosnell was rolling the dice, but this time, for a change, it was his own life he was putting on the line.

The case was now headed for a public trial that was expected to last six to eight weeks. Eight out of nine of Gosnell's co-defendants had pled guilty and at least some were expected to testify, along with a host of law enforcement officers, medical specialists, and other witnesses. Only Eileen O'Neill, a former medical student with a history of employment at shoddy abortion clinics, would be tried with Gosnell.

A total of ten jurors and four to six alternates needed to be seated before the trial could proceed, but that would not be an easy task. This case involved three aspects that would make jury selection a difficult process, including a possible death penalty, the hot button issue of abortion, and the expected length of the trial.

Jury selection involves a process called *voir dire*, a word derived from the French, meaning "to see to speak." Jurors are questioned by counsel from both sides and the judge to determine if each perspective juror has any connections to the case or the people involved. It also probes the jurors' beliefs and opinion on subjects related to the case to ensure there is no bias.

If there is reason to believe that a potential juror is unsuitable to sit in judgment, the judge can dismiss that person "for cause." Attorneys for both sides are allowed "peremptory" challenges, meaning they can dismiss someone for no stated reason.

The voir dire process allows the attorneys involved in the case to get a feel for the people of the jury and how they might respond the defendant and arguments that will be made in court; however, once a jury is seated and the trial begins, the outcome is always unpredictable. More than one attorney that thought he should have an easy win has ended up surprised by jury verdicts. One never knows exactly what will happen when a jury is involved.

Overseeing the selection was Common Pleas Judge Jeffrey P. Minehart, who would officiate the trial. Deputy District Attorneys Joanne Pescatore and Ed Cameron questioned the jury pool for the prosecution. Questioning on behalf of the defense was done by long-time Philadelphia defense attorney Jack McMahon, himself a former prosecutor.

On the first day of jury selection for the Gosnell case, already dozens of prospective jurors had been dismissed and only three jurors were selected out of a pool of 125 Philadelphians. In all, hundreds of potential jurors were questioned during the seven-day process.

One by one, jurors who expressed strong pro-life beliefs or discomfort with the death penalty were dismissed by Judge Minehart.

On March 14, the seventh and last day of jury selection, a complication arose. Circling the block around the courthouse was a motor home emblazoned with garish images and slogans calling for the conviction of Gosnell and an end to abortion. While the driver was never identified, I knew who it was. Ron Brock was a long-time pro-life activist and friend whom I worked with for years in San Diego. He gave up everything, a permanent home and a successful business as a hair dresser, to tour the country in a motor home specially outfitted on all sides with interchangeable signs and flags to draw attention to abortion and a number of other moral issues, (depending on the venue). He can often be seen at events of importance to the matters of abortion, gay marriage, pornography, and other moral issues, driving around on the streets calling the nation to repentance.

I knew Ron was only interested in exercising his First Amendment rights and was a harmless soul, but Judge Minehart did not. With safety a big concern, extra security precautions had been taken to ensure there would be no disruptions or interferences to the trial process. Jury selection was hard enough, and now there were worries that Ron's protest might further delay it by tainting the jury pool. Already it had gone beyond the date that it was first hoped the trial could begin.

Not wishing further delay, when the last available juror was questioned and five alternates had been chosen, Judge Minehart halted voir dire.

"That's it. We're going with five alternates," he said and ordered that the trial begin with opening arguments on Monday, March 18.[1]

I was watching the case closely and wanted badly to attend. I figured I would only get to go for one week, so I tried to time my trip to coincide with the testimony from Gosnell's employees. That was tough, because I could only guess when that testimony would occur. I planned to write about each day of the trial and post my stories at our primary website, OperationRescue. org. I knew there was also the possibility my stories would be picked up by pro-life news services like LifeNews.com and LifeSiteNews.com. I hoped that they might gain the attention of other pro-life leaders and perhaps the national mainstream media, which had shown little interest in the case.

I was no stranger to the inside of a courtroom. Years ago in San Diego, California, where I first became active in the pro-life movement, activists were constantly in and out of court for mostly minor infractions trumped up by pro-abortion supporters or abortion clinic workers. I was a plaintiff in a federal civil rights case against an abortion clinic for the false arrest of myself and several others. As a defendant, I spent ten years tied up in legal actions brought by abortionists over our peaceful First Amendment protests that negatively impacted their businesses. Through this experience, I became schooled in the legal process and how a courtroom functions on both the criminal and civil sides of justice.

Some of my stories were picked up and published by an independent newspaper whose target audience was pro-life Catholics. One of those involved a lawsuit filed in the 1990s by what was then the largest abortion chain in California, Family Planning Associates (FPA), a for-profit abortion business that had contracted with Kaiser Permanente to do abortions for that prominent medical group—that is until Planned Parenthood underbid them and took the contracts for themselves. This was controversial because Planned Parenthood was a non-profit business. FPA attorneys accused of Planned Parenthood of unfair business practices that had an advantage over a for-profit business because they did not have to pay taxes.

That trial ended when the California Legislature rammed through a new law while the trial was in process that allowed non-profits to compete with for-profit businesses for contracts. The judge halted the trial and ruled in favor of Planned Parenthood. But my stories detailing the case was among my first published pieces for which I was actually paid.

When I moved from San Diego to Wichita, Kansas, in 2003 to work for Troy at Operation Rescue, I honed my journalistic skills by covering tumultuous legal events related to investigations and attempted prosecutions of late-term abortionist George Tiller of Wichita and the Planned Parenthood abortion business in Overland Park. I attended and wrote about literally hundreds of legal developments, court hearings, three grand juries, appeals upon appeals, and State Supreme Court actions.

I was present at and reported on each and every hearing related to two criminal cases filed against Tiller. I attended every day of his trial and filed nightly reports on Operation Rescue's website concerning each day's testimony and other developments.

Indeed, I knew my way around a courtroom and felt that no other pro-life activist or journalist had the depth of background I had in covering legal cases related to abortion. I believed I would notice and understand what others with less experience might not. So I planned my trip carefully to maximize the few days I thought I might have in Philadelphia to coincide with the testimony of Gosnell's co-defendants.

Even so, I did not fully realize the impact my reports from the courtroom would have or what might result.

CHAPTER 11

TRIAL BEGINS

B efore I left for Philadelphia, I put out an email to a group of pro-life leaders asking if any of them wanted to join me in attending the Gosnell trial. These were men and women that worked full time fighting abortion, so I thought there would be enthusiastic interest in witnessing the proceedings first hand.

I was wrong.

Disappointed, I was still determined to cover what testimony I could even if it meant navigating an unfamiliar city by myself without moral support from like-minded friends. One person finally did respond to my invitation to meet me in Philadelphia for what I considered to be the abortion trial of the century, even bigger than the 2009 criminal trial of the nationally known late-term abortionist George Tiller. (I had also attended that trial and reported on it daily.)

Day Gardner had a keen interest in the Gosnell case. She serves as the president of the National Black Pro-life Union based in Washington, DC. A former beauty queen and body builder, Day is an accomplished woman with intelligence to match her beauty. She is a polished and articulate media spokesperson with a background in broadcasting.

Day noted that Gosnell, a black man, primarily targeted poor urban women of color, who were particularly vulnerable to abortion because of their socio-economic situation. She was also aware that abortion businesses were prone to set up shop in poor minority neighborhoods. Blacks comprise only 13.2 percent of the population in America, yet 36.2 percent all abortions are done on black women. It seemed wrong to her that a black abortionist would be responsible for inflicting so much harm on women of the black community.

I was grateful to know there would be at least one friendly face in Philadelphia, where I expected to face at least some measure of hostility once the court security realized I was with Operation Rescue.

Judge Jeffery P. Minehart would preside over the trial, a balding, yet dapper man who was one of nine Court of Common Pleas judges that were exclusively assigned to homicide cases. Minehart was a 65-year old former prosecutor who was highly regarded in the legal community as a stern, no-nonsense judge. Despite this, at least one former prosecutor once noted that the histrionics-prone judge was "an absolute jerk," and "a real prima donna." Yet, Minehart earned the respect of both sides of the courtroom for his fairness.

In January, 2010, the *Philadelphia Weekly* published a profile on Minehart describing antics that had taken place in his courtroom that gave insight into the man.

Minehart, a former juvenile probation officer, prosecutor and defense attorney, ordered 17-year-old James Canady bound and gagged at Canady's sentencing hearing after the portly, bespectacled youth—about to be officially doomed to life without parole for murdering a Logan mom-and-pop store owner in '07—called Minehart and other court officials "fucking crackers," spat in the face of his lawyer and shouted "Fuck you!" at the judge.[1]

The same article records Minehart's reflections on that incident:

We taped his mouth, they had special tape, because we didn't want him to spit again. That was disturbing to me, that someone so young had that much anger. This was a kid who robbed a grocery store owned by a hardworking Chinese immigrant, then went back and robbed it again with a handgun, and this time killed the man. This is at 15-and-a-half years of age. Then he spits in his lawyer's face, and you just ask yourself, "How did we get to this point? How did this young fellow get to this point?"[2]

***

While Minehart would preside over the Gosnell trial, it would not be held in his familiar thirteenth-floor courtroom in the Justice Juanita Kidd Stout Center for Criminal Justice. It was expected that there would be a high interest in this sensational case, so it was moved from Minehart's cramped courtroom to a larger one on the third floor that could accompany the expected droves of media and interested public. But those droves never materialized and when opening arguments were finally heard, it was to a nearly empty gallery occupied only by two or three local reporters.

Before the trial began, Judge Minehart issued a gag order on all attorneys involved in the case and ordered them not to talk about the case with the news media. He also ruled that prosecutors could not take the jury to see the squalor that has been preserved at Gosnell's run-down West Philadelphia abortion clinic. Conditions at the clinic had only deteriorated since it was shut down in 2011. The facility was unhealthy and contaminated with who-knew-what. It was infested with mold, and the ceiling on the third floor was about to cave in. Some of the prosecutors and investigators that entered the clinic most recently had fallen sick.

Because Deputy District Attorneys Joanne Pescatore and Ed Cameron were prevented from taking the jury to the crime scene, they decided to bring the crime scene to the jury. They had equipment and furnishings from Gosnell's abortion clinic brought to the courtroom and placed in the well between the attorneys' tables and the bench, right in front of the jury box. That area of the courtroom was packed with filthy, aging obstetrical equipment.

There was a rusty abortion table with a torn bed, a dirty cloth recliner used in the recovery room, a rusty, and poorly maintained suction machine that looked like something collected from a garbage dump rather than a medical office. Everything was blood-stained and filthy. The ultrasound machine was completely outdated and the ancient defibrillator looked like something from a science fiction horror movie.

On top of one piece of equipment sat plastic shoe box full of suction cannulas. These were the narrow plastic disposable tubes (intended for one-time use) that attached to the suction machine hosing. They were used during the abortions to dismember growing babies and vacuum their remains from their mother's wombs. If that alone wasn't enough to give one pause, it was the fact that the cannulas, handfuls of them, were yellowed, warped, and brittle from use on woman after woman during abortions. These instruments were impossible to sterilize and were responsible for spreading sexually transmitted infections among Gosnell's unsuspecting patients.

It was in the eerie presence of that foul abortion equipment that the jury heard opening arguments.

For those who may not be familiar with how a courtroom operates, there is an orderly process to every trial. In a nutshell, the proceedings begin with opening arguments where first the prosecution then the defense address the jury (or judge if it is a bench trial) and summarize their case. They usually briefly describe what the jurors can expect to see and hear as evidence and testimony proceeds and will make some arguments for or against conviction.

Next the prosecution will call witnesses and introduce evidence. They put on their entire case for the jury. The defense is allowed to cross-examine witnesses and make objections or motions as appropriate, but for the most part, this is the prosecution's chance to show their evidence against the accused.

Once the prosecution rests, it is then the defense's turn to make their case before the jury, with the prosecution allowed only to cross-examine the defense's witnesses.

After the defense rests, both sides get an opportunity to address the jurors one final time in closing arguments. As with opening arguments, the prosecution goes first, followed by the defense. The prosecution will also get a short time after the defense to have the last word. This is when both sides connect the dots in their case, remind jurors of the evidence and make their impassioned pleas for conviction or acquittal.

The jury then returns to the jury room and deliberates. The jury will have an opportunity to have portions of the record reread to them or send out questions to the judge. Once a verdict has been reached, the judge is notified. In turn, the judge notified the parties who all gather in the courtroom for the reading of the verdicts.

That is a simplified explanation of how a trial works. There are more complexities to the process, of course, but that is essentially how almost every trial in America is conducted.

Back in the Gosnell courtroom, the long-awaited trial finally began in earnest on March 18, 2013. The prosecution was first up, with lead prosecutor Joanne Pescatore laying out her case for the jurors. She told them, "This was a house of horrors with kitty litter and feces . . . . Babies were treated like trash, like they weren't human . . . like they hadn't taken a breath."

She explained that Gosnell probably did 200 illegal late-term abortions before he was finally caught due to the death of his patient, Karnamaya Mongar. When investigators searched his ramshackle office located a 3801

Lancaster, they discovered the remains of forty-seven aborted babies stored in the same refrigerator where employees kept their lunches.

Pescatore described Gosnell's shoddy late-term abortion practices, telling the jury that he would induce labor with drugs with women later delivering their dead babies "on the floor, recliner, in the toilet, whereever they were." Once the babies were born, he snipped their spinal cords with scissors. When asked by his staff why he snipped the backs of the babies' necks, he told them that it was "to ensure fetal demise."

Pescatore further described how Gosnell would treat white women better than his black patients, taking more personal time with them and putting them in cleaner rooms.

When defense attorney Jack McMahon took the podium to make his opening remarks to the jury, he took the prosecution to task with intensity and emotion saying, "This is nothing more than an elitist, racist prosecution of a black man."[3]

Further brandishing inflammatory arguments before a jury comprised of both whites and blacks, McMahon accused the prosecution of having brought the case against his client only because Gosnell is black and operated an urban abortion clinic that served poor women.

Apparently, McMahon hoped that the jury didn't realize that District Attorney R. Seth Williams, who brought the charges and wrote the remarkable grand jury report laying out his case for the public, was also a black man. This made any claim that a racist motive in involved in Gosnell's prosecution completely ludicrous.

The fact that Gosnell preyed primarily on poor urban women of color also must have slipped McMahon's mind.

McMahon further attacked the allegations that Gosnell's clinic was filthy and his practices fell well below even the most minimal medical standards. The able defense attorney minimized the conditions at the Women's Medical Society, as if they did not actually betray Gosnell's insensitivity to the women who were subjected to his dangerous abortions on rusty, bloodstained tables like the one positioned behind McMahon in the courtroom as he made his arguments.

"They want to put Mayo Clinic standards in West Philadelphia," McMahon argued. "If you want Mayo Clinic standards, then you go to the Mayo Clinic."[4]

He explained that the reason the bodies of forty-seven babies were found in the clinic was due to a dispute with the hazmat company that was contracted to properly dispose of the remains.

But perhaps McMahon's most important defense of Gosnell was in his allegations that none of the babies aborted at Gosnell's clinic were over the twenty-four-week abortion limit, and that none the babies born during abortions were born alive. He attempted to convince jurors that the babies were injected with digoxin, a drug that causes the pre-born baby to go into cardiac arrest, and explained that babies never survive the injections.

McMahon told the jury that none of the babies ever took a breath and that the prosecution's case was based solely on unreliable testimony from clinic workers that the babies moved. However, the grand jury report indicated that the medical examiner found no indication that the fetuses had been injected with digoxin and the drug did not show up in the toxicology screens.

"Gosnell was not skillful enough to successfully administer digoxin, late-term babies continued to be born alive, and he continued to kill them by slitting their necks," stated the report. [5]

Finally, McMahon reminded the jury of their serious responsibility by again playing the race card as if it was a straight flush. "You will be able to stop the prosecutorial lynching of Dr. Kermit Gosnell."

CHAPTER 12

FIRST WITNESSES

The first witness to testify was FBI agent Jason Huff, who was involved in the initial raid on Gosnell's clinic in 2010. He told the jury that when he entered the Women's Medical Society, he found the clinic conditions to be disorganized and unsanitary.

There were approximately six women waiting for Gosnell to complete their abortions who were walking around the clinic in drugged stupors, but in obvious pain. Gosnell only showed up for the deliveries, while unqualified workers administered drugs and supposedly monitored the women's labors. An ambulance was called and those women were transported to a local hospital.

When he finally located Gosnell, he was shocked to that see the abortionist was eating a meal while still wearing bloody surgical gloves.

"He was still wearing his bloody latex gloves. They had some holes in them. And he ate his dinner. He didn't take them off," Huff testified.[1]

The prosecution then called the first of Gosnell's co-defendants, thirty-five year old Adrienne Moton, a medical assistant who was charged with the reduced crime of third-degree murder in exchange for her testimony against Gosnell.

Moton told the court that she moved in with the Gosnell and his third wife, Pearl, while still in high school due to "family problems" and eventually ended up working at his clinic, earning $10 an hour "under the table," despite the fact that she never received any formal medical training. At the clinic, she would administer drugs, perform ultrasounds, assist with abortion procedures, and dispose of the aborted baby remains.

Tearfully, she confessed to the jury how she cut the backs of the necks of at least ten live newborn babies, then murdered them by snipping their spinal cords, just as Gosnell had taught her to do.

Moton also testified that she took photos with her cell phone of one particularly large baby boy estimated to be about thirty weeks' gestation. That baby was referred to by prosecutors as "Baby A." He had been delivered alive into a toilet where Moton said she cut the baby's throat. Gosnell later joked that the baby was so large he could have walked him to the bus stop. News reports indicated that one female juror covered her mouth in horror as the photo of Baby A was displayed on the large projection screen directly across from the jury box.

***

After Moton's emotional testimony, the mother of that baby, ShayQuana Abrams, 21, of Chester, took the stand. She said that she was only 17 when Gosnell began her abortion at a clinic in Delaware in July 2008. He instructed her to later report to his Pennsylvania clinic to finish what he told her was the termination of her twenty-four-week pregnancy. Her aunt paid Gosnell $2,750 in cash for the abortion.

Once at the grungy West Philadelphia clinic, Abrams said she was so drugged by Gosnell's employees that she had no memory of the actual abortion procedure. However, she did testify that she thought she remembered receiving an injection, presumably of the drug digoxin, through the abdomen. This was done supposedly to ensure the baby was dead before he was delivered.

After the abortion, Abrams was sent home thinking everything was okay.

But everything was far from "okay." After the abortion, Abrams testified that her health began to deteriorate.

She suffered severe pain, heavy bleeding, nausea, vomiting, and the inability to walk. She was hospitalized for two weeks with a blood clot to the heart and a grapefruit-sized abscess on her right side. She testified that she was still suffering ill effects from the abortion, including fatigue, stress, headaches, and other health issues.

I had heard women tell of abortion experiences similar to Abrams' story over and over. While every women may not suffer exactly the same complications and aftereffects, the Abrams testimony is indicative of experiences of women seeking abortions all over the country. All too often, women are given shoddy abortions with the help of unqualified, low-wage workers. They are not always told the truth about the gestational age of their pre-born babies, especially after the first trimester. Then, when they suffer complications, these women are on their own. Based on the many horrific experiences related to me by post-abortive women, and the reams of documents substantiating abortion abuses that cross my desk each day, I was fully aware that such substandard practices and callousness toward the suffering of patients are epidemic at abortion clinics across America.

***

A physician and neonatologist at St. Christopher's Hospital for Children, Dr. Daniel H. Conway, was called to the stand due to his expertise in fetal development. He was asked about Gosnell's macabre practice of collecting the severed feet of aborted babies and displaying them in his clinic. Conway took issue with Gosnell's explanation to his staff that the feet were saved in case their DNA was ever needed.

"Do you think there is any medical reason to save the foot of a baby?" asked Cameron.

"In my practice, we would have no reason to save the foot, and I've never seen that done," Conway replied.[2]

Under cross-examination, Conway testified that sometimes the creases in the bottom of a foot can be used along with other factors to aid in determining fetal age. However, he was insistent that no physician he had ever known kept severed feet for that purpose or any other.

Conway also testified about Baby A, which had been aborted by ShayQuana Abrams. Looking at the cell phone photo of Baby A taken by Adrienne Moton, Conway testified that the baby's size was consistent with twenty-seven to thirty-one-weeks' gestation. At that age, a baby has an 85 percent chance of surviving into adulthood if born alive.

He explained that in the event one of his patients birthed a baby at that gestational age range, he would be obligated to provide medical care for that baby. He referred to Pennsylvania law, which states that if any baby twenty-two weeks or older that is born with a heartbeat, respiration, or movement, a physician is duty-bound to try to save that baby's life.

Under cross-examination, Conway admitted that it was impossible for him to tell if Baby A was born alive based only on viewing Moton's photo. McMahon seized on this to conclude for the sake of the jury that Baby A had to have been born already dead because of evidence a digoxin shot had been administered.

***

The first week's testimony concluded with prosecutors questioning an expert in anesthesiology, Dr. Andrew Herlich. He stated that Karnamaya

Mongar was drugged into a coma with Demerol until her breathing stopped. Dr. Herlich noted that Demerol has "fallen out of favor" due to the number of complications associated with the drug. The dosages given to Mongar and other women were well beyond the standard dosages.

Gosnell's defense attorney, Jack McMahon, attempted to blame Mongar for her death because she left spaces blank on her medical history forms and did not tell Gosnell of heart and lung disorders discovered during her autopsy, even though she was likely unaware of her condition. Mongar was an immigrant from Bhutan who spoke little to no English and had only been in America less than a year.

It is more than likely that Karnamaya Mongar did not understand the forms and that her daughter, who accompanied her to Gosnell's clinic, had skipped over the questions for the same reason. In that case, it seemed completely negligent for Gosnell to continue ahead with Mongar's late-term abortion, not knowing her history and lacking the ability to communicate with her. I found it despicable for McMahon to blame her for Gosnell's lack of qualified staffing, his filthy facility, and criminally substandard practices.

Despicable, but nothing new. Over and over in our dealings with women who have suffered abortion complications, we hear them describe how the abortionist either tried to tell them that the complication was their fault, or that it was all in their head.

Mark Crutcher of Life Dynamics, a pro-life group out of Denton, Texas, that also collects documentation on abortion abuses, calls this the "slut or nut" defense. Abortionists accused of negligence and malpractice often defend themselves by attacking the character of the woman they injured or by simply accusing them of being crazy. McMahon was apparently well-versed in this tactic.

Dr. Herlich's testimony also introduced to the jury the fact that Gosnell offered pain relief based on a woman's ability to pay. Those who could afford it were dangerously drugged into oblivion while those who had less money were forced to endure what can only be described as physical torture as they submitted to surgical abortions without pain relief.

What kind of man could subject a woman to that kind of inhumane barbarity?

Prosecutors would bring this up over and over throughout the trial as an illustration that for the cold-hearted Gosnell, it was about the money and only about the money, no matter who suffered.

After one emotional trial day, a reporter from the local NBC affiliate caught up with McMahon on the sidewalk and asked him if Gosnell would testify in his own defense.

"Very possibly," McMahon carefully replied, mindful of a gag order that Judge Minehart had put on all the attorneys involved in the case before the trial began. "But again, we're not sure."[3]

Witnessing Gosnell testifying in his own defense was something that I simply could not miss. I felt like a race horse locked in the starting gate waiting for the bell to ring and the gates to release. I could hardly wait to get to Philadelphia!

CHAPTER 13

STATE INSPECTOR'S DISCOVERIES

Testimony was taken in the Gosnell trial on each week from Monday through Thursday. Fridays were days off in Minehart's courtroom, leaving a three-day weekend that allowed adequate preparation time for the following week's proceedings.

When testimony resumed in the trial's second week, Elinor Barsony, a Pennsylvania Department of Health employee, took the stand. The grand jury report had devoted several pages to the fact that oversight agencies turned a blind eye to complaints about Gosnell's slovenly practices, allowing him to conduct his late-term abortion horror show for decades without inspection or accountability.

Barsony's testimony detailed the devastating effects of that "hands-off" policy.

Barsony told the court that in 2010, she conducted the first inspection of Gosnell's Women's Medical Society abortion clinic in 17 years. What she found there was appalling.

Inside, Barsony witnessed a clinic crowded with women, some of whom had been drugged senseless and left unmonitored for hours. There was no privacy at all in the clinic or during recovery from Gosnell's particularly brutal abortions.

"There was no privacy, no quiet rooms, there was nothing," Barsony testified.[1]

She indicated that the staff she questioned seemed nervous about discussing their qualifications, or lack thereof, and it was easy to see why.

The so-called "doctors" who worked for Gosnell doing abortions through every stage of pregnancy had no medical licenses. One of the workers, Lynda

Williams, who substituted for the clinic's anesthesiologist, had dropped out of school in the sixth grade.

Another worker Barsony questioned was Ashley Baldwin, a fifteen-year-old high school student, the daughter of Gosnell's employee, Tina Baldwin. Ashley routinely drugged women on Gosnell's order with a one-size-fits-all cocktail of cheap drugs without regard to the woman's height, weight, or medical history. Fearful of administering an overdose, the young teenager had constructed a cheat sheet chart to help her remember how much of the powerful sedation drugs to give to women.

Barsony also found there were no nurses on staff, as required by law.

At least two of the patients present at the clinic during the inspection had no pre-abortion counseling. The state's twenty-four-hour waiting period was ignored. The emergency exit remained locked with a padlock and blocked with broken medical equipment, even though those same conditions contributed to the death of Karnamaya Mongar the year before when paramedics could not find a way to get the tiny, overdosed immigrant out of the clinic.

Jurors were shown photographs of the some of the medications that were supposed to be administered to patients after anesthesia, most of which had expired in 2007.

The general condition of the clinic itself was as appalling as the gross lack of qualified staff and adherence to state-mandated medical safety practices. Barsony found "filthy, corroded" tubing attached to what appeared to be the suction abortion machines.

Records were not properly maintained. Barsony testified that she spent long hours inspecting the abortion clinic into the night, finishing up at 2:00 am. A few days later, Barsony returned to the clinic. The unmistakable odor of cleaning solutions permeated the air and she noticed that necessary equipment that the facility had lacked was now present. Nevertheless, Barsony asked Gosnell to voluntarily close his clinic, but he had no intention of doing so. Gosnell believed that the whole affair would soon blow over and he could return to business as usual.

Thankfully, that was not to be.

On February 22, 2010, the Pennsylvania State Board of Medicine temporarily suspended Gosnell's medical license, barring him from the practice of medicine. The following month, the Pennsylvania Department of Health took action to ensure that no other abortionist will begin operating at Kermit Gosnell's West Philadelphia abortion clinic because unsafe conditions at the facility itself posed a danger to the public.[2]

With its facility license revoked, the Women's Medical Society finally shut down for good, something that should have happened years ago.

The lack of enforcement up until that time had allowed Gosnell's abortion business to deteriorate.

I knew this to be human nature at work. When people think no one is watching, at first they will behave. Then slowly, as they begin to realize that there are no consequences for bad behavior, they will relax, and begin acting in ways they otherwise might not. Without the threat of negative consequences, most people can be counted on to misbehave, and to eventually sink into to the lowest possible level of depravity.

For example, if there was no law against theft, most people would steal left and right. The same would happen if theft was illegal, but there was absolutely no consequence for breaking the law.

We have seen that scenario played out during televised news coverage of street riots. When police stand by and allow rioters to loot and destroy property without being arrested, such as was the case during the 2015 Baltimore, Maryland, riots, soon that behavior intensifies and expands with larger numbers joining in the fray. However, when police immediately arrest those who break the law, the violent behavior is often curbed. The arrests, a negative consequence to illegal behavior, deterred others from participating in similar acts.

The degradation of conditions and practices at Gosnell's clinic was the predictable outcome of a lack of enforcement by the state. Unfortunately, there are many states to this day that refuse to exercise oversight when it comes to abortion clinics, and the outcome of that refusal is frighteningly inevitable. That means there are more "Gosnells" out there. They just have yet to get caught.

CHAPTER 14

FIGHT BREAKS OUT

Surprisingly, the next witness called by the prosecution was known to me. Dr. Timothy Rohrig, a toxicologist and director of Sedgwick County Regional Forensic Science Center in Wichita, Kansas, who was set to testify about drug levels found in the body of Karnamaya Mongar.

At first I wondered why the prosecution would use a Kansas forensic scientist instead of someone from a nearby east coast city, but I soon realized that Rohrig was the likely choice. He was one of the few toxicologists in the nation who had experience with a high-profile, politically charged abortion death case.

In 2005, an abortion patient died from complications to a botched third-trimester abortion at George Tiller's late-term abortion facility in Wichita. Having received a call on January 13, 2005 from local pro-life street activists that an ambulance had arrived at Tiller's Women's Health Care Services, I grabbed my video camera and rushed to Wesley Medical Center in time to witness the EMTs off-loading a young woman from an ambulance and rushing her into the emergency room.

While there were regular ambulance runs to and from Tiller's large, high-volume late-term abortion clinic, I knew this incident was different by the uncharacteristically panicked looks on the faces of the emergency personnel. Soon, Troy Newman received a tip that this patient had passed away.

Pro-abortion politicians, including then-Governor Kathleen Sebelius, who later served in the Obama administration as Secretary of Health and Human Services, attempted to block us from obtaining information about this case. However, I was able to discover the identity of the deceased patient, who was a nineteen-year old Down syndrome teenager named Christin Gilbert. Having her name opened up the door for us to access her autopsy report and learn more about what kind of complication led to her tragic death.

Autopsy reports usually take about six to eight weeks to complete, but the Gilbert case was anything but usual. Because of the complicated political implications related to ongoing criminal investigations of Tiller by the State Attorney General's office, along with a pending bill in the legislature that would have made abortion clinics comply with minimum safety standards, Gilbert's autopsy took eight months.

When it was finally released, it was a sanitized report, scrubbed of all references to Tiller, his abortion facility, and the physician who we believe was actually responsible for Gilbert's fatal abortion, LeRoy Carhart, another nationally known abortionist who worked for Tiller on a part-time basis.[1]

It was Rohrig that signed off on the toxicology findings included in the autopsy report of Christin Gilbert, which analyzed the amount of drugs in her system at the time of her death, including the drug digoxin, a drug that would play a prominent role in the Gosnell trial.

In Philadelphia, Rohrig was set to testify about the concentration of Demerol in Karnamaya Mongar's blood, but defense attorney Jack McMahon loudly objected to Rohrig testifying at all and challenged the science behind Rohrig's analysis of Karnamaya Mongar's blood that was drawn from her heart after her death. He argued that there was no scientific basis for Rohrig's conclusions regarding the presence of certain drugs or the levels of those drugs in her system when she died.

What started as a heated exchange between McMahon and prosecutors Joanne Pescatore and Ed Cameron over the admissibility of Rohrig's testimony soon degenerated into an angry shouting match between McMahon and Judge Jeffery Minehart. On the verge of getting out of control, Minehart ordered McMahon to sit down.[2]

McMahon motioned for a Daubert hearing. The Daubert standard is an evidentiary rule that allows testimony to be prohibited if it is based on so-called "junk science." It originated from the 1993 *Daubert* Supreme Court case, which established a standard by which judges could evaluate the credibility of expert scientific testimony, but was later expanded by subsequent cases to apply to all testimony.

Judge Minehart granted McMahon's motion, then halted the trial and dismissed the jury until he could hear further arguments related to the admissibility of Rohrig's testimony.

According to a local news report, minutes after the argument between McMahon and Judge Minehart, McMahon exchanged angry words with prosecutor Joanne Pescatore in the hallway outside the courtroom that also escalated to the point of shouting.

To determine whether to allow Rohrig's testimony, Minehart called on Rohrig to explain his findings without a jury present. After McMahon's five-hour attempt to prevent Rohrig's testimony from reaching the jury Minehart ruled that Rohrig should be allowed to testify.

The jury was returned to the courtroom in the afternoon and finally Rohrig took the stand. He testified that the toxicology results revealed that 710 micrograms-per-liter of Demerol were present in Mongar's system after her death. While the exact dosage was unclear, the results indicated she was given more than the 150 mg of Demerol that Gosnell's defense attorney claims.

"It was more than 150 and probably a lot more than 150," Rohrig told the court.

Upon cross-examination, McMahon attempted to discredit Rohrig's conclusions about the content of Demerol in Mongar's system, arguing that they were flawed because heart blood was used instead of femoral artery blood, which McMahon believed was more reliable.

McMahon fought tooth and toenail to keep Rohrig's testimony from the jury because of the damning nature of it. Mongar, 41, weighed barely 100 pounds when Lynda Williams, an unqualified and unsupervised employee of Gosnell's with just a sixth-grade education, fatally overdosed her.

Williams essentially ran amok at the clinic before Gosnell came to work. If women complained too much or generally just bothered her, Williams would inject more drugs to shut them up. It was just easier for her to get through the day without hassles if all the women were drugged unconscious or nearly so.

The maximum adult dosage recommended for Demerol is 100 mg intramuscularly every 4 hours, but Mongar was a slight woman, weighing barely 100 pounds. A legitimate physician would have modified her dosage downward based on her weight.

Another incriminating factor was the incomplete medical history for Mongar that Gosnell's staff failed to attempt to flesh out. This was problematic, since there are several contraindications for the use of Demerol, including asthma or other respiratory disease. If anyone had bothered to ask, Mongar had spent years in a primitive Afghanistan refugee camp where cooking was done over an open fire. After years of breathing smoke from those fires that were so necessary for the survival of her family, Mongar had unknowingly developed a lung disease as a result. The possibility that Mongar could have had such a disease might have been suspected, had anyone taken a proper history or stopped to learn more about her. To be on the safe side, another drug should have been used.

Rohrig's testimony about the high content of Demerol present in her post-mortem blood essentially ensured that the jury would have to hold Gosnell accountable for the avoidable death of Karnamaya Mongar.

Rohrig also testified that there were no puncture wounds consistent with an injection needle found in any of the babies' bodies recovered from Gosnell's clinic, nor was there any trace of digoxin in any of the remains. This testimony further eroded Gosnell's defense, which took the position that no baby was ever born alive at the Women's Medical Society.

CHAPTER 15

CONTROVERSIAL HOMICIDE DETERMINATION

As the second week of testimony wrapped up in the Gosnell trial, emotions ran high as another argument broke out in court between McMahon and Medical Examiner Dr. Gary Collins, who was called by the prosecution to testify concerning his decision to classify the overdose death of Karnamaya Mongar as a homicide.

Dr. Collins explained that he initially assumed that Gosnell operated a proper medical clinic and therefore concluded that Mongar's death was the result of "accidental overdose." He noted as much in an August 13, 2010, report. However, once the grand jury began to investigate, it provided Collins with additional information as it was uncovered.

Collins was shocked to learn of the wretched conditions and substandard practices to which Gosnell and his unqualified staff subjected vulnerable women. This prompted him to revisit Mongar's case, and on December 17, 2010, Collings changed the official designation of Mongar's cause of death to homicide.

"From the get go, the circumstances (described) were inaccurate—totally inaccurate. That made it sound like everything was being done above board," Collins testified concerning the limited information he was given access to when first evaluating the events surrounding Mongar's death.

"You would think you would have people trained in CPR and actual nurses, registered nurses, if you are doing abortions," Collins said. He had based his initial cause of death finding on those erroneous assumptions.[1]

Then Collins learned that Gosnell had none of those things.

Most people probably share Dr. Collin's naiveté when it comes to abortion as it is currently practiced in America. The reality is that abortion clinics across the nation are filled with untrained staff members who conduct medical duties for which they are not qualified in abortion clinics that are poorly equipped to handle the medical emergencies that occur all too often. These conditions are the rule, not the exception.

***

In recent years, the number of abortions has dropped to new lows not seen since the 1973 *Roe v. Wade* decision decriminalized abortion in America. As those numbers continue to decrease, competition for every abortion dollar has increased. In many places, raising the fee for an abortion to offset the lower volume is not an option from a business standpoint since a competing abortion business could easily undercut them and take away their customers. The solution employed by many abortion providers to this decreased demand for their services is to cut corners. Some abortion clinics can only survive by hiring the cheapest workforce, buying the least expensive medications and supplies, and decreasing certain services that were once standard.

Gosnell was the chief corners-cutter, if there ever was one. As already mentioned, he used dangerous drugs like Demerol because they were cheaper than the safer ones. He reused disposable surgical instruments meant for one-time use. He hired unqualified, needy men and women who had trouble finding employment elsewhere and paid them scant wages under the table to avoid paying payroll taxes. He took steps to ensure that his employees were so dependent on him that they could never quit.

While Gosnell was an extreme example, I have seen elements of Gosnell's shoddy practices in abortion business across the United States through volumes of inspection reports and other documents that cross my desk every day.

For example, I have seen evidence that one large east-coast abortion chain dramatically cut expenditures, even some of the most necessary costs, at the expense of women's health and safety. The chain stopped paying for routine maintenance on such necessary equipment as the autoclave, which is used to sterilize surgical equipment. When one of the facilities was infested with roaches, the clinic administrator was ordered not to call the exterminator. Employees themselves stepped in and attempted to mitigate the pest situation using money out of their own pockets.

Abortion was becoming very dangerous in America, but hardly anyone had yet realized it.

***

McMahon engaged in a heated cross-examination of Collins over his decision to amend Mongar's cause of death, promoting Judge Minehart to issue a warning. McMahon grew angry as an agitated Collins surprised everyone in the court room when he suddenly jumped from his seat, tore off the large sheet of paper displayed for the jury that contained McMahon's version of the timeline of events leading to Mongar's death, and began scribbling his own timeline on the exhibit.

Judge Minehart stopped the witness, who later apologized to the court for overstepping. The judge cautioned the jury to "focus on the evidence, not the histrionics of lawyers, witnesses, and 'sometimes a judge,'" according to one news report.

With most of the preliminary expert witnesses out of the way, it was time for me to get to Philadelphia before the real fireworks began.

CHAPTER 16

THE JUANITA KIDD STOUT CENTER
FOR CRIMINAL JUSTICE

I deplaned at the Philadelphia airport and scanned the unfamiliar surroundings. I had been to Philadelphia once for a brief protest one evening in 2004, during what we called the "Prayer for Life Tour." Operation Rescue had joined with several other activist groups on a tour of cities in Pennsylvania and Ohio, two important swing states, in the weeks just prior to the 2004 presidential election. We had gathered at a union hall somewhere in Philadelphia to protest Democratic candidate John Kerry for his support of abortion.

But that was years ago. The Philadelphia stop had only been for a few hours in the increasing darkness of a fall evening in late October. It was as if I had never been to Philadelphia before. I took a cab to my over-priced downtown hi-rise hotel and checked in. It was early Monday afternoon by the time I was able to catch another cab downtown to the courthouse where Gosnell stood trial for murder.

I soaked in my first good look at the Juanita Kidd Stout Center for Criminal Justice. It was an impressive, modern gray building essentially indistinguishable from the other skyscrapers that crowded the Philadelphia skyline. I entered the rotating doors and found myself in a spacious foyer. A security checkpoint featured the expected x-ray machines that scanned bags for anything that might be considered a weapon similar to those found at nearly every courthouse in America these days. The officers were pleasant and I soon made my way through security and toward the bank of elevators that would take me to Judge Minehart's courtroom.

I did not know that Gosnell's trial had been moved to a courtroom that could accommodate larger numbers of members of the media and curious public, so I pushed the button for the thirteenth floor and prepared myself to step into a trial already in progress.

But what I found instead raised my anxiety level in this unfamiliar setting. Minehart's courtroom was empty. I thought for a moment that something had happened, the trial was over, and I had just missed everything. However, a note on the door soon informed me that Judge Minehart was presiding over a case in Room 304. Reassured, I headed back to the elevator and down ten floors.

I've been in some pretty ratty courthouses before, so my expectations for this big-city court weren't very high, but I was pleasantly surprised to find that the third floor was actually quite clean and beautiful, with its white polished marble floors, dark wood molding, and other federal-period appointments that reminded me I was in the historic birthplace of our nation.

A secondary security station had been set up just outside the courtroom, but no one was manning it at the time, so I cautiously made my way into the courtroom, hoping to slip in unnoticed and praying there would be a seat for me.

There was no trial in progress, but I did notice that the front of the courtroom was filled with what appeared to be furnishings and equipment from a medical office. A couple of bailiffs who were shooting the breeze in the otherwise empty courtroom stopped their conversation, turning my way with mildly annoyed expressions.

"Is this where the Kermit Gosnell trial is being held?" I asked. It had to be, I thought. What other courtroom would be filled with abortion tables and suction machines? But where was everybody?

The bailiffs were nicer than I expected them to be and told me that court was cancelled for the day because Gosnell's attorney, Jack McMahon, had caught a nasty head cold. However, he was expected to be well enough to continue the trial the next day. They suggested that I should come back tomorrow.

As I hailed another cab down on the busy, narrow street outside the courthouse, I was both disappointed and at the same time relieved. I had been looking forward to hearing testimony that day, but was glad I hadn't missed anything. I'd be back early tomorrow in plenty of time to stake out a good seat. For me, the trial was just beginning.

The next morning, I arrived at the courthouse to a very different scene. The lobby was packed with people. Two lines of individuals, from attorneys to obvious defendants reporting for court appearances, snaked through roped lines and into the security checkpoint bottleneck. I wondered how long it would take me to wind my way through and hoped I would not be late for the start of the day's proceedings.

Once through the security checkpoint, I blended into the sea of humanity that packed the cramped elevator area. I soon realized that if I politely waited my turn, I would never catch an elevator. People from all walks of life quickly shoved their way into each car as the elevator doors opened, loading them to what had to be maximum capacity. It was like seeing how many people would fit into a Volkswagen. I tamped down a rush of claustrophobia and looked for another way to be one of the lucky ones to catch a ride.

I soon learned that if I scooted along the wall, I could squeeze through the crowd right up to an elevator door. As the door opened and most of those exiting the car spilled into the hallway, I could just roll around the doorway and right into the elevator with no problems at all! After a few days, I got pretty good at catching an elevator quickly no matter how much competition there was for space.

Unlike yesterday, the small security station outside the courtroom was manned with a couple of officers. I set my purse on the table and watched as a bailiff rifled through my belongings. Then she held up my cell phone.

"Ma'am, do you have a press pass?" she asked.

No, I didn't, I replied, wondering what all this meant.

She informed me that no cell phones were allowed into the courtroom, with the exception of credentialed media. I would have to get rid of my phone if I wanted to observe the trial. I wished someone had told me that the day before and wondered out loud what I was supposed to do. The bailiff told me that there was a Marriott Hotel across the street and that sometimes the Front Desk would allow people to check their cell phones there while they attended court.

I was thankful for the information and rushed down the elevator. Dodging cars, buses, and taxis that sped down the bustling city street, I made my way to the Marriott, where I begged a favor from a nice man at the counter.

With my phone checked, I ran back into the courthouse, snaked my way through security, then rolled into the first elevator that opened, hoping I wasn't too late and that there would still be a seat for me.

The bailiff again checked my hand bag and finally I was cleared to enter the courtroom.

I was surprised once again when I realized that the observers' gallery was nearly empty. Seated dutifully in the front row behind the defense table was a man whose press pass identified him as a reporter with the NBC television news affiliate. Behind the prosecution table sat a middle-aged reporter with the *Philadelphia Inquirer* named Joe Slobodian. That was it. I laughed to myself about how I had needlessly worried about getting a seat.

I settled into an aisle seat on row two behind the prosecution table, readied my pen and notepad, and waited for the action to begin. Now I had a chance to really take in my surroundings.

It was hard to keep my eyes off the court's well that was filled with abortion equipment brought in from Gosnell's clinic. There was the rusty and torn abortion table that was pictured in the grand jury report. It looked every bit as menacing as it did in the photo. There was also a dingy plaid cloth recliner, an ancient ultrasound machine, a rolling table for equipment, and a dirty yellowish suction abortion machine. Everything looked so rusty, I thought. Then I realized what I was looking at wasn't all rust. Some of it was dried blood that seemed to be spattered on every piece of equipment in the room. I shuddered.

Then I noticed on the wall over the witness stand was a chart with rows of photos. I immediately recognized the pictures as the now-familiar mug shots of Gosnell and his co-defendants, but there were a couple of pictures I didn't recognize. I squinted in vain to read the names.

Soon, a slender, suited woman with shoulder-length brown hair entered the court room and an older gray-haired gentleman in a dapper gray suit and began flitting around the prosecution table. This was my first look at lead prosecutor Joanne Pescatore and her co-prosecutor, Ed Cameron. They causally laughed and joked as they readied for another day of trial.

At the defense table sat a woman I recognized as Eileen O'Neill, the only one of Gosnell's co-defendants to reject a plea bargain in favor of a trial. O'Neill looked older and thinner than her mug shot. Her ill-fitting bright purple shirt seemed to hang from her frame. She sat quietly facing forward, rarely looking beyond the perimeter of the defense table.

Soon, I was met in the courtroom by Day Gardner, leader of the National Black Pro-Life Union. Day's professional good looks struck me as she entered the court room and took the seat beside me. She was carefully attired in a tasteful gray skirt suit and her gorgeous long reddish-brown hair fell in perfect spirals around her shoulders. A former beauty queen, Day has the distinction of serving as Miss Delaware in 1976 and was the first African-American woman to become a top ten finalist in the Miss America pageant.

During the Gosnell trial, we became fast friends. As mentioned before, she was the only pro-life leader that offered to join me in Philadelphia. She provided me with much-appreciated insight into what it is like to be a black woman in America and issues related to abortion within the black community.

Day was particularly interested in Gosnell as a black abortionist who focused his practice on poor urban women of color. To Day, this was another example of black-on-black crime that was tearing the African-American community apart.

Jack McMahon entered the courtroom room along with O'Neill's attorney James Berardinelli. In a way, I almost felt sorry for Berardinelli, who had his work cut out for him. Who really wanted to represent a defendant that was sitting next to Gosnell, and have their case tainted with all the testimony against him? I completely understood why the rest of Gosnell's co-defendants took plea bargains in exchange for the hope of reduced sentences once everything was over.

Meanwhile, prosecutors Pescatore and Cameron were having a laugh over a joke about an exhibit they were preparing. Being deaf in my right ear, I was not able to catch the punch line of their joke, but whatever it was, I was pretty sure it was off-color, considering the nature of the exhibit. In two glasses of water on their table they had placed a synthetic cervical dilator and a cervical dilator made from a natural seaweed substance called laminaria.

These dilators resemble tampons, but are only about as wide as a pencil lead. Usually, several are placed into a woman's cervix on the first day of a late-term abortion. They absorb moisture from the woman's body and slowly expand, opening the cervix overnight wide enough to accommodate the abortion instruments that would be used to extract the baby's body, which was often removed one piece at a time. Women who are more advanced into their pregnancy may need to return to have the first round of dilators removed and a second set inserted in order to get enough dilation for a bigger baby.

But I forgot about the joke when Kermit Gosnell entered the room, escorted by a bailiff from a holding cell on the other side of a door near the defense table.

It was the first time I had seen Gosnell in person. As he entered the room, he looked around at the gallery and noticed Day and me as new faces in the courtroom. He smiled warmly at both of us, making sure he established eye contact. It was if he was trying to form a connection with us or disarm us with his "charm." Repulsed, I averted my gaze, but Day was unabashed. She locked eyes with him and stared him down.

After observing Gosnell throughout the following days, it was my impression that he truly believed he hadn't done anything wrong and that he would be exonerated. It was hard to imagine how he could be so self-assured, considering that he was accused of doing, unless he was living in a delusion of his own making.

Once Gosnell was seated, Judge Minehart called in the jury. In single file, the jurors entered the jury box located on the right-hand side of the courtroom and took their seats. They were an eclectic group that appeared to be comprised of just ordinary citizens. There were some older men and women along with a few younger ones. The jury was about equally split between blacks and whites. Yet, these ordinary people were being asked to do an extraordinary thing.

I didn't have much time to further assess them at that moment, though, because Pescatore had just called her first witness of the day.

CHAPTER 17

HOW ABORTIONS ARE DONE

D r. Karen Feisullin raised her right hand, swore to tell the truth, then seated herself in the witness box. She testified that she was a practicing OB/GYN who for the past seven years had worked in a hospital setting, but she didn't name the hospital. She then told the court why. She occasionally did "procedures," a sanitized way of saying she was an abortionist. However, a simple Google search performed later revealed that she worked at Abington Memorial Hospital in Philadelphia, so her place of employment was hardly a secret.

Feisullin testified that she does between two and four second-trimester abortions per week, 95 percent of which are for fetal anomalies. As if to justify her abortion practice, she testified that she only performs abortion in babies with "defects" up to eighteen or nineteen weeks' gestation. She testified that her department only offered abortions if a prognosis is, in their assessment, "incompatible with life" or the baby would require many surgeries after he or she was born.

That didn't make me feel any better about her participation in abortion, but in this context, I just had to let it go. I understood the prosecution would need to call an abortionist in order to put testimony on the record about how abortions are done in a "reputable" setting. It was necessary to hear her testimony in order to lay the groundwork for later proving that Gosnell's practices were dangerously outside medical standards and were in fact illegal.

Yet, Feisullin was not testifying as an expert, and thus avoided the probing questions about her qualifications that might come with that designation.

In response to questions from Pescatore, Feisullin used a pointer to explain the non-pregnant female anatomy on a chart showing a cross-section diagram of a woman's torso.

She explained to the jury what was meant by an ectopic pregnancy. That is when a fertilized egg, now called a blastocyte, implants in the wall of the fallopian tube rather than in the nourishing lining of the uterus. Such pregnancies are doomed, since the fallopian tube is incapable of stretching enough to accommodate a growing embryo. If the baby grows too big, the woman's fallopian tube will rupture, causing a life-threatening condition for the woman.

Because the ectopic baby has no future and places the mother's life in jeopardy, pro-life supporters do not consider the removal an ectopic pregnancy to be immoral. In fact, it would be immoral and unmerciful not to treat a woman suffering an ectopic pregnancy.

Feisullin then went on to explain the types of abortion. This was to help the jury develop enough of an understanding of the vocabulary and process so they could fully comprehend testimony about abortions done by Gosnell that was planned to be presented later in the prosecution's case.

A spontaneous abortion was a miscarriage that occurs naturally, Feisullin explained.

Induced abortions are done by providers using surgical techniques or abortion-inducing medications.

She told the jury that medication abortions are done using drugs called Methotrexate, misoprostol, and mifepristone. Medication abortions are done before the ninth week of pregnancy. However, Feisullin was quick to point out that such abortions have a failure rate of five percent and that anyone that did them needed to back up that could do surgery to finish incomplete abortions.

I was aware from my own research that there are over 200 abortion facilities in the US that conduct abortions only using the medication option. The vast majority of those facilities are operated by Planned Parenthood. There are no surgical abortions done at these facilities for various reasons; some for economic considerations since surgical abortions require equipment and specialized staff that can be expensive to purchase. Others do not conduct surgeries because they cannot comply with minimum standards that surgical abortion facilities must meet. In most states, an office that only dispenses abortion drugs does not have to be licensed or inspected—ever.

These medication abortion offices are not equipped to perform surgical abortions. Their abortion providers rarely qualify for hospital privileges of their own; neither do they have anyone on call to provide surgeries to that 5 percent of their medication abortion customers who will require the procedures due to incomplete abortions. Their game plan for such a complication is to tell the woman to go to the hospital emergency room. Sometimes women are even told to tell the ER staff that they are having a miscarriage, and to say nothing about their abortions. This practice means that abortion complications are not recorded, allowing the abortion clinics to continue to claim that abortions are "safe."

***

When it came to explaining surgical abortions, Feisullin described the abortion process in graphic detail, referring to several charts with a pointer to help the jury understand the dilation of the cervix and the dismemberment of the child in the womb during a Dilation and Evacuation abortion, used in the second trimester.

She discussed the process of first dilating the woman's cervix using dilators like the ones displayed on the defense table submerged in glasses of water. The dilators come in three sizes of two, seven, and eight millimeters, which are recommended for use in abortions processes taking at least two days. This allows the cervix to slowly open as the dilators absorb bodily fluids and expand. This is done to prevent tears to the cervix that can occur by trying to force the muscular aperture open too rapidly.

Feisullin cautioned that a certain skill level is required for the successful insertion of the dilators, sometimes referred to generically as "laminaria." Push too hard or too far in, and the laminaria can rupture the membranes and cause complications.

***

I listened to Feisullin's testimony with great interest. I was very familiar with this complication. It had resulted in a dramatic life-threatening medical emergency in Albuquerque, New Mexico, just a couple of years earlier. We worked closely with Bud and Tara Shaver, who had interned with us for a year at our national headquarters in Wichita, Kansas, before moving to Albuquerque, where the nation's largest late-term abortion facility, Southwestern Women's Options, was located. They hoped to employ methods they learned during their internship with us to make Albuquerque abortion-free.

Tara had requested copies of recordings and Computer Aided Dispatch (CAD) print-outs for all 911 calls placed from Southwest Women's Options over a time span of six months.

We were surprised to learn that eight such calls related to serious medical emergencies had occurred during that time frame. But one incident stood out from the rest.

On May 12, 2011, an ambulance was summoned to the late-term abortion clinic to transport a twenty-six-year old woman whose uterus had ruptured during an abortion at 35 weeks' gestation. We were shocked! Thirty-five weeks was practically full term! There is no scientific doubt that a baby born at that time will easily survive outside the womb.[1]

Tara and I filed complaints, and after overcoming strong pushback from the New Mexico Medical Board, our complaints were finally accepted and the abortionist, late-term abortion specialist Shelly Sella, was charged by the NMMB with negligence during the woman's abortion. Described only as M. L., the patient had a previous history of a recent Caesarian section delivery, making her labor high risk affair, one that is not recommended for an outpatient clinical setting like Southwestern Women's Options. The concern was that during the stress of labor, the uterus could rupture at the site of the C-section scar, which would be weaker than the rest of womb. Southwestern Women's Options was ill-equipped to handle life-threatening complications of that magnitude.

Because I was a co-complainant in that case, I flew to Albuquerque to attend the public hearing, which was expected to last two days. When abortionists and clinic workers talk, one never knows what they will say or what information they will drop that can be used to expose the truth about abuses that take place at abortion clinics. I wanted to hear the testimony for myself, in much the same way I wanted to hear the clinic workers testify at the Gosnell trial.

However, while I was in the air on my way to Albuquerque, the NMMB ordered the hearing closed to the public. When I got to the location of the hearing, a security guard literally locked the door in front of me!

Not being allowed to attend that hearing was disappointing, to say the least, but Tara was later able to obtain a full transcript of the hearing. From that we learned much more.

M. L. had traveled to Albuquerque for a late-term abortion of her thirty-five-week-old baby at the recommendation of her New York physician, who had diagnosed her baby with an abnormally large head and brain. The baby's head was estimated to be the size of a baby at forty weeks. Sella agreed to do the abortion on the basis of the "fetal anomaly" and the supposed distraught mindset of the patient.

Sella argued strenuously that obstetric standards and warnings issued by the American College of Obstetricians and Gynecologists simply did not apply to abortions. ACOG does not support the trial of labor after cesarean (TOLAC) in a non-hospital setting and prohibits the use of misoprostol to induce or augment labor in women with histories of previous cesarean deliveries.

Misoprostol, also known as Cytotec, was originally developed to treat stomach ulcers but was later discovered to have the unfortunate side effect of initiating uterine contractions in pregnant women. Misoprostol use in abortion is unpredictable and can cause intense uterine contractions.

Despite the risks, misoprostol is used in two ways during a third-trimester abortion. First it is administered vaginally to "ripen" the cervix and prepare it for the delivery of the dead baby. Secondly, it is administered buccally (between the cheek and jaw) to induce or augment labor.

Women who have had previous C-section deliveries like M. L. are at greater risk for uterine rupture during labor. Misoprostol dramatically increases that risk because of the particularly strong and unpredictable nature of the contractions it induces. That is why ACOG considers it to be too dangerous to use on these women.

Sella claimed that protocols developed by Wichita abortionist George Tiller should be used for the standard of care for third trimester abortions rather than the tougher obstetrical, ACOG standards.

However, Dr. Gerald L. Bullock, an expert witness for the Board, testified that obstetrical standards are appropriate because there is essentially no difference between the procedure used in a third-trimester abortion and an instance of a women in her third trimester whose baby has spontaneously died in the womb. Obstetrical standards are the unquestioned standard in the latter circumstance.[2]

Sella learned to do the third-trimester abortion procedure from the late George Tiller. Sella testified that she worked for Tiller at his infamous late-term abortion clinic in Wichita, Kansas, from 2002 until his death in 2009. Tiller developed the controversial abortion process and was considered the national authority on third-trimester abortions.

Not mentioned in the Sella disciplinary proceedings was the fact that Tiller faced an eleven-count petition for illegal late-term abortions brought by the Kansas State Board of Healing Arts due to a complaint I had filed that would likely have cost him his medical license, had he not been murdered by an "lone wolf" shooter in May 2009.

However, another Tiller associate that also worked with Sella in Wichita, Ann Kristin Neuhaus, did in fact have her medical license revoked in 2012 on a nearly identical petition based on my complaints. In Kansas, a second physician was required to certify that abortions after twenty-two weeks posed "substantial and irreversible harm" to the woman if she continued her pregnancy. Neuhaus had certified that eleven third-trimester abortions that were done on minor girls were medically justified for mental health reasons, even though she was unqualified and incompetent to arrive at those conclusions. It would have been impossible for Sella not to have known of Neuhaus' incompetence, which allowed Sella to conduct late-term abortions that should have been illegal, if the law had been correctly followed.

The testimony at Sella's disciplinary hearing revealed a time line of events that led to M. L.'s uterine rupture and subsequent transfer to UNM hospital for emergency surgery. It paints a graphic picture of what can go wrong when abortionists consider themselves exempt from accepted medical standards.

On the morning of May 10, 2011, M. L. arrived at Southwestern Women's Options (SWO) in Albuquerque for her first appointment. M. L. had been interviewed by a telephone "counselor" (likely an unlicensed and unqualified clinic worker) who took information about her state of mind and medical history, including her history of previous cesarean section, and relayed it to Sella and her associate, Susan Robinson, who also does third-trimester abortions at SWO. The two consulted and agreed that M.L. was a good candidate for the Induction abortion used at SWO.

On the day of M. L.'s arrival, Sella initiated "fetal demise" by vaginally injecting digoxin into M. L.'s fetus. This drug stops the baby's heart. After an ultrasound confirmed that the baby was dead, the patient's cervix was packed with laminaria, the seaweed sticks that slowly expand and dilate the cervix in preparation for labor and delivery. Sella then administered 100 micrograms of mispropstol vaginally for the purpose of "softening the cervix."

Dr. Bullock testified on behalf of the prosecution that the standard dosage of misoprostol generally used for induction of labor is 50 micrograms, half of the dosage given by Sella when there was no intention of inducing labor. Afterwards, M. L. was sent to her hotel where no monitoring of her condition occurred. Dr. Bullock considered this a serious breach in the standard of care.

Sella testified that she intended to use the frequent dosing of misoprostol along with numerous laminaria insertions and removals to prepare M. L.'s cervix for labor induction on the fourth day. Sella denied that she was inducing labor by administering misoprostol vaginally on the first day.

To that, Dr. Bullock responded, "Well, yeah, I would agree that she probably intended to soften the cervix, but whether you intend to induce labor or not, that is what it did, and the lady came back in the second day in the late evening in active labor, and you can't call that spontaneous labor. This was Misoprostol-induced labor. If the lady had stayed at home and hadn't been at the clinic, she would have never gone into labor that day."[3]

On the second day, May 11, M. L. returned to the clinic in the morning. Sella changed out her laminaria, gave her another dose of misprostol, and again sent her back to her hotel with instructions to take yet another dose of the drug at 3:00 pm. M. L. took the drug as instructed.

At about 5:00 pm that same day, M. L. returned to the clinic for another laminaria change and misoprostol dose. However, while Sella was inserting new laminaria, she inadvertently broke her bag of water.

While it is unknown exactly when M. L.'s contractions began, Dr. Bullock testified that this incident likely stimulated the onset of labor. In fact, there was great debate from expert witnesses about the times and dosages of Mispropstol and other medications administered to M. L., due to confusing medical records kept by the clinic, including some inaccurately recorded dosage times.

The onset of labor prompted M.L. report back to the clinic for a third time on May 11, near the midnight hour. Sella was forced to scrap her plan to begin labor on the fourth day of the abortion and took steps to manage M. L.'s labor in preparation for an early delivery.

Shortly after midnight on May 12, Sella checked the progress of M. L.'s cervical dilation and again administered Misoprostol. At the same time, Sella began to give her patient Pitocin, another uterine stimulant that is not supposed to be used simultaneously with Misoprostol.

It is estimated that the misoprostol was in M. L.'s system along with the Pitocin for 3 1/2 hours. Meanwhile, M. L. was given pain medication, sedated, and placed in the gurney room. She was supposed to sleep through the night in mild labor and be checked for progress again around 7 am. There was never any testimony concerning how well M. L. actually did through the night or what her pain/comfort level was during this ordeal.

The large size of the baby's head created an increased risk of uterine rupture, a fact was apparently ignored by Sella, as noted in the Board documents. M. L. had received a lower transverse incision during the surgical delivery of a previous child. That incision type is supposed to be less likely to rupture that the classical vertical incision, but even so, that did not prevent the Sella's reckless practices from inflicting harm.

In the morning of May 12, Sella removed the laminaria and checked M. L.'s cervix. Sella had intended to collapse the skull in order to make it smaller and easier to deliver. However, she could no longer feel the baby's head as she had expected. She conducted an ultrasound and discovered that the baby was now lying sideways in the womb. At that moment, she suspected that the uterus had ruptured.

Sella had an office worker call 911 and request an emergency transport for M. L. to UNM. Since Sella has no hospital privileges, she had to call one of three abortionists from the UNM Center for Reproductive Health, a stand-alone abortion clinic affiliated with the UNM Medical Center, to treat M. L. at the hospital.

It took twenty-four minutes from the time 911 was called for M. L. to arrive at the emergency room.

Once there, M. L. was rushed into surgery, where her dead baby was removed and her uterus repaired. An unknown hospital physician noted on her chart that the baby weighed 7.5 pounds. Sella vigorously disputed that assessment. She opined that the baby was never weighed and that ultrasound measurements placed the baby's weight at 5 pounds, 13 ounces. We may never know the truth.

There was little difference whether the baby weighed 7.5 pounds or just under 6 pounds. This was a baby that was the size of many full-term babies. The entire revolting discussion on the record attempting to justify the abortion of a thirty-five-week baby struck me as completely barbaric.

Dr. Bullock noted that the rupture occurred when the baby's over-sized head came down and stretched the C-section scar where the uterus was weak. The head broke through the scar and tore the uterus, forcing the baby, at least partially, into the woman's abdominal cavity.

"Well, you know, everybody was really lucky this time, because quite often, particularly the way this rupture went, it was a thousand wonders that it didn't extend another centimeter into the uterine arteries, which would have had a horrendous bleeding episode if that had happened," he said.[4]

Dr. Bullock described M. L.'s injuries and the harm done to her:

Yes, the understood harm is going to be another cesarean, a scar that went caddywhompus, the scar that went crossways . . . all the way down to the cervix, which will make it more hazardous. In fact, one of the doctors at UNM said that she should not get pregnant again.[5]

A document containing closing arguments submitted to the Board of Healing Arts by prosecutor Daniel Rubin argued that no specific national standard exists with respect to late-term abortions and that obstetrical standards should be applied in this case.

Rubin concluded that Sella's testimony and that of her expert witness confirmed that all third-trimester abortionists are engaging in horrifically dangerous procedures with drugs that should not ever be used in settings where there is no access to immediate emergency care.

In the end, despite the recommendation of the NMMB to discipline Sella for gross negligence for breaching the standard of care during her treatment of M. L., Sella was inexplicably cleared. Today, she continues to abort babies in New Mexico throughout all nine months of pregnancy.

M. L.'s unfortunate experience has revealed a shadowy world of regulatory gaps where abortionists make up their own rules. In the abortionist's world, time-tested standards of care do not apply; they simply make up their own. This is a world where abortionists can subject women to dangerous practices that would not be tolerated in any other medical discipline, yet demand that they treated like they walk on water.

That was never illustrated better than in the case of Kermit Gosnell.

By filing complaints against Sella, Tara and I had attempted to close those gaps and return the abortionists to the real world of medical accountability and ethics.

I had high hopes that the Gosnell case would succeed where the Sella case had failed. The grand jury report had excoriated Pennsylvania state oversight agencies for failing to monitor Gosnell and turning a blind eye to his horrific practices. I hoped a conviction would finally force change and bring down the abortion culture that covered up for abortionists who hurt women or violated the law.

Back in the Gosnell courtroom, Karen Feissulin was helping to do just that, whether she realized it or not, by delivering her most damaging testimony against Gosnell.

***

Feisullin was directed by Pescatore to the ultrasound machine that had been brought into court from Gosnell's abortion facility. She testified that the machine was so old that she had never seen one like it. She put on latex gloves before hesitantly picking up the abdominal and vaginal transducers, which were discolored and filthy. Feisullin testified that she was not even sure where the monitor screen was on the ancient device.

Feisullin then discussed ultrasound images found in three of Gosnell's abortion charts. Each record contained two to three sonogram images showing babies that would have been between twenty-four weeks six days and thirty weeks gestation, keeping in mind that the upper limit for abortions under the Pennsylvania Abortion Control Act is twenty-three weeks six days.

She testified that the ultrasound photos were of such poor quality that she could not see the anatomical landmarks needed to ensure that the measurements of the babies' heads were accurate. In one case, the measurement of the baby's head diameter, which is used to determine gestational age, was done in the wrong place, making the measurement completely unreliable.

In the record of each case, Gosnell had written in his own hand that each baby was twenty-four weeks six days, no matter how big the heads measured. This was an indication that he did not have an accurate view of the legal abortion limit in Pennsylvania, which was twenty-four weeks. None of the images contained fetal ages that were within the state's legal limits.

By adding a week, Gosnell unwittingly incriminated himself in the commission of illegal late-term abortions.

Gosnell's defense attorney disputed a diagram of the Partial Birth Abortion process that was shown in court. Partial-birth abortions were outlawed nationally after the Supreme Court upheld the 2003 Partial Birth Abortion Ban Act in 2007. McMahon insisted that the process shown in the diagram was still legal while Feisullin testified that it was not. She insisted that because that procedure was illegal, she would not use it. McMahon strenuously objected, prompting one of several sidebar conferences that day.

A sidebar conference is when attorneys approach the judge's bench and make arguments concerning points of law off the record, and hopefully out of earshot of the jury.

Minehart allowed the testimony to stand and Feisullin continued her testimony describing a late-term abortion.

According to Feisullin, first, a baby in the late second or third trimester would be terminated through the intrauterine injection of potassium chloride, which kills the baby immediately, or digoxin, which can take up to twenty-four hours to end the baby's life. Laminaria are inserted and the woman is given misoprostol to aid in the dilation process.

Once the woman is ready for her abortion to be completed, she is hooked up to monitors that track her blood pressure, respiration, and oxygen saturation levels. Once the patient is anesthetized, the laminaria is removed and metal dilators are used under ultrasound guidance to complete the dilation process.

A disposable cannula or curette like the ones sitting in a plastic box in the courtroom would be attached to the suction machine and the amniotic fluid surrounding the now-dead baby would be drained away in order to decrease the risks of the fluid, creating an embolism in the woman.

Feisullin was shown the box of reused, yellowed curettes that had been found at Gosnell's clinic and testified that plastic was never reused since it is impossible to sterilize due to the porous composition of the plastic.

Feisullin described how the baby would then be removed piece by piece using forceps. However, if for some reason the baby was born alive (Feisullin had never seen that happen) the baby would need to be treated as a patient.

"As a human being, you would offer comfort care," she testified, noting that resuscitation measures could also be taken.

Feisullin also noted that as the pregnancy advanced, risks would increase. Since the uterine wall thins out later in pregnancy as it stretches to accommodate the growing baby, risks of uterine rupture increase exponentially.

Pescatore asked Feisullin if she knew of any reason that a physician would keep in jars the severed the feet of aborted baby, as had been found at Gosnell's abortion facility.

"No, I can't think of a reason to remove feet and keep them in bottles," she testified.

That's because there wasn't a reason; not a sane reason, anyway.

CHAPTER 18

ABORTED BABIES "TESTIFY"

Crime Scene Investigator John Taggart, who had earlier testified, was recalled to the stand to discuss photos he had taken during his investigation of crime scenes at the Gosnell clinic and Gosnell's two residences. As testimony continued, photos of the bodies of several aborted babies were shown to the jury, each with a gaping wound in the back of their necks.

The babies, which varied in size but were generally smaller than ShayQuana Abrams' baby, were all intact and had the appearance of being partially mummified or dried, possibly from having been frozen for an extensive period of time in the clinic's refrigerator. The brownish-black skin had shrunk as it dried, revealing the upper spinal column that authorities say was pierced with scissors in order to snip the spinal cords of newborn babies born alive during abortions by Gosnell.

Photos of the remains of Karnamaya Mongar, the woman who died as a result of an overdose by Gosnell's untrained, unqualified staff, were not shown to the jury due to an objection by Gosnell's defense attorney Jack McMahon.

Also shown were photos of babies' feet in jars, one of which had been severed just below the hip and included the entire leg. A photo of a two-inch foot severed above the ankle was shown next to a ruler.

During the gruesome display, Gosnell sat attentive but emotionless, sometimes making notes.

Other photos showed the cramped and cluttered maze of rooms at Gosnell's Women's Medical Society, graphically revealing how it earned the moniker of "House of Horrors." The three-story structure has metal poles on the top floor holding up the leaky, decaying roof. Taggart indicated that he believes the structure is unstable and that the roof will soon collapse.

Taggart pointed out the significance of each photo as it was projected onto the screen directly across from the jury box. In essence, Taggart became our tour guide as his photos directed us through the maze of cluttered hallways and cramped rooms then up and down the winding stair cases that connected the aging structure's patchwork floor plan.

There was cramped junky lab area with a sign above the sink that read, "Please do not dispose of speculums," referring to the plastic, single-use instruments that Gosnell reused to the extent that he was spreading STDs amongst his patients.

There was the dirty bathroom with a tub full of kitty litter and feces, although Taggart testified that he never saw a cat.

Narrow halls were inexplicably lined with empty milk jugs, wilted plants occupied every nook and cranny, and a dirty fish tank still held large angel fish. There was even a bedroom with a small television on the third floor.

Everywhere, there were safes scattered about. Lots of them. Gosnell did a predominately cash business, and was much more careful when it came to locking away the day's receipts than he ever was about basic sanitation.

Gosnell's clinic had two small abortion rooms that were claustrophobic, disorganized, and dirty. They were called the Monet Room and the O'Keefe Room after the cheap painting reproductions that hung in each. It was Taggart that had gathered the furniture and objects from the clinic that were displayed in the courtroom. Each piece of equipment was identified by Taggart, who didn't bother to filter is disdain over their appalling condition.

Several members of the jury rose and leaned over to get a better look at the ancient and filthy equipment and furnishings as they were identified by Taggart.

Pictures were also projected showing Gosnell's two large homes, his boat and private boat dock, and his newer model F-150 extended cab pickup truck. While his possessions were being displayed, Gosnell smiled broadly and nodded in proud acknowledgement of his possessions.

It is estimated that Gosnell made millions aborting babies while his financially struggling patients were subjected to the reuse of disposable instruments and other dangerously shoddy corner-cutting practices inflicted upon them by Gosnell and his unqualified, low-paid staff.

However, a photo of his gaudy deep purple bedroom at his Philadelphia home was revealing of the confusion with which Gosnell constantly surrounded himself. In it, belongings were strewn about and piled everywhere, and appeared much as one would expect a hoarder's house to look, resembling the general junky appearance of his abortion clinic rooms.

A crash cart was discovered under a bed in Gosnell's house and was now displayed in the courtroom. Taggart testified that there was no crash cart found inside his clinic.

A few days prior, Taggart had returned to the clinic and retrieved one final item which was also in court. It was a large garbage disposal that was under the sink in the wash room that was between the O'Keefe and Monet abortion rooms; the same washroom where he had earlier made the ghastly discovery of those jars containing the severed feet of aborted babies. When asked why the garbage disposal was brought to court, Gosnell's attorney objected, prompting yet another out-of-earshot sidebar discussion. Judge Minehart sustained the objection and Taggart was not allowed to tell the jury the significance of the garbage disposal.

However, I knew why the garbage disposal was brought to court.

After Taggart was dismissed, he sat down on the bench in front of me to observe more of the proceedings. I leaned forward and whispered, "I know why you brought the garbage disposal."

He look at me quizzically.

"I know because we have one just like it. It was in an abortion clinic we bought a few years ago," I said.

Taggart nodded. He knew what I meant.

In 2006, Operation Rescue had the opportunity to purchase a building that housed Central Women's Services, an abortion facility in Wichita, Kansas. The clinic had been struggling financially. There was no local doctor willing to do abortions for them, so they hired an older abortionist who lived in the Kansas City area. Because it took 2 1/2 to 3 hours to drive each way, the abortionist only agreed to do abortions for them one day per month. That just wasn't enough to pay the bills. The abortion business started underpaying their rent. The building owner had no patience for losing money, so he put the aging building on the market.

For years, Troy had dealt in real estate, flipping houses for extra money to support his family while he ran Operation Rescue. He was tipped off by one of his contacts that the Central building was for sale. At the time, our offices were in a double-wide trailer, which was unsuitable for our needs. I told Troy that I was all for buying the building and kicking the abortionists out.

We purchased the building through a third party. We were pretty sure that if the abortion business or owner knew it was us, they would cancel the deal. The abortion clinic was told that we could not retain them as tenants. Deeply in debt with no place to go, Central Women's Services shut down and moved out.[1]

When we finally received the keys to our new building, we couldn't wait to get inside and look around. Upon opening the door, the first thing that struck us was the stench. We followed our noses to a washroom between two small abortion rooms similar to those described by Taggart at Gosnell's abortion clinic.

Under the sink, we found the source of the reek. It was the large garbage disposal under the sink where the bottles from the suction machines were rinsed after each abortion. This disposal was from the "Bone Crusher" series. (We couldn't make that up!) It was designed for industrial kitchens that needed an efficient way to dispose of chicken and fish bones.

The garbage disposal in the former abortion clinic was clogged with a slimy substance that could be nothing except decaying human remains from the aborted babies. It had apparently been that way for some time, because in every room in the building we found cans of air freshener to tamp down the nauseous scent of death.

Gosnell had been grinding up what aborted baby remains would fit down the disposal and flushing them into the city's sewer system.

***

John Taggart described the condition of Gosnell's abortion building where metal poles held up a leaky roof and the stench of death and cat urine lingered. Those conditions had only continued to deteriorate as the clinic stood idle over the previous two years. The leaks in the roof had expanded. The ceiling and drywall is moldy and coming down. Exposed electrical wires create a safety hazard. It has become so unhealthful to enter the building that Prosecutor Joanne Pescatore told the judge that she got sick the last two times she was there. Taggart said he expects the building to fall in soon.

At the end of the day, the jury was dismissed and Gosnell was ushered in and out of the courtroom by Sheriff's Deputies.

I looked at Day and sighed. It was a lot to process. I told Day I would see her in the morning then caught a cab back to my hotel where I began to write the first of many stories to come.

ABORTED BABIES DRAMATICALLY TESTIFY AGAINST GOSNELL AT MURDER TRIAL my headline proclaimed. And so they did.

CHAPTER 19

BLOOD EVIDENCE
AND A 911 CALL

The next morning, I arrived downtown, checked my cell phone at the Marriott's front desk then began the ritual of winding my way through the security line, scooting along the wall and rolling into the elevator that would take me to Gosnell's court room.

I cleared security with no problems and settled into my favorite aisle seat in the second row behind the prosecution table. Day Gardner soon joined me. Day made a point of introducing herself to all the reporters that were in and out courtroom, which never seemed to exceed a half-dozen at any given time. It was great for her to do that. She made a wonderful media spokesperson, and her perspective was unique and compelling.

However, I was trying to keep a low profile. I was concerned that if court officials realized I was an activist with Operation Rescue, they might make things tough for me or even block me from attending the trial as the New Mexico Medical Board had done in the Sella disciplinary case.

But in any case, my cover was already blown. On a break, John Taggart had asked me where I was from. When I told him I came in from Wichita, Kansas, he asked, "Are you with Operation Rescue?"

I don't know why I was so surprised that he figured me out so quickly. After all, he is an experienced, detail-oriented crime scene investigator. But Taggart said they had been told to expect me. I remembered that I had mentioned my trip to Philadelphia to the FBI agents that come by our office from time to time, and reckoned they had told them I would be there.

But pleasantly, Taggart didn't hassle me and I was glad to know that I would be able to observe without worry of being locked out of yet another courtroom.

Taggart was the first witness of the day and was cross-examined by Jack McMahon. He testified that after he had sketched the layout of the Women's Medical Society, seized evidence, and collected samples, he returned to the location once a week to feed the fish and turtles that had been left behind and to "check on the place."

In late July, he took his evidence to the grand jury investigating Gosnell.

He testified that the photos that he took of the crime scenes were shown in court were taken about four months after the initial FBI raid.

McMahon accused Taggart of bringing to court only the equipment that was in the worst shape while leaving similar equipment that was newer or in good condition.

When prodded by McMahon, Taggart refused to say that the floors were clean or that the clinic was in good condition; however, he admitted that Gosnell did have his clinic "cleaned" and painted after Mongar's death. It didn't do much good, though, based on the photographic evidence that had been presented so far.

When the subject of the baby feet that were found in jars by Taggart came up, the prosecution dropped a bombshell.

The jars were in court and available for examination by the jury.

I think I audibly gasped when I heard that. What would be the jury's reaction to seeing those severed feet? I wasn't even sure what my own reaction would be, although I had already seen a photo that was included in the grand jury report. Witnessing such a gruesome thing in person was quite a different thing than viewing pictures.

But McMahon immediately jumped up and called for another sidebar conference, where Judge Minehart ruled that the feet would not be shown.

I was relieved and disappointed at the same time. Part of me didn't want to see them, but another part of me wanted the full extent of Gosnell's depravity to be put on display for all to see, and let the chips fall where they may. But that was not to be.

Questioning then returned to the matter of blood that was present in the clinic and even on a lot of the furnishings and equipment that were present in the courtroom. Taggart testified that blood was found throughout the clinic.

"Did you take swabs of any of the blood?" asked McMahon.

Taggart said that he did not swab the blood because there was nothing to compare it to.

McMahon saw an opening and pounced on it.

"Then how do you know it was blood and not something else?" asked McMahon who was trying to leave the impression with the jury that there was some doubt about whether Taggart actually discovered blood.

This peeved Joanne Pescatore to the point where the tension was palpable. She questioned Taggart further about the blood, allowing him to explain that the purpose of swabbing blood at a normal crime scene is to compare it to the victim or suspect's blood, but he pointed out that this was not a normal crime scene. There was no reason to swab the blood.

"If I asked you to swab the blood on the evidence in this courtroom over the break, would you do it?" she asked, prompting Taggart to answer in the affirmative.

Pescatore wasn't afraid of the findings. She showed the jury she was confident that tests would positively indicate the presents of human blood. In fact, blood really was everywhere, including on the furnishings right in front of the jury. Even an untrained eye could see that.

***

The next witness called was a paramedic with the Philadelphia Fire Department who gave testimony about his experience at Gosnell's abortion clinic when he responded to a Code Blue call for help in November 2009.

Derek Smith, a young paramedic with a two-year Associates of Arts degree, told the court that an emergency call came in around 11 pm that night, so he and his partner, Dana Kucma, rushed to 3801 Lansing to render assistance.

Smith was the first paramedic to arrive on the scene. He was taken through the maze of cluttered rooms and hallways to an abortion room where he found Karnamaya Mongar laying on an abortion table naked from the waist down with her legs still in the stirrups. She was bleeding slightly from the vagina, but was in full cardiac arrest. Mongar had no IV when Smith arrived and he was told by a staff member that she had just had an abortion. Smith said that Mongar had "flat lined," meaning there was no detectible electronic pulse in her heart with no blood circulating. Her skin was pale.

An effort was made to get information about the drugs the patient was given from Gosnell's staff, but that effort was unsuccessful. Gosnell was in the area, Smith said, but he did not offer any help.

An IV was inserted into Mongar's arm by Smith and after fifteen to twenty minutes of intervention, he was able to eventually restart her heart through the use emergency drugs, chest compressions, and a defibrillator that he bought with him. He then asked one of the firemen at the scene to find him a way out.

Mongar had to be put on a Reeves board, which is a flat board with straps and handles that must be hand-carried. This was because the gurney that normally would have been used would not fit through the cramped hallways. Extricating her from the clinic was complicated and delayed her transport to the hospital. The narrow hall leading to the back emergency door was obstructed by piles of junk, and the door was locked with a chain and padlock. Employees ran through the office searching for a key to unlock to door, but one was never found. Bolt cutters were finally used to cut the chain, so Smith was finally able to extract Mongar from the clinic.

Smith testified that no clinic employee accompanied Mongar to the clinic and that no medical file or other paperwork that may have had useful medical information was transferred to the hospital with the patient.

Mongar later died from what a toxicology witness said was an overdose of Demerol, leading to Gosnell being charged with third-degree murder in her death.

CHAPTER 20

ELIZABETH HAMPTON

Smith was the first piece of the puzzle for the prosecution in making the case against Gosnell for the murder of Karnamaya Mongar. The second piece was Elizabeth Hampton, a former employee of Gosnell's who was called to testify about her role at Gosnell's clinic and about events on the night that Mongar died.

Hampton, a heavy-set black woman in her early 50s, is the foster sister of Gosnell's wife, Pearl, and common-law wife of twenty years to James "Jimmy" Johnson, a maintenance man also employed by Gosnell, who later would give his own testimony. Hampton was arrested and charged as one of Gosnell's co-defendants in January 2011. Hoping for leniency at sentencing, Hampton was testifying as part of a plea bargain agreement with the prosecution.

She and Johnson were living in a home owned by Gosnell, whom she referred to as "Barron." Hampton explained that she received a disability check each month that she signed over to Pearl, who would take $600 in payment for rent and return the balance to Hampton in cash.

She talked about how her husband, Jimmy, came into the clinic to repair things that were broken. An item he frequently repaired was one of the abortion beds. The legs on it kept breaking. Jimmy also did odd jobs for Gosnell at his numerous other properties, including his beach house, a small apartment building, a house in Brandywine, his Mantua home, the house she lived in, and the house next door.

Hampton noted that Barron and Pearl traveled frequently and loved vacationing in Jamaica and Rio de Janeiro, Brazil.

Hampton testified that she worked for Gosnell twelve hours a day, five days a week at the abortion clinic answering phones and "cleaning," although no one could really understand what it was she supposedly cleaned. She was paid $10 an hour cash and a bonus of $20 for each second- or third-trimester abortion done during her work shift. Her bonus money would earn her an extra $60 to 80 per night. She didn't seem to like working shifts with her foster-sister Pearl, however, because when Pearl came in she would "boss everybody around."

Throughout Hampton's testimony, I noticed that Gosnell smiled warmly and attempted to make eye contact with her. I found this to be creepy, perhaps sinister in some way, as if he was trying to exert some kind of emotional control over her, as he had apparently done throughout the years.

As Hampton sat on the witness stand, she became emotional and tearful. With some difficulty, she told the court that she had worked on and off for Gosnell since 1999. Since 2002, she suffered from alcohol abuse, perhaps due to her work at the late-term abortion clinic. When she was drinking, Hampton said she tended to become violent. Thankfully, she was finally able to get clean and sober in 2006.

By now Hampton was openly weeping. She explained how she had quit working for Gosnell that year due to a dispute with him after she saw "something" at the clinic she "could not go along with."

Whatever that "something" was, it must have been unspeakably horrible and extremely traumatic. Hampton said it caused her to "fall off the wagon" and return to drinking for a time, but she eventually was able to return to the life of sobriety that she currently enjoyed.

Apparently, whatever this dark secret was that Hampton harbored obviously had been discussed ahead of time, probably with the judge, because Pescatore cautioned Hampton that she was not allowed to say what that "something" was.

It was hard to imagine, too, given the previous testimony that included severed feet, bloody murder, and squalor that would have gagged a Billy goat. But Hampton was allowed to keep her secret, and maybe that was for the best. Some things are so horrible that they should be left unsaid. Nevertheless, I confess that I remain curious about it even now.

Later, Pearl approached Hampton and asked her to come back to work at the clinic. She really didn't want to, now that she had regained her sobriety, but she felt somehow deeply obligated and guilty about saying "no." Both Gosnell and Pearl called her and pressured her to come back, but she continued to refuse until the Gosnell's served her with an eviction notice. In October 2009, she relented and returned to Gosnell's employment "to preserve her household."

When she returned to work, conditions at the clinic were worse than she had ever seen them. It was dirty. It smelled. The stench of dried blood and cat urine and feces filled the air. She said she used Febreze to try to cover the unpleasant odors, but Gosnell made her stop using the air freshener because, remarkably, he didn't like the way it smelled.

Hampton said she took it upon herself to separate the dirty tools from the "clean" ones. To help out, her husband, Jimmy, would come in and take out the trash and mop up. Even though Jimmy was Gosnell's maintenance man, he didn't fix the leaky plumbing or the porous roof.

"The leaks just kept leaking," she said.

Now somewhat more composed than she had been a few minutes earlier, Hampton continued to describe her daily duties at Gosnell's Women's Medical Society. In addition to cleaning, she answered phones, cleaned the fish tank, washed the windows, and generally acted the part of a security guard.

Her cleaning duties included the large bottle on the suction machine that would fill with blood and fetal remains during first trimester abortions. She testified that she would dump the bloody contents of the bottle into a wash sink located between procedure rooms then turn on the garbage disposal (the same one present in the court room as evidence) and grind and flush the contents down the drain, even though it was illegal in Pennsylvania to dispose of bloody remains in this way.

Often, she said, she was just there, doing as little as possible. She knew if she just showed up, she would get paid, and that was really all that mattered to her.

Hampton understood that white women were treated differently than those she described as "Afro-Americans." She said that Gosnell was friendlier to white women and allowed them to wait in "Dr. Steve's" office. She was referring to Steven Massof, who held himself out to Hampton and other staff as a licensed physician. It was later learned by Hampton that he was not. She said white women were put in Massof's office because it was a cleaner area of the clinic.

Hampton testified, "He [Gosnell] wasn't mean to Afro-Americans, but they never got in that room."

But somehow, Hampton said, it really didn't bother her that whites were treated different from black women.

Hampton clearly remembered Karnamaya Mongar, who was already in the middle of labor at the Women's Medical Society when Hampton reported for her evening shift late in the afternoon of November 20, 2009. Hampton said that she was asked by another employee, Tina Baldwin, to administer Cytotec to Mongar so Baldwin could go home at 5:00 pm.

Hampton said she found two pills in an unmarked envelope paper clipped to Mongar's chart, which contained no dosage instructions, then located Mongar in the recovery room. Mongar was sitting in a recliner without an IV. She was already in such a drugged stupor that she was unable to take the medication herself. Hampton then placed a pill between each cheek and gum then left Mongar unattended as she returned to the front desk.

The dosage was twice the recommended amount.

Sometime later, Hampton noticed a commotion in the clinic as two other employees made multiple calls to 911 while running though the building, pulling out drawers in search of the key to the back door, the only entrance that would accommodate a gurney. Hampton then went into the procedure room and saw Gosnell standing near Mongar, just looking at her as she laid on the abortion table with her legs still in the stirrups. Hamilton noticed that her head was off to the side and her mouth was open. Yet, Gosnell did not attempt to provide her any medical assistance.

Gosnell then asked Hampton bring the family members to him who were waiting for Mongar at the clinic. According to her testimony, Hampton obeyed and while blaring ambulance sirens drew closer, she escorted two women she described as Mongar's daughters to "Dr. Steve" Massof's office, which was one of the cleanest rooms in the clinic.

In the meantime, paramedics and firemen arrived and eventually transported Mongar to the hospital where she was pronounced dead.

Hampton testified that Sherry West took Mongar's chart and accompanied the ambulance to the hospital, but this testimony was in direct conflict with the earlier testimony of paramedic Derek Smith, who said no one from Gosnell's clinic accompanied them to the hospital and that no medical record was available.

Personally, I believed Mr. Smith. He had no reason to lie about the charts. But on the other hand, Hampton had great interest in making it look like they tried to care for Mongar and follow proper protocols. After all, this was a murder case, and she considered Gosnell a family member she was obligated to protect.

After the emergency responders left, Gosnell went back to work, completing several more abortions as the rest of his staff returned to business as usual.

Over the next few days, news circulated among the staff at the Women's Medical Society that Karnamaya Mongar was dead. Gosnell ordered that the clinic be cleaned from top to bottom. Hampton did an extra thorough job cleaning the surgical tools while Jimmy Johnson was ordered to paint all the walls on the first floor. Gosnell bought new blue waiting room chairs as well as new chairs for the front desk. She noted that it was unusual to have such a "big cleaning spree."

"Things get bloody in an abortion place, correct," she testified in answer to a question about the cleaning.

All this was done, Hampton thought, to impress a woman from the National Abortion Foundation who later visited the clinic.

About three months after Mongar's death, Hampton was sitting at the front desk at around 8:30 pm when the FBI and other law enforcement agencies raided the clinic just a few minutes after Gosnell had arrived for work.

Hampton testified that agents with the FBI and DEA segregated all the employees and interviewed each of them.

Frightened, Hampton admitted she lied to them to cover up for Gosnell and the rest of the staff, including herself. She told agents that as Mongar was being loaded into an ambulance for transport to a nearby hospital, Hampton spoke with one of Mongar's adult daughters. Hampton later admitted she lied when she said that Mongar's daughter spoke English very well. In truth, Mongar's daughter, also a refugee from Bhutan, spoke very poor English. Hampton said she "was storying" when she told agents that Mongar's daughter had told her that Mongar had taken "many pills" prior to going to the clinic for the abortion in an effort to self-abort her nineteen-week pre-born baby. None of that conversation actually happened. It was a vain attempt to blame Mongar for the drug overdose that killed her.

The day after the raid, the clinic opened to business as usual, like nothing untoward had ever happened. Three or four days later, while several women at the clinic were awaiting abortions, police officers came with the order for them to close.

After that, Gosnell again ordered most of his employees to once again clean and paint the clinic. He even replaced more of the furnishings. Hampton explained, "If he said to do something, we did it without questioning."

But the work to make Gosnell's dilapidated clinic appear at least somewhat respectable was a wasted effort. The Woman's Medical Society would never again open for business.

***

About a year later, Hampton was arrested and charged with perjury, repeating the lie she told to the FBI to the grand jury investigating Gosnell. She entered into a plea agreement that would have the potential to reduce her expected fifteen-year sentence in exchange for her cooperation and honest testimony against Gosnell.

Now in court, under oath with the possibility of a tough prison sentence hanging over her head, Hampton tearfully fessed up to her deception and claimed she was now telling the truth because she wanted to correct the "mess" she had made of things. She did not know what her sentence would be and was not promised anything by the prosecution. Everything depended on the quality and truthfulness of her testimony.

Since all the witnesses were not allowed to hear any other testimony, Hampton had no idea about Smith's previous testimony that impeached hers on the matter of Sherry West taking Mongar's medical record to the hospital. While I thought she might be in trouble with the prosecution, I reminded myself that each person that witnesses an event will recall things slightly differently. Hampton's fate rested in the hands of a judge who would determine an appropriate sentence after the Gosnell trial was over.

Meanwhile, a disagreement broke out between prosecutors and defense attorney Jack McMahon over exactly what Hampton had lied about. McMahon tried to convince the jury that Hampton's original story about Mongar taking pills prior to her abortion in an unsuccessful effort to self-abortion was the truth.

Judge Minehart dismissed the jury for the day, then rebuked the attorneys for not reaching agreements about such disputes prior to coming to court. Afterwards, McMahon got into a verbal confrontation with Assistant District Attorney Ed Cameron. McMahon argued he had notes taken previously that indicated Hampton lied about only part of an incident that occurred between her and one of Mongar's daughters on the night of Mongar's death. Cameron asked McMahon to produce the notes, which he could not. The two began shouting at each other until lead prosecutor Joanne Pescatore got physically between the two men loudly ordered them to "stop it!"

Judge Minehart later reminded the jury that Hampton's story about her conversation with Mongar's daughter was an admitted lie, and that Mongar never took any pills prior to the abortion.

This wasn't the last time that emotions would boil over. The most gut-wrenching testimony was yet to come.

CHAPTER 21

RAINING FETUSES

Day Gardner was upset. The testimony so far in this case was disturbing, to say the least, and exposed serious but scarcely reported problems with the abortion industry. Why wasn't there more news coverage of this trial? She decided we should hold a press conference outside the court during a noon break and call attention to the atrocities that were being uncovered in that courtroom.

Day invited Rev. Clenard Childress Jr., Founder of BlackGenocide.org to attend make comments to the media. I invited Rev. Pat Mahoney, who had probably participated in more press conferences than anyone in America over his four decades of activism. Pat always seemed to be in the middle of some major news story and no one was better at addressing controversial issues before the news media than Pat with his intelligent, articulate, and often entertaining delivery.

Also in attendance were two women who regretted their abortions. The few reporters present were drawn to those women's compelling stories and essentially ignored the rest of the speakers. I was the last to make comments, and by then the reporters already had gotten their stories and had rushed away to file them. I addressed only a handful of pro-life supporters who attended the press conference about the fact that many of Gosnell's appalling practices could be found in nearly every abortion clinic in the country.

In the end, the press conference caused barely a ripple in the dearth of media coverage of the Gosnell trial. It was a pity, too, especially after the shocking testimony that had just been heard earlier that morning when former Gosnell employee Steven Massof took the stand.

Massof's testimony concerning the inner workings of Gosnell's shoddy abortion business lasted all morning and into the afternoon. He described a chaotic office where conditions continuously deteriorated over the time he worked there.

Massof, 50, had been incarcerated since his arrest with Gosnell and seven others in 2011. He was escorted by marshalls into the court room wearing an ill-fitting green prison jumpsuit that seemed to swallow his short, thin frame. He appeared in court unshaven. His partially bald head sported a large square bandage covering what he dubiously told bailiffs was the result of a "slip on a ladder."

I thought it was much more likely that another inmate had beaten the tar out of him. That was the kind of effect he had on others. For me, his shifty-eyed mannerisms, generally creepy demeanor, and disheveled unkempt appearance, was nothing less than shudder-inducing. I instantly disliked him.

Massof spoke eerily, in a slow and deliberate manner, almost over-articulating his words. He seemed to take an odd sarcastic glee in relating the illegal activities and filthy conditions under which he worked for approximately five years. If there was remorse, it was only for having been caught.

Using his odd manner of enunciation, Massof told the court that because he faced between 180 and 880 years in prison if he was convicted on all initial counts, he had entered into plea agreements with both state and federal prosecutors. He had already pled guilty to two counts of third-degree murder related to the deaths of babies born alive after abortions. On the federal side, he had pled guilty to thirty of the numerous drug charges pending against him for dishing out illegal narcotics prescriptions. He still faced a possible sentence of 120 years in prison and up to $7.5 million in fines. He indicated that he understood his sentence would be determined by a judge based on his cooperation in testifying against Gosnell on both the state and federal cases.

I appreciated the fact that the details of Massof's plea agreements were made known to the jury ahead of time. It helped them understand the kind of unsavory character they were hearing from and could filter his testimony through that knowledge.

Massof told the court that he earned a degree in biology and chemistry and spent some time doing research in the field of immunology before attending medical school in the West Indies. After his graduation from St. George School of Medicine in Granada, Massof was unable to find a residency program that would accept him. He turned instead to the "bar and restaurant" industry to make ends meet.

Finally, Massof was introduced to Gosnell by a friend in the "pharmaceutical industry." I couldn't help but wonder if that was his smart-mouthed way of referring to an illegal street drug dealer. In any case, the two met in 2003, and Gosnell offered Massof a "residency," failing to inform him that it was not a sanctioned program. But since Massof was never licensed to practice medicine, his indignation at the apparent slight by Gosnell seemed hollow and hypocritical.

It was becoming obvious that Gosnell had a habit of seeking out employees among misfits or those in desperate circumstances. Once they were dependent upon him for their living, he would exploit them by extracting maximum work for minimal pay. Massof certainly fit the profile. He testified that he received no pay at all for his first two weeks of work for Gosnell, then received a salary of only $200 to $300 per week thereafter.

For the first couple of months of his employment, Massof shadowed Gosnell in the family practice side of his business in order to learn from Gosnell's experience. After that, he began seeing the family practice patients without supervision. After Gosnell gave Massof a signed prescription pad, Massof flippantly remarked, "I got a *lot* more patients coming to me."

Massof said he would sometimes leave patient files for Gosnell to sign, even though it was Massof that was treating them. It apparently was to give an air of legitimacy to what Massof knew quite well was his illegal practice of medicine.

But Massof wasn't the only one with a pre-signed prescription pad. He testified that Eileen O'Neill also had one and used it outside of Gosnell's presence, even though he knew she wasn't licensed to practice medicine either.

Massof testified that he had an interest in abortion and a curiosity about it. Ever drawn to the abortion part of Gosnell's business and wanting to become more involved in it, Massof began "helping move patients around" from one area of the clinic to the next. Later he began doing first-trimester procedures and eventually took on the "second tris."

Massof testified matter-of-factly that he saw over 100 babies born alive who had their necks snipped in what he said was "literally a beheading. It is separating the brain from the body."

During busy times, when the women were given drugs to induce contractions all at once, Massof discussed the chaos that often ensued. He told the court that "it would rain fetuses. Fetuses and blood all over the place."

"I felt like a firemen in hell. I couldn't put out all the fires," he said.

Massof testified that Gosnell told him that the legal limit for abortions was twenty-four weeks, but they would see women over that limit at least once a week and usually more. No one was turned away because they were too far along. Massof insisted that the latest abortion he witnesses was twenty-six weeks, but he had earlier told the grand jury that no abortions were done past twenty-four weeks.

There was the unmistakable impression that Massof simply wasn't telling the whole truth about anything. Sure, his testimony was damaging to Gosnell, but there was a real sense that Massof knew a lot more than he was telling, even while trying to save his own hide from serving over 100 years in prison.

As for the over-the-limit abortions at the Women's Medical Society, Massof explained how he was trained to manipulate the ultrasound transducer to make it appear that the baby was under twenty-four weeks. Using hand gestures to illustrate, Massof showed the court how one could raise the transducer in order to take fetal measurements on the wrong plane. Just as objects appear smaller the farther away they are, so an ultrasound image can easily be manipulated to make a fetus appear smaller, and therefore younger.

While this testimony may have surprised some, I knew this to be true. Troy and I suspected that workers employed by George Tiller at his infamous third-trimester abortion mill in Wichita, Kansas, were falsifying fetal ages in a similar way. In the fall of 2008, we were determined to prove it.

We found a volunteer who was in her twenty-fifth week of pregnancy that was willing to pose as a woman considering abortion. We sent her to Tiller's clinic, where she received an ultrasound examination. When the first measurements taken during the sonogram showed her baby past the threshold of viability, a Tiller employee threw those measurements in the trash. She then came up with a lower measurement. Shaye was scheduled for an abortion in violation of Kansas law, which set the legal limit at twenty-two weeks.

That same day, we sent her for an ultrasound at an independent business called Baby Waves, then to a hospital for a third ultrasound. All showed her pregnancy well beyond the legal limit for abortions in Kansas *except* for the second ultrasound from Women's Health Care Services, which had been clearly manipulated. We obtained copies of each ultrasound image and submitted a complaint to the Kansas Board of Healing Arts. Unfortunately, it went nowhere. The local news media refused to cover the release of our evidence that clearly proved manipulation by Tiller's staff for the purpose of breaking the law.[1]

Now, Massof was corroborating our findings under oath in court. This wasn't an issue just confined to Gosnell's Women's Medical Society or Tiller's

Women's Health Care Services. It was happening at abortion clinics all over the country; and it was as illegal as the day is long.

***

Massof testified that quit his job at Gosnell's clinic in June 2008, after a dispute with the father of Ashley Baldwin, the fifteen-year old high school student who helped with abortion procedures at the clinic. His account of his relationship with Ashley seemed suspicious, leaving me with the uneasy the impression that there was more to it than the inappropriate jesting that Massof related to the court.

Massof related an altercation he had with Ashley's father, who was supposedly angry after he found out that Massof nicknamed his daughter "Fartzilla."

"He threatened to beat me within an inch of my life," Massof said. "I ran away as fast as I could."

Massof also referred to each of the mug shots displayed on the wall of all Gosnell's employees and told the court the duties of each one.

Madeline Joe, one of Gosnell's employees arrested with him, was a receptionist that directed patients either to the family practice side or for abortions. She became the manager of the clinic, kept financial records and ordered supplies.

Pearl Gosnell, Kermit's wife, helped with what little cleaning was actually done.

Kareema Cross, who was not arrested with the others, processed blood and worked in the procedure room. Cross was set to testify later in the trial.

Adrienne Moton took vital signs, according to Massof. Tina Baldwin was a medical assistant who took vitals, processed blood, and was later promoted to a position as receptionist. Latasha Lewis was also a medical assistant who helped with abortion procedures.

Massof explained that Lynda Williams had come to Gosnell's employment from the Atlantic Women's Medical Services in Delaware, where Gosnell also occasionally worked for owner, Leroy Brinkley. Williams supposedly helped with sterilization, starting IVs, and monitoring patients in recovery.

Somewhat surprisingly, Massof testified that he never worked with Sherry West. It was customary at Gosnell's clinic for the employees to be seen there as patients, but Massof never knew West as a patient, either.

However, he did know , Jimmy Johnson. Jimmy would help dispose of the fetuses on Monday mornings, but what Jimmy did with them, he did not say. Jimmy would have plenty to say about that for himself when he later took the stand.

Massof had something disturbing to say about Liz, which added another perspective to her as a person. During her earlier testimony, she admitted her duties included "providing general security" at the clinic. But Massof told the court that it was Elizabeth Hampton who would help "hold down the women" who were "uncooperative" during abortion procedures.

Did he mean she held down women against their will? Massof never clarified.

This statement was troubling to say the least and begged the question of whether some of these abortions were forced. I certainly thought that was plausible. Forced abortions are more common at American abortion clinics that most people would ever think. I knew many women tried to withdraw their consent, or never gave it in the first place, but were given abortions by force nonetheless.

For example, my friend, Jennifer McCoy, told me of her forced abortion when she was only sixteen years old. It nearly ruined her life. I wrote about her experience in order to expose her scofflaw abortionist, Alberto Hodari of Michigan, who eventually was forced to surrender his medical license many years later.[2,3]

Jennifer was sixteen years old in 1988, when she discovered that she was pregnant; news that she welcomed, since she believed that she was in love with her baby's father. She had no thought of abortion because she believed it was wrong. However, the baby's father was one of her high school teachers who was about forty years old, married, and had a family of his own. Their relationship qualified as statutory rape.

Jennifer's mother found out about the relationship, but instead of reporting her daughter's sexual abuse to the authorities, she called the teacher and threatened to expose him if he did not help her persuade Jennifer to have an abortion.

Jennifer was taken by him to one of several abortion clinics operated by Alberto Hodari under the pretense of receiving prenatal care. "I didn't even know what an abortion clinic was," she said.

Once at the clinic, she was asked to sign some papers. She signed all the parts related to medical care, but refused to sign anything that discussed abortion. "That's not why I'm here," she repeatedly told the clinic staff.

Jennifer was then given an ultrasound examination. She asked to see her baby, but her request was refused. "It really isn't necessary," she was told.

She was placed in an examination room, and after a long wait, Hodari entered the room. She told him that she was just there for an exam. She had been told by the clinic staff that she had to get an exam in order to determine how far along she was.

"He told me, 'If you change your mind, then we can do whatever else you decide you want to do,'" she said.

Hodari began the exam. "Then all of a sudden I was in excruciating pain," Jennifer recalled. "I tried to sit up, and I heard a machine turn on, like a vacuum, and I realized what was going on."

"I tried to get up from the table. I actually tried to sit up, and he pushed me back down on the table and told me if I moved I could die. It would be over in five minutes and I could go on with my life. I was scared to death at that point that what he said was true, and so all I could do is lay there and cry."

"And when it was over I remember being taken by a nurse into another room where I was crying violently, and I remember her saying, 'Did you do everything you thought you could?' I then remember throwing something at her because I could not believe that she would say something to me when there was nothing I could do from that point on."

Hodari had forced an abortion on this unsuspecting teenager, then handed her back into the hands of her rapist.

Jennifer left the clinic and headed straight to the Southgate Police Department, just up the street from the abortion mill, to file charges against Hodari for aborting her baby against her will. A few weeks later, she went to court. Hodari's attorney produced papers from the abortion mill, and told the court that Jennifer's mother had signed the necessary consent forms for the abortion.

"He said since I was a minor, that it wasn't necessary for me to sign the paperwork, nor even know what they were going to do," she said. To her frustration, the case was dismissed.

Jennifer later confronted her mother about signing the paperwork behind her back, but her mother would never say if she did. "To this day, I have doubts that she did that," said Jennifer. "She wasn't even there."

Through all of this, no one, including Hodari, ever reported Jennifer's sex abuse at the hands of her teacher, which continued for four more years. Once the school discovered it, Jennifer's teacher was quietly asked to resign, and the matter was swept under the rug.

Because of the abortion, Jennifer had thoughts of suicide. Her relationship with her mother remained strained for years. Her life spun out of control.

Finally, Jennifer found forgiveness and healing through her renewed faith in Jesus Christ. She is now living in Wichita, Kansas, is married and the mother of ten children. She spends what extra time her large family allows trying to help women who are considering abortion to choose life for their babies. She wants to warn others of abortion's dangers.

"I know if he did this to me, he's done it to others," said Jennifer. Hodari, who has since retired, was never held accountable for what he did to her.

I thought again of what Massof said about Liz Hampton holding down the uncooperative women. That wasn't really the focus of the trial, and it was a point that prosecutors glossed over in presenting their case. Whatever else might happen to Gosnell and his cohorts in crime, none of them would ever be held responsible for any abortions they may have forced on women.

Forced and coerced abortions remain a very real problem today that is mostly ignored by prosecutors and media alike. That is something that desperately needs to change.

***

Of all Gosnell's co-defendants that had so far testified, Massof appeared to be the least sympathetic. Gosnell had exerted emotional control over Adrienne Moton, who Gosnell once took into his home during a difficult time in her life. Liz Hampton was a family member that was pressured, then coerced to work for Gosnell out of obligation. It's not that these people didn't make their own choices in life. They certainly did. But Gosnell undeniably exerted control over them by encouraging their dependence on him. It was eerily similar to how a cult leader controls his flock.

Massof's situation was something different. He had more options in life than the others. Massof had a ghoulish interest in abortion and had intentionally sought involvement in the late-term abortion side of Gosnell's business. While the women were tearfully emotional, Massof appeared almost emotionally detached and resigned to his fate. Yet, he was coldly remorseful, at least at some surface level. He related grisly details of his involvement in violent late-term abortions and the callous murder of living babies in a way that gave the appearance that he may have thought there was some macabre humor in his horrific experiences, almost as if it was all a sick joke on him.

If he thought any of that was funny, he was the only one. I don't have any medical training, but it was my honest impression that Massof urgently needed to be evaluated for mental illness.

***

Unfortunately, my first trip to Philadelphia was at an end and I reluctantly made my way to the airport. I wanted to return for the rest of the trial, but I understood that Operation Rescue had limited resources. It was expensive for me to travel from Kansas and stay in downtown Philadelphia where a bowl of oatmeal for breakfast cost what I thought was an outrageous amount of $15, not counting a tip.

I called Troy from the airport and told him how badly I wanted to come back. He assured me that he would find a way to get be back in that courtroom. Thankfully, he kept his promise.

CHAPTER 22

NO OUTLIER

I did not want to return to the courtroom without a press pass. It was such a hassle to check my phone at the Marriott across the street, no matter how gracious they were about allowing me to do so. Besides, I felt vulnerable being without the ability to communicate, and I wanted to be able to tweet information about the trial on the breaks.

Troy made a phone call to Dick Bott, founder of the Bott Radio Network, an influential network of Christian radio stations that broadcast throughout the Midwest. Troy had become fast friends with him during our early days in Kansas as we began to uncover governmental corruption that was protecting abortionists from investigation and prosecution. Mr. Bott even offered to air regular one-minute commentaries produced by Troy throughout his network.

Troy explained the situation to him, and Mr. Bott was more than willing to help me. Before long, I was in possession of an official Bott Radio Network press pass, complete with a recent professional photo of me. This was a huge help and allowed me to keep my cell phone and my iPad with me in court so I could communicate via social media with the outside world up-to-the-minute happenings throughout the day.

During breaks in the court proceedings, I had numerous conversations with the local reporters who were in and out of the courtroom. One such conversation was with Steve Volk of *Philadelphia Magazine*.

When I introduced myself to him, he seemed surprised. "I was wanting to call you!" he said.

We discussed the conditions at Gosnell's clinic and some of the other appalling practices, which I explained were more common at abortion clinics than is generally known. This was obviously a new thought for him. He was convinced that Gosnell was an outlier and that other abortion clinics were clean and safe, providing excellent medical care.

I pulled out my iPhone, (thanks my new Bott Radio Network press pass), and began to show him photos we had recently obtained through an open records request that were taken by the Muskegon, Michigan, health officials. The photos depicted conditions at an abortion clinic operated by abortionist Robert Alexander.[1]

The pictures showed a filthy abortion office filled with clutter, almost indistinguishable from Officer Taggart's photos of Gosnell's clinic that had been shown in court. One may have thought that the rusty suction machine at Alexander's clinic was the same one sitting before us in the courtroom, which had been seized from Gosnell's "House of Horrors." A closer look at that picture revealed something as horrifying as anything seen during Gosnell's trial.

The picture from Muskegon showed the suction machine had a glass bottle that was filled with blood and tissue – the contents of the last few abortions that had been done by Alexander prior to closing his clinic for a one-week Christmas break. Attached to the rust-covered machine was a brownish-yellow suction tube that, when the machine was in use, would have been connected to a cannula that was inserted into the woman' uterus during an abortion procedure. That filthy, contaminated tube was and laying on the dirty floor that looked as if it hadn't been mopped in six months, if ever.

The Muskegon Fire Marshall immediately posted a closure order for Alexander's abortion clinic. It never reopened and Alexander's medical license was eventually placed on indefinite suspension.[2]

I know it must have been hard for Steve to grasp what I was telling him. He described himself to me as being "pro-choice," and had never questioned the pro-abortion rhetoric that abortion was safe and legal. However, he was honest enough to admit what he was seeing in that courtroom was making him seriously reconsider his position.

I had more evidence in the form of reams of official inspection reports that proved many conditions and practices at the Gosnell clinic were replicated elsewhere, and not just confined to one other isolated clinic in Michigan.

Despite the fact that so many facilities have serious safety and sanitation issues, the abortion lobby continues to fight common-sense clinic safety standards, such as those that would ensure emergency workers have gurney access to procedure rooms. They ludicrously complain that safety rules are onerous and nothing short of an evil plot by anti-abortionists to "deny women heath care."

In truth, if Gosnell's clinic had complied with such rules that have since been enacted in Pennsylvania and elsewhere, Karnamaya Mongar might still be alive today.

Photos of conditions at Gosnell's facility that were displayed in court showed the only "handicapped" exit was at the end of a hallway crammed full of broken office furniture and other debris. On the night Mongar died, the door was locked with a key that frantic clinic workers could not find as firemen sought a way to get their code blue patient out of the facility and into an awaiting ambulance.

In fact, when Pennsylvania began inspecting clinics in that state, they found an enormous number of deficiencies. Two abortion clinics immediately closed rather than clean up and others have since followed suit.

Pennsylvania wasn't alone.

In January 2010, pro-life activists in Birmingham, Alabama, photographed emergency responders hand-carrying two abortion patients out of the New Women All Women abortion clinic down broken stairs and into a trash-strewn alley. An inspection by the Alabama Department of Public Health discovered seventy-six pages of clinic deficiencies, including evidence that medical tasks that were done by untrained, unqualified staff. The state forced the abortion clinic, a repeat offender, to close.[3,4]

None of the employees at Gosnell's abortion clinic were properly qualified for their jobs, including the two, Eileen O'Neill and Steven Massof, who held themselves out to be licensed physicians when they were not. Massof testified that his first experience seeing patients was his first day of work at Gosnell's clinic. Yet, within two weeks, he was seeing patients with no supervision and prescribing drugs.

Untrained, unqualified staffing is a major problem that can be found in almost every abortion clinic across the country. Examples of this are numerous.

In Southern California, abortion clinic owner Bertha Bugarin and her sister, Rachel, were caught illegally doing abortions at the now defunct Clinica Medica Para La Mujer De Hoy abortion clinic chain in 2009. Neither of them had any medical background and held no licenses to practice medicine.[5]

A third abortionist who worked for Bugarin, Laurence Reich, had his medical license revoked in 2006 for sexually molesting his abortion patients. A year later, when police raided one of Bugarin's Los Angeles abortion facilities, we were informed by police that the unlicensed and disgraced Reich was found still doing abortions.[6]

In the summer of 2009, four former employees of nationally known late-term abortionist LeRoy Carhart come forward and related very much the same story as told by Gosnell's workers of drug violations, unqualified medical practices, dirty conditions, falsified ultrasounds, and other abortion abuses. In fact, these women all admitted in signed affidavits that they were unlicensed and unqualified for many of the medical tasks that Carhart made them perform. The ladies also testified to witnessing the falsification of ultrasound images in much the same way that Steven Massof had described.[7]

Filthy conditions and the reuse of dirty surgical equipment at Gosnell's clinic shocked the public when it first became known. Gosnell was accused of spreading sexually transmitted diseases from one patient to another because he did not clean surgical instruments between patients. However, similar conditions are well documented throughout the abortion industry.

A former Kansas City abortionist, Krishna Rajanna, lost his medical license after photos surfaced that showed blood-stained carpets in procedure rooms, reused surgical equipment, and the storage of employee's lunches in the same refrigerator as the aborted baby remains, the same conditions found at Gosnell's clinic. In addition, Kansas City Police Detective William Howard testified on March 15, 2005 before the House Committee on Health and Human Services as a neutral observer of conditions he witnessed while responding to a call to Rajanna's abortion mill on September 18, 2003. He stated in part:

> In a statement to me one witness/suspect related how Dr. Rajanna was a filthy man who did not properly sterilize his equipment. The medical equipment was cleaned with Clorox and water then put in a 'dishwasher'. The aborted fetuses were placed inside Styrofoam cups and put in the refrigerator freezer next to TV dinners. The female witness went on to describe of how she and other girls actually witnessed Rajanna microwave one of the aborted fetuses and stir it into his lunch. I have heard that some Middle Easterners eat the placenta from birth and that they believe that this adds longevity to life. I thought: Maybe this could be what she was referring to. This witness claimed other employees who had seen him do the very same thing—Bear in mind, I am an experienced police officer who has worked in every aspect in law enforcement and had spent my last five

*years in the homicide unit where I worked countless community deaths. I
thought I had heard and seen every vile, disgusting crime scene but was in
for a new shock when I started this investigation.*[8]

Elsewhere in Kansas, a Wichita abortion clinic bought and closed
by Operation Rescue revealed dirty, roach-infested conditions, a leaky
roof, moldy ceilings and walls, and blood-spattered wash room where the
contents of the abortion suction machine bottles were dumped down a
sink and ground up in that industrial garbage disposal in conditions
nearly identical to those identified by CSU officer Taggart and employee
Liz Hampton.[9]

These examples are just the tip of the iceberg. Numerous documents of
abortion clinic deficiencies have been compiled by Operation Rescue and can
be read at AbortionDocs.org.

But perhaps most disturbing are the allegations that babies were born
alive on a routine basis, then intentionally killed. That earned Gosnell's
abortion clinic the "House of Horrors" moniker and designation as a charnel
house. It was the conclusion, drawn by the few media outlets that bothered to
cover the grisly Gosnell case, that this never happens elsewhere.

Apparently, none of those people had ever heard of Florida abortionists
Pierre Renelique or James Scott Pendergraft IV.

On July 19, 2006, when eighteen-year-old Sycloria Williams sought out
Renelique's services at his North Miami abortion clinic. She was twenty-three
weeks pregnant. Renelique inserted laminaria, gave her a drug that would
stimulate uterine contractions, and sent her home with instructions to report
to A Gyn Diagnostics in Hialeah the following morning, where he would
complete her abortion.

When Williams arrived at the Hialeah clinic at 9 am the next morning,
she was already experiencing cramping, but Renelique was nowhere to be
found. Clinic co-owner Belkis Gonzalez, a woman with no medical training,
directed Williams to wait in the clinic's recovery room, where she was given
additional medication. As the minutes and hours ticked by, Williams began
feeling worse. She suffered severe contractions and nausea. Her complaints
were met by stern orders for her to sit down and keep her legs shut, even
though Williams instinctively knew that her baby was coming. Williams
was told that Renelique would be there by 2:00 pm, but as the hour passed,
Renelique still was not responding to pages. At that point, Williams lifted
herself out of the recliner and birthed a baby girl.

The tiny baby was writhing, her chest rising and falling as she struggled for her first breaths. At that point, pandemonium broke out inside the clinic. Gonzalez grabbed a pair of orange-handled desk scissors and severed the baby's umbilical cord, but did not clamp it. She shoved the baby into a red biohazard bag along with caustic chemicals meant to speed decomposition, and tossed the body onto the roof of the clinic.

When Renelique arrived at the clinic at 3:00 pm, he finally attended to Williams. At a hearing of the Florida Medical Board held in February, 2009, Renelique testified that he was so confused and unaware of William's condition that he started an abortion procedure on the sedated woman even though she had delivered her baby an hour earlier.

"That's when one of the employees came to me and said, 'Dr. Renelique, what are you looking for?' I said, 'I'm looking for a fetus.' And she said, 'What fetus?'" Renelique said.[10]

Renelique and his associates then falsified the patient's charts to indicate that he had conducted the abortion and discharged her at 12:05 pm, even though Williams did not give birth until 2:00 pm and Renelique did not arrive at the clinic until after 3:00 pm.

An informant sneaked out to a nearby pay phone and called the police to report the murder of baby Shanice Denise Osbourne, as her mother would later name her. The police arrived and searched the clinic but could not find the baby. On second search, the body of Shanice was found. The abortion clinic was closed by the state and Renelique's Florida medical license was revoked.

After a huge outpouring of public pressure instigated by Operation Rescue, Belkis Gonzalez was eventually arrested and charged not with murder, but with practicing medicine without a license. After an unbelievable three years of delay, all charges against her were dropped.

In another well-documented example of babies being born alive during abortions, a woman named Angele made an appointment at James Pendergraft's EPOC abortion clinic in Orlando, Florida, for a twenty-two-week abortion. Her baby was supposedly injected with digoxin, after which Angele was induced into labor and delivered her baby into a toilet inside the abortion clinic.

To her horror, Angele realized that her son, who she named Rowan, was gasping while his little chest rose and fell with each breath. Grabbing her cell phone, she called her friend that was waiting for her in the clinic's waiting room, and begged her to call for help. Her friend called 911, but when paramedics arrived, the clinic workers told them there was no emergency and sent them away. Angele held Rowan in that restroom stall until he died from extreme prematurity.[11]

So well documented was Angele's story that it was made into short 2009 movie directed by Angel Manuel Soto called *22 Weeks*.[12]

More recently, in July 2015, David Daleiden of the Center for Medical Progress, began releasing a series of undercover videos that contained prima facie evidence of Planned Parenthood's involvement in the illegal sale of aborted baby parts to biologic companies that, in turn, sold them to commercial and medical laboratories.

Troy served as a founding member of the board for the Center for Medical Progress and was privy to Daleiden's nearly three-year investigation.

One particular video featured Holly O'Donnell, a former organ procurement specialist with Stem Express, which contracted with Planned Parenthood in California for the harvesting of fetal organs. Stem Express' organ procurement specialists would be sent to certain Planned Parenthood clinics and conduct the harvesting and shipping of the organs of babies aborted at Planned Parenthood.

Holly related how one day, she was working at the Planned Parenthood abortion facility in San Jose when she was asked to procure a baby's brain. O'Donnell was training with another StemExpress employee identified as "Jessica" when the Planned Parenthood abortionist emerged from the delivery room, "really frustrated" that one distraught woman could not be calmed down enough to do the abortion procedure. The patient could not be medicated because her fetus had been selected for organ harvesting. Certain drugs render fetal "specimens" useless to researchers.

"Finally the woman, she calmed down and the doctor went in to perform the abortion. It takes a little while and I'm in the hallway. I see the jar come out. Goes into the path lab. And Jessica, I can hear, is preparing it," explained O'Donnell, reliving the memory step by step.[13]

She continued:

So then I hear her call my name. "Hey, Holly! Come over here. I want you to see something kinda cool. It's kinda neat!" So I'm over here and the moment I see it I'm just flabbergasted. This is the most gestated fetus and closest thing to a "baby" that I've seen.

And she's like, "Okay, I want to show you something." So she has one of her instruments and she just taps the heart and it starts beating. And I'm sitting here, and I'm looking at this fetus, and its heart is beating and I don't know what to think . . .

I knew why it was happening. It's because of the electrical current was— the nodes were still firing, and I don't know if that constitutes—it's technically dead? Or it's alive?

It had a face. It wasn't completely torn up. And its nose was very pronounced. It had eyelids and its mouth was pronounced. And then, since the fetus was so intact, [Jessica] said, "Okay, this is a really good fetus and it looks like we can procure a lot from it. We're going to procure a brain."[14]

O'Donnell then described how Jessica began the harvesting process by cutting through the lower jaw and into the face with scissors, then instructed O'Donnell to finish cutting through the face so she could extract the brain. Dutifully, she complied.

So, was Gosnell an outlier as the media likes to state, or are newborns being murdered at other abortion clinics in America? While it seems unlikely or shocking, it is true that Gosnell is not alone. Evidence suggests that live newborns are being intentionally killed at other abortion clinics across America more often than anyone would have ever guessed.

The primary difference between Gosnell's "House of Horrors" abortion clinic and so many others around the country seems to be that he was caught by law enforcement officials that had no political agenda on abortion. They saw the dead babies, and for them, there was no doubt that it was murder. Americans can only wonder with dread how many other Gosnell-like clinics continue to operate under the protection of political climates like those described in the Gosnell grand jury report that encourage regulators to ignore abortion abuses in order to protect abortion businesses no matter the cost.

In America today, women, especially the poor urban women of color like those that comprised the majority of Gosnell's abortion business, are preyed upon by shoddy, unscrupulous abortionists who profit financially while the women are rushed to emergency rooms in droves around the country.

It is my firm belief that abortion continues only because Americans have been denied the truth about the abuses that go on every day in our country's abortion clinics. When something negative does come out about an abortionist or clinic, the pro-abortion liberal media responds in one of three ways: It refuses to cover it, it acts as if it is an anomalous incident, or it flat-out lies to make the public believe it never happened then attacks the pro-life group that exposed the abuse in the first place.

Abortion lobbyists cry about "burdensome" health and safety laws as if they hurt women, when in reality, those laws are necessary to protect women from harm and exploitation by abortionists who only pretend to champion the rights of women. The only real way to protect women from the abuse inflicted upon them by those like Gosnell is to close every abortion clinic and relegate the barbaric practice into the trash heap of history where it belongs.

CHAPTER 23

WEST AND WILLIAMS

Sherry West, 53, was brought into the courtroom wearing a green prison jumpsuit. She had been incarcerated since being arrested in the overnight raid in January, 2011, when police took Gosnell and eight of her co-workers into custody.

Her hair was longer now than her mug shot, which had captured her with cropped reddish hair and a "deer caught in the headlights" look. She wore it pulled back into a pony tail.

West told of her loyalty to Gosnell, who was her doctor for 20 years. In 2007, West said she lost her job as a "surgical technician" doing prep work in an operating room at the Veteran's Administration hospital after she developed mental issues and suffered a "nervous breakdown."

Adding to her troubles, West said she developed hepatitis C due to her work with the VA and tried unsuccessfully to get on disability. She had not had a paycheck in nearly two years and was financially desperate when Gosnell offered her a job at his clinic in 2008.

West told the court she hated working at the Women's Medical Society and especially hated working in the abortion rooms, but did so because she needed the money.

West called the babies she helped to abort "specimens" because it was "easier to deal with mentally."

Appearing uncomfortable at having to relive the memory, she recounted a particularly horrific experience for the court. She was nearby a procedure room when one baby, whom she described as eighteen to twenty-four inches long, was born alive. Other workers called her into the room for help.

"There was this clear glass pan, and I saw it, and I thought, *What do you expect me to do?*" West told the court.

"It wasn't fully developed," she said, according to the *Philadelphia Inquirer.* "It didn't have eyes or a mouth, but it was like screeching, making this noise. It was weird. It sounded like a little alien . . . It really freaked me out, and I said, 'Call Dr. Gosnell,' and I went back out front."

Her testimony about a baby that was nearly two feet long not having eyes or a mouth did not ring true. If he didn't have a mouth, how could he "screech" like an "alien?" The fact that the baby did screech was in indication his lungs were fully developed.

A quick Google search revealed that a baby at thirty-seven weeks' gestation could be expected to be eighteen inches long while a twenty-four-inch long baby would be considered a very large full-term infant. In reality, it is scientifically factual that facial features begin developing in a growing baby in the womb at around six or seven weeks' gestation, and are fully formed shortly thereafter.

I got the impression that West was unsuccessfully trying to minimize how truly developed the baby was in order to somehow mitigate the consequences of killing him. West did have a history of mental health issues so I guessed another possibility was that the event was so traumatic that she blocked the memory of the baby's face.

The grand jury report that painted an uncomplimentary picture of West and her cohort, Lynda Williams, who were described as heartless women who ran roughshod over helpless patients, drugging them when they complained or were annoying in some way. Because of this insight, it seemed more likely that West was just trying to engage in damage control, to the extent she could.

Prosecutor Joanne Pescatore questioned West about events surrounding the death of Karnamaya Mongar. West used a pair of reading glasses to refer to inadequately kept clinic records, which rarely noted who administered drugs or how much were given. She was frequently responded to Pescatore's questions with, "I don't know," leading Pescatore to walk her through a written transcript of a previous interview. Only that would seem to jar loose her memory of events.

The questioning moved on to the topic of the death of Karnamaya Mongar.

West had already entered a plea agreement with the prosecution. She pled guilty to third-degree murder and delivering drugs that resulted in death for her part in the overdose death of Mongar. She also admitted to the charges of conspiracy and participating in a corrupt organization. As she sat there in court, West faced a maximum penalty of 70 to 100 years at sentencing. Her testimony, as with her other co-defendants, was being given in exchange for the hope of leniency at the time of sentencing.

West described the atmosphere at the clinic the night Mongar died as "hectic."

She admitted that she had administered some of the sedative that later killed the diminutive immigrant during her nineteen-week abortion then described the chaos that gripped the staff as they ran about the office trying to find a key for the locked back door so paramedics could get a gurney into the clinic once Mongar's heart stopped beating.

West said that after Mongar's death, Gosnell held a staff meeting to ease any concerns from his employees, but he never changed his protocols for administering drugs. Everything very quickly returned to business as usual.

However, under questioning by defense attorney Jack McMahon, West broke down on the stand and tearfully recanted her guilty plea. She told the court that she didn't think she was guilty and that she took the plea bargain out of confusion. She later contradicted that testimony when she confirmed that she did so willingly with the hope of receiving a lesser sentence.

West's testimony was troubling on several points. It was horrific to think of a helpless baby that was born alive and shrieking, knowing the brutal fate he faced. West's cold and callous way of dealing with the babies through denial and dehumanization was disturbing and reminiscent of how, for example, the Nazi's dehumanized Jews in order to not only justify murdering them, but to assuage their consciences when they did.

Abortionists have several ways of dehumanizing babies. They call them "products of conception" or deny that they are alive. They convince themselves that the woman's life is more important than the "potential life" of the baby. Some even deny that the babies are even human. All are arguments that defy science, reason, and morality.

***

Lynda Williams was also wearing prison garb as she was escorted onto the stand to testify against her former boss. Williams sat quietly, staring blankly ahead. Her demeanor seemed so strange. Was she drugged or suffering some kind of mental health issue?

Williams, who dropped out of school in the sixth grade and never went back, began working for Gosnell at his West Philadelphia clinic in 2008. She had met Gosnell while employed at Atlantic Women's Medical Services in Delaware, where Gosnell also worked.

Williams needed a change of scenery after her husband was murdered in 2007. She told a jury that Gosnell was aware she suffered from bipolar disorder and depression when he hired her to work at his abortion clinic in West Philadelphia assisting with late-term abortions. In fact, she was being treated by Gosnell for the mental illnesses.

Initially, Williams was told it would be her duty to clean surgical instruments, but soon, she was anesthetizing patients, assisting with late-term abortions, and even snipping the spinal cords of the bigger babies in the manner in which Gosnell had shown her.

According to the grand jury report, it was actually Williams who had administered the fatal doses of Demerol, promethazine, and diazepam that ultimately took Karnamaya Mongar's life. This was perhaps unsurprising, given the grand jury testimony of several of William's co-workers, including Ashley Baldwin and Kareema Cross. According to them, Williams frequently mixed her own cocktail of drugs when medicating women, then would leave them completely unmonitored. The year before Mongar's death, Cross went to Williams and scolded her for overmedicating women, but Cross's concerns were dismissed by Williams, and complaints to Gosnell himself went unheeded.

Williams and West rode to work together every day and worked the same hours. West seemed to be heavily influenced by Williams. According to the grand jury testimony of other Gosnell workers, this led to an intolerable situation that was described in the grand jury report:

> According to [Latosha] Lewis, Gosnell hired Sherry West when she lost her job at the Philadelphia Veterans Administration Medical Center after contracting hepatitis C. Yet, despite her hepatitis, West regularly failed to wear gloves when treating patients. In fact, [Kareema] Cross testified that she never saw West wear gloves, even though West worked in the procedure room with the doctor and inserted patients' IV connections.

> Cross also said that Williams and West did not know how to give injections correctly, and that patients regularly came in to complain because their arms swelled up after injections as a result of improper technique.

> Even more dangerous was West and Williams' reckless attitude toward medicating patients. Cross, Lewis, and Ashley Baldwin all described West and Williams as incompetent. Although medicating patients based on a

predetermined chart is in itself astonishingly reckless, West and Williams did not even follow the chart when medicating patients. Neither seemed to understand – or care about – the grave risk to patients that their haphazard approach posed. Latosha Lewis testified: "It was a game to them." Lewis said that when they were supposed to be administering medications, West and Williams were "just goofing off and playing around."

According to Kareema Cross, Williams was especially dangerous because she imagined that she was the doctor. Williams seemed to feel it didn't matter what she did, because Gosnell didn't care. Cross, Lewis, and Ashley Baldwin all testified that Williams routinely overmedicated patients. This happened because she paid no attention to the chart when she drew up the drugs in a syringe, and because she failed to keep track of or to record what she administered. West, who had told Gosnell that she wasn't comfortable medicating patients, ended up following Williams' lead.

After Steven Massof stopped working for Gosnell, it fell to Williams to snip the necks of babies when Gosnell was absent, and even sometimes when he was present, according to the grand jury report:

> *When Massof left the clinic in 2008, Lynda Williams took over the job of cutting baby's [sic] necks when Gosnell was not there. Cross saw Williams slit the neck of a baby ("Baby C") who had been moving and breathing for approximately twenty minutes. Gosnell had delivered the baby and put it on a counter while he suctioned the placenta from the mother. Williams called Cross over to look at the baby because it was breathing and moving its arms when Williams pulled on them. After playing with the baby, Williams slit its neck.[2]*

Before coming to court, Williams already pled guilty to conspiracy and two counts of third degree murder for killing babies, including Baby C, via Gosnell's neck-snipping procedure. As the other Gosnell employees, by testifying against Gosnell, she hoped for leniency at the time of sentencing. She faced the possibility of 100 years in prison.

One news report described Williams as testifying "in a flat, emotionless voice and at times seemed catatonic, taking several seconds before reacting to questions."

Williams told the court that when she began assisting with the later abortions, Gosnell taught her how to turn the babies over and snip their spinal cords with surgical scissors. That practice was "routine" at Gosnell's clinic as a means of ensuring "fetal demise."

Assistant District Attorney Joanne Pescatore asked Williams if she knew what she did was murder. To that Williams responded, "No, I didn't."

"I only do what I'm told to do," she told the court. "What I was told to do was snip their neck."

After prodding, she related how Gosnell was absent one day when an abortion patient spontaneously delivered her baby into a toilet after heavy doses of Cytotec.

As instructed by Gosnell, Williams turned the baby onto his tummy and inserted the scissors into his neck.

"It jumped, the arm," Williams testified, demonstrating the arm motion to the jury.

The *News Journal* further described William's testimony:
When Assistant District Attorney Joanne Pescatore initially pressed Williams to describe what she saw when she cut the neck of the child delivered in a toilet, Williams responded with a blank stare and silence.[3]

Williams also responded the same way when asked about seeing Gosnell cut the necks of babies who were delivered before abortion procedures, admitting after reviewing earlier statements that she had seen Gosnell do this at least thirty times.

Williams was also present during Karnamaya Mongar's abortion and testified that she repeatedly administered Demerol to her because Mongar was in pain. During the abortion, Williams mentioned to Gosnell her concern that Mongar's breathing had slowed and she had turned gray. According to Williams, Gosnell continued with the abortion procedure then began to administer CPR. Finally, he told Williams to call 911.

Williams also testified that Gosnell would often alter medical records to make it appear that the babies he was aborting were under the legal limit in Pennsylvania of twenty-four weeks. She said that drugs were often out of date and ineffective. Williams told the court that if a woman squirmed in pain during the procedure, Gosnell would slap her leg hard enough to leave a handprint.

When it was McMahon's turn to cross examine Williams, he attempted cast doubt on whether the baby whose arm had jumped was actually alive at the time his neck was snipped by Williams.

She admitted that Gosnell told her that because of the drugs administered earlier in the abortion procedures, that the babies were already dead. But that begged the question of why the neck-snipping was even necessary.

McMahon tried to convince Williams that the arm movement she noticed was just an involuntary nerve spasm. Williams admitted that she never saw the baby actually breathing and observed no other movements besides the arm jumping as she thrust the scissors into his neck.

"The baby didn't appear to be alive to you?" McMahon asked.

"No," answered Williams in a monotone while she stared into the distance.[4]

Williams' testimony that the baby appeared dead was unconvincing to me. There seemed little doubt that babies were being born alive only to meet their demise at the sharp end of a pair of surgical scissors.

I hoped that the jury saw that, too.

McMahon ended his questioning of Williams by asking her about a note she scrawled on a police statement when she was initially questioned. She admitted that she had written, "I just want this to all end. He [Dr. Gosnell] done nothing wrong!!!"[5]

As disturbing as West and Williams' testimony was, there was one commonality that caught my attention. West had admitted to suffering from mental health disorders, including a history of anxiety and depression. Williams suffered from mental illnesses as well. An alarming pattern was beginning to emerge.

CHAPTER 24

MENTAL ILLNESS

The Gosnell trial highlighted a little discussed yet extremely troubling aspect that appears to be relatively common throughout the abortion cartel, and that is the problem of mental illness. Gosnell sought out employees among those with little education who were in desperate circumstances, and in some cases, suffering from mental illness and/or substance abuse. Gosnell would take them in, treat them as patients, perhaps house them, and create in them a sense of dependency on him. In this way, he could exert control over them and keep them working long hours under the most horrendous of conditions.

Elizabeth Hampton, a foster sister to Gosnell's third wife, Pearl, had testified she suffered from depression and anxiety in addition to alcohol abuse, and that she once had a "nervous breakdown." She attempted to sever ties with Gosnell's business after her involvement in a traumatic episode there that caused her to relapse into alcoholism. She was pressured by the Gosnell's to return to work at the clinic, and she eventually succumbed to that pressure "out of obligation," even though she hated the work. Liz lived rent-free in one of Gosnell's homes and had her paychecks filtered through Pearl. Even her common-law husband, Jimmy, relied on the Gosnell's for employment. This placed Liz's life almost completely under Gosnell's control.

Sherry West was also financially desperate and admitted to mental health issues, including an anxiety disorder for which she was medicated with Prozac. Like Liz, she also experienced a "nervous breakdown." She was essentially unemployable—except at Kermit Gosnell's abortion business. West had a deep loyalty to Gosnell and attempted to defend him even from the witness stand.

Lynda Williams could aptly be described as a basket case. She met Gosnell while working at an abortion clinic in Delaware where Gosnell conducted abortions on a part-time basis. After the murder of her husband, she found herself in a financially desperate situation. She admitted to suffering from mental illnesses, including bipolar disorder, an anxiety disorder, and depression that caused her to be heavily medicated with at least three kinds of drugs. Gosnell took her in and was treating her as a patient, prescribing drugs for her mental conditions. She soon developed a dependency on Gosnell for her drugs and her livelihood, which led her to adamantly defend his practices. She repeatedly told police he did nothing wrong.

Steven Massof was a misfit with an inordinate fascination with abortions, particularly the late-term variety. He earned a medical degree in a third-world Caribbean nation that lacked the same medical standards as found in the US. After failing to qualify for a residency in America, Massof agreed to work long hours for low wages for the opportunity to abort late-term babies. While undiagnosed, I highly suspected from his strange demeanor in court and ghoulish fascination (or perhaps obsession) with later abortions that he also suffered some kind of mental illness. He, too, fell under Gosnell's control, but to a lesser degree than some of the women.

While Adrienne Moton did not admit to mental health issues, her testimony indicated that Gosnell did exert some control over her. She had lived with the Gosnell family during a trying time in her young life, and she felt beholden to him.

It seemed odd that so many people could witness the cold-hearted murder of live babies and work in the squalid conditions, yet show so little concern. If anyone did question the murder of infants, Gosnell would reassure them that this was how things were done and that the babies, despite moving, crying, or otherwise struggling for life, were already dead.

He was the doctor, so they believed him.

But mental illness amongst abortion workers is a phenomenon that is not confined only to Gosnell's abortion staff. Abortion facilities experience high rates of employee turnover due to the grisly nature of the business. This has made abortion businesses willing to hire workers that legitimate medical practices would never consider. Because abortion businesses must repeatedly draw from a very shallow pool of workers, abortion facilities are often staffed with poorly educated workers who find it difficult to obtain employment elsewhere. Some of them are plagued with addiction issues and/or mental health conditions.

In addition, abortionists with addiction and psychological problems tend to gravitate to the abortion business, probably because they can continue to work and even flourish at abortion clinics where there is very little accountability. While their deteriorating mental conditions and physical skills would be noticed and reported at a legitimate medical practice, at abortion clinics they may go without notice.

Abortionist Robert Alexander ran that horrifically filthy abortion clinic in Muskegon, Michigan that rivaled the squalor to Gosnell's West Philadelphia "House of Horrors." I shared photos of the conditions at his clinic with reporters during Gosnell's trial to prove that Gosnell was not the only abortionist to maintain dangerously unsanitary conditions.

Before the horrors at Alexander's clinic were discovered by law enforcement, Operation Rescue had filed a complaint against him based on information provided us by a former employee. As the result of that complaint, which suddenly took on new urgency after conditions at the Muskegon mill were publicized locally, Alexander was later called before a disciplinary hearing, where local activist Lynn Mills described his behavior as "bizarre." She recounted a conversation outside the hearing room where Alexander tried to convince her that he had converted to the pro-life position when it was obvious he had not.

His bizarre behavior soon had an explanation. Alexander testified in his own defense for slightly under an hour, detailing his battle with bipolar disorder since he was nineteen years old. Alexander read a lengthy list of symptoms experienced by those with that mental illness and told the administrative judge that he is heavily medicated in order to manage his condition, taking Lithium three times per day and Prozac twice a day. Alexander claimed to be under the regular care of a psychiatrist and a psychologist.

Alexander also inexplicably maintained that he should be allowed to continue practicing under the Americans with Disabilities Act, despite his serious mental illness. The judge who oversaw the proceeding was shocked.

"I mean, to be honest with you, as I listen to Dr. Alexander tell me about all the various symptoms that a person may have, I question whether anyone should be practicing medicine with a lot of those symptoms," the judge said.[1]

Thankfully, Alexander's medical license was suspended indefinitely and conditions were placed on him that should make it impossible for him to ever practice medicine again.

***

Gary T. Prohaska, 78, was a long-time California abortionist who had once worked for a Planned Parenthood abortion facility in San Diego. As time went by, it became apparent that something wasn't quite right with him. According to disciplinary records, someone noticed his unfit mental condition and reported to the Medical Board that Prohaska was suffering from symptoms consistent with early dementia.

Prohaska underwent a mental health evaluation that confirmed the onset of dementia. The Medical Board of California filed a petition on August 12, 2014, to revoke the medical license based on his diagnosed mental impairment.

The petition stated that Prohaska had suffered "moderate severity cognitive impairment" according to a psychiatrist who examined Prohaska at the California Medical Board's request. It further stated that Prohaska's "impairment is permanent and renders him unsafe to practice medicine."[2]

Prohaska voluntarily surrendered his medical license rather than pay for the costs associated with revocation proceedings. One can only wonder how long Prohaska had been operating with his dangerous mental impairment, and how long he would have continued to operate had someone not been brave enough to report him.

***

Kimberly Marion Walker's story is a tragic one. Her mental illness began to manifest in 2005, three years after graduating from medical school at Drexel University and during her residency at St. Peter's Hospital in New Jersey. The New Jersey Professional Assistance Program diagnosed her with "cannabis dependence and possible paranoid delusions."

After her diagnosis, Walker voluntarily entered an inpatient treatment program where doctors found that her paranoia led her to believe that "people were following her and attempting to harm her." She was suicidal. During her treatment, she was diagnosed with a mood disorder, prescribed medication for that condition only, and released.

But without the anti-psychotic drugs she apparently needed, her condition only worsened.

On October 26, 2006, during her leave of absence from a residency program in which she sought treatment for her mental illness, Walker strolled into St. Peter's Hospital, pointed a loaded handgun at a security guard, and fired repeatedly.

Miraculously, the gun failed to discharge and no one was hurt, but Walker was arrested and stood trial for attempted murder. She was found not guilty by reason of insanity and was admitted into the Ann Klein Forensic Center where her delusions, such as thinking the radio and television were speaking directly to her, continued to manifest. She was even wrongly convinced that she had murdered her boyfriend.

Three mental health evaluations conducted after her arrest produced three different—but all very serious—diagnoses, according to records obtained by Operation Rescue from the Maryland Board of Physicians. Those diagnoses were: Bipolar II with Psychotic Features; Schizoaffective, Bipolar Type; and Schizoaffective, Bipolar Type with a differential diagnosis of Schizophrenia, Paranoid Type.

She was treated and prescribed an anti-psychotic drug that seemed to stabilize her condition by 2008. However, when Walker would reduce her medication dosage on her own, her symptoms would return.

Now living on her own and working part-time jobs, Walker began to believe that her medication was the cause of her mental health issues. She reduced her medication dosage and finally stopped taking it altogether on July 8, 2009.

A week later, she applied for a medical license in the State of Maryland.

Unsurprisingly, without her medication, Walker's symptoms returned. It was during this time, in July or August of 2009, that she first met Steven Chase Brigham through a "help wanted" ad on his website. Brigham indicated he wanted to hire her as soon as her medical license was approved and offered to train her to do abortions.

The medical license application process took longer than anticipated, so in January 2010, Brigham told Walker report to his Elkton facility three to four times per month, apparently for the purpose of observing abortion procedures.

In another parallel to the Gosnell case, Walker later told Board investigators that Brigham's abortion clinic "nursing staff" appeared to be comprised of "foreign medical graduate[s]" with doctorates, who were unlicensed just as she was. Gosnell employed similar workers, such as Steven Massof and Eileen O'Neill. Like Gosnell, who paid his unlicensed "doctors" a shockingly low salary, Brigham paid Walker just $50 per session to cover "gas and tolls."

On August 2, 2010, Walker was informed that her medical license application was rejected due to her mental instability. The Board determined that she posed a danger to the public, yet she continued to observe abortions at Brigham's Elkton facility.

Walker was not present on August 9, 2010, when a patient known as D. B. suffered a perforated uterus and pulled bowel during a late-term abortion at the Elkton facility that required emergency surgery to save her life. Walker was informed of the botched abortion incident by Brigham a few days later. He warned her that there would be in investigation and told her not to come in the following week because the Elkton clinic would be closed. It is more likely that he didn't want her around because he didn't want investigators to find out she had no valid medical license.

Indeed, there was an investigation. Among those records seized by police was a patient log that indicated "Dr. Woaker," a misspelled reference to Kimberly Walker, had provided recovery care after abortions for patients at Elkton on August 4, 2010, two days after her application for licensure had been rejected by the Maryland Board of Physicians.[3]

Walker denied treating any patient and said she did not know why her name was on the patient log, a denial that may or may not have been the truth since Brigham also falsely denied treating women. She indicated that she witnessed Brigham conducting abortion and other medical duties, but never knew Brigham was unlicensed in Maryland, and just assumed that he was.[4]

One might expect that this episode would have been the end of Walker's medical career, but surprisingly, despite her serious mental illness, despite her attempt to murder a hospital security guard, despite her history of not properly taking her medication, and despite her involvement with Brigham's illegal late-term abortion business, the Maryland Board of Physicians issued Kimberly Walker a conditional license to practice medicine on February 26, 2013.

By October of 2013, it became obvious that Walker had failed to live up to the conditions the Board placed on her. In violation of her consent agreement, Walker entered into a contract for employment at an unspecified "medical clinic" and provided "patient services" without notifying the Board or gaining their approval. Walker's medical license was revoked for a period of two years. The revocation order was signed on December 30, 2013.

Two weeks later, Kimberly Marion Walker was found dead at the age of thirty-six from a self-inflicted gunshot wound to the head.

An autopsy conducted on January 14, 2014, noted that a toxicology screening revealed that she had no drugs or alcohol in her system at the time of her suicide. Her mental illness had taken its final toll.[5]

***

Alexander, Prohaska, and Walker are certainly not alone. Operation Rescue has documented many other incidents of mental disorders suffered by those who work in the business of abortion. Those are the ones that have been documented. It stands to reason that there are many more mentally unfit or addicted workers currently staffing abortion clinics around America.

This issue is yet another argument in favor of greater accountability for abortion providers and businesses, as if the crimes of Kermit Gosnell are not enough.

CHAPTER 25

DEAD OR ALIVE

D efense attorney Jack McMahon skillfully used his cross-examination of witnesses as an opportunity to pose Gosnell's primary defense theory. As mentioned, McMahon made bold attempts to convince the jury that all the babies aborted at Gosnell's clinic were already dead when their spinal cords were snipped.

McMahon pressed former Gosnell employee Lynda Williams concerning her duties at Gosnell's abortion facility, which included cleaning up and disposing of babies born after late-term abortions, many of which were beyond the legal gestational limit of twenty-four weeks.

Williams had testified under direct examination concerning a baby that was delivered into a toilet at the clinic in Gosnell's absence. She told the court that when she saw the baby moving, she picked him up and stabbed the back of his neck with surgical scissors, as Gosnell had taught her to do.

Later, under McMahon's cross-examination, Williams testified that Gosnell reassured her that the baby was dead already and that any movement was "involuntary movement, a last breath." He told her drugs given to the woman earlier had already killed the baby.

Williams and others testified that the snipping of spinal cords was to "ensure fetal demise" as if this gruesome technique was used as an insurance policy to make sure the baby was actually dead. Yet all the snippings took place after the babies were born.

If the babies were already dead, why snip the spinal cords of their dead corpses?

This was an important point. Once babies leave the birth canal, they are no longer considered fetuses, but are in fact newborn babies, which have legal protections under the law. Killing them is murder in every moral and legal sense.

The grand jury report noted that an unnamed neonatologist testified before the grand jury saying that what Gosnell told his people about the babies already being dead prior to the snippings was absolutely false.

"If a baby moves, it is alive. Equally troubling, it feels a 'tremendous amount of pain' when its spinal cord is severed," stated the neonatologist, according to the report.[1]

The drug Gosnell claims to have used to initiate fetal death was digoxin, a medicine once widely used to treat heart attacks. Late-term abortionists routinely inject digoxin into the fetus or the amniotic fluid around the growing baby to induce the equivalent of a heart attack. Digoxin paralyzes the heart muscle, thus killing the baby.

This became a common practice after the US Supreme Court in *Carhart v. Gonzalez* banned the use of the partial-birth abortion method, in which the baby was still living but only partially delivered when an abortionist would open the skull and evacuate brains. This evacuation was done to allow the skull to collapse and the dead infant to slip easily from the birth canal.

McMahon stated in court that babies never survive digoxin injections. However, Operation Rescue has documentation that McMahon's statement was simply not true. In fact, literature on the subject of the efficacy of digoxin injections to accomplish "fetal demise" indicate that the injections fail about 13 percent of the time, even under the best circumstances, and if the drug is injected into the amniotic sac instead of the fetus, the failure rate on the first try can be as astronomically high as 70 percent.[2,3]

One example of the failure of digoxin to kill a baby on the first effort is the well-documented second-trimester abortion of Michelle Armesto (Berge)'s at twenty-four weeks five days. Armesto testified before a Kansas Legislative Hearing in 2007 about her abortion four years earlier at Women's Health Care Services in Wichita, Kansas. She provided Operation Rescue with a copy of her abortion records, which clearly indicate that the digoxin had to be re-administered on Day 2 of her procedure after the first injection on Day 1 had failed, as evidenced by the detection of fetal heart tones.[4]

Another verified example of digoxin survival is "Baby Rowan" case. Rowan was aborted at twenty-two weeks gestation with the use of digoxin at James S. Pendergraft's EPOC Center in Orlando, Florida in 2005. Pendergraft has publicly discussed his use of digoxin in late-term abortions, and claims to be an expert in its use.

However, when Rowan's mother delivered him in a toilet inside the abortion facility, she noticed that he was moving and gasping for breath. Baby Rowan died of extreme prematurity in his mother's arms.[5]

These examples are consistent with the earlier testimony of Dr. Karen Feisullin, who explained that it can take up to twenty-four hours for digoxin to actually kill a pre-born baby, depending where the injection is made.

In addition, toxicologist Dr. Timothy Rohrig, had testified that there was no evidence of puncture in any of the fetuses seized from Gosnell's clinic were examined by him. He further testified that there was no trace of digoxin in any of the toxicology screenings done on the fetal remains.

Feisullin and Rohrig's testimony was devastating to the defense claims that every baby had been injected with digoxin, and that survival of the injections was not possible. Either Gosnell incompetently administered digoxin, or more likely, he never bothered with it in the first place.

"At Gosnell's abortion mill, the lines of legal conduct were blurred and the boundaries of ethical conduct seemed non-existent," Troy Newman said in a statement. "Gosnell relied on undereducated, inexperienced workers who would fall for his phony semantics to help him get away with murder."[6]

The prosecution continued to dismantle Gosnell's primary defense by calling one of his former patients to the stand. Shanice Manning, 20, tearfully told the court of her late-term abortion experience with Gosnell when she was just fifteen years old. Manning said she was taken to Gosnell's clinic by her mother for a late-term abortion she regretted. She was not given any counseling nor was the Pennsylvania twenty-four-hour waiting period law observed.

Manning did not remember any injection prior to the insertion of the laminaria at the beginning of her late-term abortion. However, she did remember asking Gosnell the sex of her baby.

"Well, if you're a good girl, maybe I'll tell you," she said Gosnell told her.

Manning suffered complications and ended up at the hospital where her baby was stillborn.

Baby Manning was twenty-nine weeks' gestation at the time of death. According to the medical examiner who inspected the body, there was no evidence of puncture wounds, bolstering the prosecution's case that Gosnell never administered the digoxin injections and falsified medical records when he noted that he did.

It is improbable that so many of Gosnell's employees would have pled guilty to murder and agreed to testify if the babies were in fact dead.

Gosnell's defense was falling apart.

***

Misrepresenting the use of digoxin injections is tragically not unique to Kermit Gosnell's case. Steven Chase Brigham lost his medical license after authorities discovered that he was engaged in an illegal bi-state abortion scheme in Maryland very similar to Gosnell's operation in Philadelphia. Brigham would begin the late-term abortions in New Jersey, then finish them at a secret, and quite illegal, abortion clinic in Elkton, Maryland. Medical records from Patient D. B., who nearly died from a botched late-term abortion at the Elkton facility, contained a form titled "Laminaria Insertion & Induction of Fetal Demise." That form was completed at Brigham's Voorhees, New Jersey, facility on August 12, 2010. On that form, Brigham documents a pelvic exam and laminaria insertion, but the section of the form that was supposed to document the digoxin injection was left blank.[7]

Like Gosnell, Brigham attempted to tell authorities he had injected D.B.'s baby with Digoxin, but records and evidence indicated that he had lied. Brigham was later arrested and charged with murder in Maryland. The late-term abortions themselves were not forbidden in Maryland; however, if anyone kills a pre-born baby during the commission of a crime in Maryland, the perpetrator may be charged with murder for that death.

Unfortunately, the charges against Brigham were dropped when the prosecution's expert witness withdrew from the case due to pressure from outside sources, presumably within the abortion cartel.

Meanwhile, in Houston, Texas, another late-term abortionist quietly aborted late-term babies in a manner consistent with Gosnell's practices. He would have continued the practice in relative anonymity had it not been for one of his own employees who contacted Operation Rescue. But that is a story for another time.

Nevertheless, the evidence against Brigham and others infers that more late-term abortionists than Gosnell cut corners (and costs) by skipping the tricky Digoxin injection. This leads to one logical, but horrifying conclusion: babies are being born alive and intentionally killed in America – and the murderers are getting away scot free.

CHAPTER 26

TWEET-UP

I f there was one question I was asked more than any other about what I was witnessing at the Gosnell trial, it was, "Why am I not seeing any of this in the mainstream media?"

The case has all the elements of a trial that might attract wall-to-wall coverage on certain cable news stations. It was sensational. It was grisly. It was unbelievably horrific, every bit as much as any serial killer trial that has ever been covered. There was even a sexual component with the strange (and largely unspoken) relationship between unlicensed abortionist Steven Massof and the fifteen-year-old Ashley Baldwin. There were rumors as well of Gosnell's affair with at least one of his employees.

***

With a mostly empty court room, the answer was obvious: there was no interest in a murder case that involved abortion, no matter how sensational, macabre, or newsworthy. Some news outlets defended their lack of coverage with the excuse that this was just a local murder case with no national implications. They were wrong.

Brian Kemper, the head of a pro-life youth group, Stand True, and social media guru Andy Moore, creator of AbortionWiki.org, noticed the lack of media interest and decided to do something about it. Together with Troy Newman, they hatched a plan to launch a #Gosnell "tweet-up" that would focus on challenging media outlets to cover the trial and prove that there was a broad-based public interest in it.

For those few not familiar with Twitter, it is a social network that allows posts up to 140 characters. The hash tag (#) is used to draw attention to a subject of interest and allow other users on Twitter to follow a topic by following the tagged subject's stream of hash-tagged comments.

Trending topics show up on a user's Twitter app or page, drawing even more attention.

Troy, Bryan, and Andy looped in other pro-life leaders who had been reading my reports and created a Facebook page to promote the event. We were surprised when we saw that very quickly over 10,000 people on Facebook signed up to participate.

The #Gosnell Twitter campaign was launched during the fourth week of the trial. The campaign exceeded all expectations. Soon #Gosnell was trending on Twitter, first as the Number Ten trending topic, then rapidly climbing up the rankings to the coveted Number One spot.[1]

"I couldn't hit the 'new tweets' button fast enough. At one point there were about 100 tweets coming as fast as I could push the refresh button," Troy told me.

Two important things then happened that launched the campaign into the stratosphere.

A Philadelphia-area columnist with the Bucks County Courier Times, J. D. Mullane, posted a photo he secretly took from inside the Gosnell courtroom showing rows of completely empty gallery pews on which were posted signs reserving them for the media. That photo embodied our message. Retweets caused the image to spread like wildfire through Twitter, Facebook, and other social media platforms as proof that the media was ignoring this important story.

Almost simultaneously, Kristin Powers, a columnist with *USA Today*, penned an article that appeared on Page One on April 11, 2013. She took *The New York Times*, *The Washington Post*, and television news networks to task for ignoring this extraordinary trial. In the process, Powers reached a national audience who were hearing about Gosnell's atrocities for the very first time.[2]

The tweet-up was successful beyond our dreams. The timing, coupled with Mullane's incriminating photo and Power's *USA Today* piece, all worked together to make this one of the most successful social media campaigns we had ever seen.

It helped us bypass the mainstream media and educate vast numbers of Twitter users that otherwise would never have heard of Gosnell. But more importantly, it shamed the media into covering the story and proved that a unified pro-life effort could be more powerful than we ever thought.

The tweet-up accomplished its goal, as I witnessed for myself on Monday morning at the start of the fifth week of court proceedings. For the first time, the Gosnell court room was filled with members of the media. There was

Fox News' Kimberly Guilfoyle, and Sara Hoyt from CNN, and a host of other reporters too numerous to remember. Several media outlets to begin publishing stories, many for the first time. Anderson Cooper of CNN broadcasted a noteworthy segment on the Gosnell story that was remarkably fair considering Cooper's leftist ideology.[3]

Fox News produced a one-hour special report hosted by Bret Baier about Gosnell that aired before the trial was even over, which angered Judge Minehart to no small degree. He was concerned the jury may have been contaminated by it. Thankfully, no one had seen it and the trial was allowed to resume, but not without Minehart admonishing the gallery with one of his now familiar stern lectures.[4]

But the media attention, unfortunately, would not last long. As court took its morning break on Tuesday, April 15, 2013, I checked the messages on my iPhone, which had sat quietly in my purse on mute. What I saw stunned me. Troy had texted me that there had been an explosion at the Boston Marathon and that people had died.

I leaned forward to the Reuters reporter sitting in front of me waiting for his own cell phone to boot up, and asked him if he knew about that yet and showed him the message I had received. He hadn't, but was worried enough to head for the hallway to make a call.

Soon, all the reporters were notified of the horrific news of the terror attack in Boston. When court resumed, the Gosnell courtroom was mostly empty as all but a handful of reporters were quickly reassigned to this breaking story.

***

In the media coverage that ensued, several news outlets, including Fox News, referred to testimony given the previous week by Ashley Baldwin, who, as a fifteen-year-old high school student had worked 50 hours a week for Gosnell, helping out with grisly late-term abortions.

For the first time, national media detailed how the teenager began working for Gosnell because her mother, Tina Baldwin, was employed by him. While Ashley was not charged with any crimes, her mother faced numerous charges, including "corruption of a minor" for allowing her daughter to be a party to Gosnell's criminal enterprise.

Ashley Baldwin, who was twenty-two by the time of the trial, testified that she saw at least five babies born alive moving, and in one case "screeching" as Gosnell applied surgical scissors to the back of the neck then severed the newborns' spinal cords.

"They just looked like regular babies," she had said.[5]

She testified that one of the victims was so large, Gosnell joked that "this baby is going to walk me home." That joke bothered her to the extent that she discussed it with her mother and fellow co-worker.[6]

Baldwin told the grand jury that even though she was still a high school student at the time, she was left "in charge" before Gosnell arrived at the facility. She cared for women in active labor, administered sedation, and phoned Gosnell to let him know when he was needed at the clinic.

Sometimes she sent women to deliver their late-term babies into the toilet.

Baldwin told the court that she received very little training. Gosnell taught her basics about how to insert IVs, do lab work, and how to operate the ultrasound machine. Ashley seemed to shrug off the fact that, as a teen, she was conducting medical tasks that required months or years of education and training. Most of them were "not that hard," she said.

Gosnell assured her that it was all perfectly legal because he "had her grandfathered in." He supplemented her "training" by giving her medical books to read on her own. Gosnell had shown her how to administer sedation to patients and gave her dosages that were to be used. However, the dosages did not take into consideration a patient's height and weight or her medical history. At Gosnell's abortion business, sedation was a one-size-fits-all proposition. In order to keep from getting confused, Ashley Baldwin drew a color-coded chart with drug names and dosages and posted it on a wall for her reference.

Despite her lack of training, she began assisting Gosnell during the abortion procedures themselves, sometimes handing him surgical implements or applying pressure to the woman's distended abdomen.

The younger Baldwin was also present when Karnamaya Mongar died. Baldwin testified that when Mongar turned gray and stopped breathing Gosnell began giving her chest compressions and told Baldwin to get the defibrillator.

"I got a small shock when I plugged it in," she told the court. "It didn't work."[7]

Less media attention was paid to the testimony of Tina Baldwin, who began working for Gosnell in 2002, primarily as a receptionist answering phones. Tina job also included administering contraction-inducing drugs to abortion patients to send them into labor. While Baldwin was charged with several offenses, she was never charged with murder, as were some of her co-defendants.

Tina Baldwin testified that she believed Eileen O'Neill, who sat next to Gosnell at the defense table, as being a caring person. Gosnell had promised to help her get her medical license, but Baldwin thought he was stalling. Nevertheless, Baldwin testified that she often saw O'Neill illegally write prescriptions for patients on a prescription pad that had been pre-signed by Gosnell.

On the night of the FBI raid, Tina Baldwin was off, but both O'Neill and Tina's young daughter, Ashley, were working at the clinic. Tina testified that O'Neill called to tell her she had slipped out the back door and was worried, not for Ashley, but because she left her coat and purse behind, including her driver's license.

Tina Baldwin, like most of the clinic staff, was black woman. She talked of Gosnell's preferential treatment of white women. Because O'Neill kept her office somewhat cleaner than the rest of the facility, Gosnell often used her office for white patients.

"Nine out of 10 times, if the patient was white" Gosnell would not allow Baldwin to administer the drugs she routinely gave to the black abortion patients. "He wanted to meet with them himself," she testified.[8]

Baldwin said that Gosnell was apologetic to the rest of his staff about the special treatment white patients received, but explained "that's the way it is."

But even though the media missed some of the most important testimony, the case had captured their attention. When it came time for closing arguments, the courtroom that had been occupied for weeks by just a few of us, would be standing-room only.

CHAPTER 27

"EXPERT" ABORTIONIST

The fifth week of Kermit Gosnell's capital murder trial began with an admonition to the jury. Judge Minehart remarked on the increased media coverage in the case and instructed the jury members to avoid media coverage.

Later in the day, Judge Minehart learned of J. D. Mullane's photo of the empty media seats inside the courtroom that had swept like wildfire over Twitter and other social media networks. This time, Minehart made his wrath well known.

"Jurors are intimidated enough," he lectured, causing me to wonder whether there had been some act of intimidation that went unspoken in open court, or if the abortion aspect of this case was taking its toll on the jury.

Minehart also vented his anger concerning a cell phone that had loudly rang out in court earlier. Minehart threatened to ban phones from the courtroom if any further infractions took place. The bailiff later backed up his boss by threatening to confiscate any offending electronic devices, which he promised to flush down the nearest toilet.

All across the room, reporters (including me) were seen reaching for their devices and double-checking to ensure they were off, lest they suffer further wrath from the bench.

Testimony for the day began with the prosecution calling Dr. Charles David Benjamin to the stand. Benjamin told the court that he was a Doctor of Osteopathic Medicine, or D. O., who was Board Certified as an Obstetrician and Gynecologist.

But the unsaid truth was that he was an abortionist.

Benjamin, a stocky, balding middle-aged man, testified that he had conducted over 40,000 abortions since 1978. He had twenty-five years of experience as an abortion provider in a clinic setting, the past twenty years of which were focused primarily on abortions. He was on staff at Albert Einstein Medical Center in Philadelphia, where he trains residents how to do abortions.

Benjamin was presented as an abortion expert over the objections of Gosnell's attorney Jack McMahon.

Benjamin worked in private practice and as an abortion provider with the local Planned Parenthood, where the vast majority of his abortions were done. Benjamin testified that he conducts abortions through 21.5 weeks in a hospital setting but limits in-clinic abortions to seventeen weeks and under. He said that 60 percent of his abortion cases used financial assistance raised by non-profit groups that promote abortion.

As with the testimony of Karen Feisullin, I had no issue with Benjamin giving his "expert" testimony on behalf of the prosecution. I understood it was necessary to bring in someone with abortion experience to explain to the court how Gosnell's practices differed from standard practices of other providers. It isn't every day one gets the opportunity to hear an abortionist talk freely about how he manages his abortion business. I listened carefully for anything I could learn from the "horse's mouth," so to speak.

It didn't take long before Benjamin was forced to admit that he had a run-in with regulators over a drug-handling issue in his office. Drugs had been tampered with or were missing and had to be replaced. It was a minor violation, to be sure, but I could tell he hated having to discuss it from the stand under oath.

Benjamin also had to admit that he had a patient death in his practice. He attempted to minimize it by telling the jury that the patient was actually his partner's patient. She died thirty years ago from sepsis, a systemic blood infection. Even though the patient wasn't his, it was still considered a death within his practice.

Benjamin admitted he was familiar with Gosnell, but denied ever referring patients to him. Benjamin testified concerning Gosnell's grossly outdated sonogram machine, his use of drugs in abortion procedures, and the dispensing of pain and sedation drugs by Gosnell's unqualified workers in his absence.

Benjamin discussed his own use of anesthesia and sedation, telling the court that the amount and type of sedation he gives depends upon a woman's Body Mass Index (BMI). This allows the dosages to be tailored to each woman's size. Abortions on obese patients, who required extra sedation, were done in the hospital.

Unlike Gosnell, who did not actually employ nurses, Benjamin did have licensed nurses, but they were not allowed to administer sedation in his private practice. The Planned Parenthood where he worked employed a nurse anesthetist that was responsible for sedation.

Benjamin also discussed the use of Cytotec, or misoprostol. Gosnell had allowed his unlicensed and unqualified clinic workers to administer one dosage after another to women undergoing second- and third-trimester abortion, then left them unmonitored.

Benjamin stated that he only uses Cytotec in patients twelve weeks gestation or later. He said he never leaves women who have been given Cytotec unmonitored because of the possibility of strong contractions, which can not only be extremely painful, but can cause physical damage to some women.

As far as emergency equipment was concerned, the only crash cart Gosnell apparently owned was not stored at his clinic, but found by police under his bed at his residence. While Gosnell risked the lives of his patients by conducting his shoddy brand of abortions without access to a crash cart, Benjamin said that the crash cart in his office checked to make sure it is stocked and working properly on a monthly basis.

Likewise, Benjamin's autoclave, a machine used to sterilize reusable medical equipment, is tested weekly and receives routine maintenance yearly. Gosnell's autoclave did not work properly.

Gosnell's ultrasound machine was so old that Benjamin could not even guess when it had been made. It sat in the courtroom covered with grime with an internal inducer yellowed from being used for years without a sanitary cover to protect women from infection. Gosnell allowed unqualified workers to take ultrasound measurements, but Benjamin said that he performs all ultrasound exams himself.

While Benjamin testified that he does not use digoxin to cause "fetal demise" in his own practice, he is familiar with its use. He indicated that a standard dosage of digoxin administered into the fetus or amniotic fluid is .5 ml to 2 ml. When asked about a dosage of five grams, the amount believed to have been administered to Karnamaya Mongar, Benjamin responded saying it would be a "very high dose." He testified that it was 500 times the normal dosage or more.

He noted that digoxin causes death for the baby in the womb 95 to 97 percent of the time. This was a disturbing figure because of its implications. The percentage left room for the possibility that the drug could "fail" and lead to babies being born alive during late-term abortion perhaps as much as five percent of the time.

We know what happened to babies when they were born alive at Gosnell's facility. But what about the other clinics where late-term abortions are routinely done? I knew that there were more late-term abortion facilities in the US than is usually stated, but exactly how many facilities were doing these procedures at viability or later when digoxin was more likely to be used? The questions haunted me.

March 2016, I directed my assistant at Operation Rescue to conduct a telephonic survey for the purpose of finding out how many abortion facilities in the US do abortions at twenty weeks' gestation or older. What she found surprised even me.

Out of the 511 surgical abortion facilities operating in America at the time of the survey, we found that 162 locations conducted abortions at 20 weeks gestation or later. Out of the 162 late-term facilities, 122 facilities, about 76 percent, would not provide abortions after 24 weeks.

Interestingly, the vast majority of abortion facilities that offer abortions at twenty weeks or later are not affiliated with Planned Parenthood. Only 18 out of 162 late-term facilities are Planned Parenthood facilities. The remainder, 144 facilities, were independent or have other affiliations.

Despite research that shows viability may occur as early as twenty-two weeks, abortion businesses consider viability at twenty-four weeks of pregnancy. There are forty abortion facilities in our country that openly do abortions at twenty-four weeks or later.

There were five abortion facilities that openly conduct abortions throughout all nine months of pregnancy. These extreme late-term abortion facilities include:

- Southwestern Women's Options in Albuquerque, New Mexico.

- Pro-Choice Medical Center in Beverly Hills, California.

- Boulder Abortion Clinic in Boulder, Colorado.

- Germantown Reproductive Health Services in Germantown, Maryland.

- Women's Med Center in Kettering, Ohio, a suburb of Dayton.

All of these facilities use what I call the Tiller Induction Abortion method. This late-term abortion process was not invented by the infamous late-term abortionist George Tiller of Wichita, Kansas, but it was certainly "perfected" and popularized by him. It is a 3- to 4-day procedure that involves the use of digoxin to stop the baby's heart prior to the induction of labor.

While it is likely that five third-trimester facilities surely experience an occasional abortion where the baby is born alive, it could be happening at 157 others as well.

This is an issue that was the subject of concern during the investigation conducted by House Select Investigative Panel on Infant Lives in 2016. That panel, chaired by Rep. Marsha Blackburn, found evidence that babies were indeed being born alive during abortions, but it wasn't just do to negligence as it was in Gosnell's case. Within fifteen referrals made by the Select Panel at the end of their investigation, they noted that evidence suggested that late-term babies were allowed to be born alive during abortions so the abortion business would have the freshest and most intact organs for sale to middle-man organ procurement companies or research laboratories. In two referrals, they detailed practices of a Texas abortion provider so appalling that it evoked the name of Kermit Gosnell.

CHAPTER 28

MORE DEAD BABIES

After Benjamin was dismissed from the witness stand, the prosecution called Dr. Sam Gulino, Chief Medical Examiner for the City of Philadelphia. His office had been tasked with examining the body of Karnamaya Monger in 2009, and later, the forty-seven human baby remains that were discovered at Gosnell's abortion facility.

The matter of Karnamaya Mongar's death certificate was raised. There were actually three death certificates issued that each listed a different cause of death. Her first certificate stated that the cause was "Undetermined." Once the medical examiner's office was able to get a little more information, the second certificate was issued that amended the cause of death to "Accidental."

It was only after the office received yet more information from the grand jury months after Mongar's death that Gulino reviewed the case and approved yet another change. This time, Mongar's cause of death was listed as "Homicide."

Of course, McMahon attempted to ascribe sinister motives to the homicide determination, but his arguments made little traction, at least with me. He implied that the District Attorney's office convinced Gulino to designate Mongar's cause of death a homicide for political reasons after the case began to gain publicity. Gulino denied it.

However, it was Gulino's testimony related to his examination of the remains of forty-seven frozen fetuses seized by law enforcement authorities from Gosnell's abortion clinic that turned out to be the most important of the day.

The remains arrived at the medical examiner's office in three sets. The first arrived on February 20, 2010, after the initial raid on Gosnell's ramshackle facility. The second group arrived on September 24 of that same year.

These two groups contained the remains of forty-two babies, which were frozen and stored in a variety of containers, including milk jugs, cat food cans, and even a cherry limeade container, all mixed together with discarded gloves, cervical dilators and paper.

The containers were each in their own bags, and those bags were discovered within three large red bio-hazard bags. Several containers contained the "fragmented" remains of several babies. Ages were estimated from less than twelve weeks up to twenty-two weeks. It took Dr. Gulino five days just to catalog the contents before examinations could even be done.

A month later, in October, 2010, Gulino's office received the third macabre delivery of remains, which consisted of five jars of severed feet and other body parts that had been collected by Officer Taggart. These were not frozen, but were preserved in formaldehyde. Each of those jars were labeled with the patient's name and date of the abortion, which all took place from December 5 through 9, 2009. Two of the jars were from the same patient and contained a right and left foot of the same baby. Using the measurement of the feet, Dr. Gulino estimated the fetal ages to be fourteen to nineteen weeks' gestation.

Gosnell's defense attorney argued that the extremities were preserved in the event that DNA evidence was needed and as proof of fetal age. However, Gulino testified that the severing of both feet and a hand would be unnecessary even if this were the case.

The prosecution had its own disturbing theory about why the hands and feet were collected. Serial killers often engage in the practice of taking mementos from their dead victims as trophies of their kills. The prosecution believed that the feet and hands were collected by Gosnell and displayed as trophies of his ghastly handiwork.

During the trial, there was never a definitive answer given to the question of why Gosnell collected the severed hands and feet of his tiny victims. The answer to that question remains locked away in his obviously depraved mind and it is doubtful that the public will ever be privy to the truth.

***

According to Dr. Gulino, this case was unprecedented. He could not find a colleague who had ever dealt with frozen fetal remains of this nature. Since frozen remains decompose quickly when thawed, he had to come up with a new protocol for thawing the remains for examination without destroying them.

Because thawing the fragile remains was a tricky process, the tissue samples were damaged to some extent. Testing to determine whether a baby breathed air was rendered inconclusive. Because of this, there was no way he could say for sure that any of the babies were actually born alive.

However, Gulino testified that it is possible that they were alive at birth or had been birthed into water such as into a toilet. Several former employees, including Ashley Baldwin, testified that they saw babies born into toilets at Gosnell's clinic.

Gulino stated that there would be no reason to sever the babies' spinal cords if they were dead prior to birth, as the defense claimed.

A series of photographs taken by Gulino's office of the bodies were then displayed on the large viewing screen across from the jury.

For the first time, photos of Karnamaya Mongar's dead baby were shown to the jury. Designated as "2J," Mongar's baby was a little girl estimated to be sixteen to nineteen weeks' gestation. Photos of both the back and front were displayed. The baby's skin was bright red, (a condition later described as the early stages of decomposition), and sported a head of dark brown hair.

She was awkwardly positioned. Her arms were up, but her legs were bent as if they were broken. A close-up photo of her back showed a deep gash approximately an inch long in the neck at the base of the skull. The placenta and bloody gauze were found with her remains. The Medical Examiner found no fetal anomalies when he examined the baby's body. In other words, Mongar's baby had been perfectly healthy.

It was frankly disturbing to hear the condition of Mongar's baby, who died in 2009, and the fact that the body was still in a freezer at the Women's Medical Society when the clinic was raided in 2010. It was hard not to be overcome by grief and horror while contemplating the child's last painful moments of life that expired while her mother lay dying on that rusty, tattered abortion table.

But there were soon images of other babies that filled the projection screen, and emotions had to be set aside if I was to properly document what I was witnessing, a horrendous display that those outside of the courtroom would likely never see.

The bodies of a baby boy and a baby girl in the twenty-first to twenty-second weeks of gestation were displayed in grisly color. These babies, designated "1D" and "1C," were described as possibly viable.

Baby 1B was a little boy whose remains weighed 950 grams. There were no apparent fetal anomalies. Gulino gave a conservative estimate of fetal age at twenty-eight weeks. This baby also had the one-inch slit, often described by Gulino as a "defect," in the back of his neck.

Baby 1C was a little girl with brown hair and fused eyelids. Like Baby 1B, she, too, had a slit in the back of her neck consistent with Gosnell's "snipping" practice. Her body showed no evidence of fetal anomaly.

Both babies, along with Mongar's child, were checked for evidence of breathing after birth. Their bodies were X-rayed and their lungs were removed and put in water to see if they would float. Floating is an indication of aeration, or air in the lungs. But none of the lungs floated and there was no X-ray evidence of air in the lungs or stomach. Air was detected by X-ray in the large intestine of Baby 1B, and in his abdominal cavity.

Gulino cautioned about taking the test results as evidence the babies were dead prior to birth. He noted that a fetus born into a toilet or bathtub would not show aeration even if it was breathing. He testified that the tests were inconclusive and suggested that the freezing and thawing processes may have caused blood vessels and cells to burst. The likelihood of such damage made the testing unreliable. Decomposition is also known to cause false positives and negatives for air in the lungs.

As more coroner photos flashed across the screen, I found the display both revolting and riveting. I scribbled notes of each image as fast as I could.

Baby 3-E-1 had an estimated gestational age of twenty-two weeks, considered the lower limit of viability.

Baby 3-F was estimated to be twenty-one weeks' gestation at the time of death.

Baby 2-E's head was collapsed, and no brain was evident. Gulino surmised the missing brain could have been due to the removal of the brains by suction or from the head being crushed. It was also suggested that brain matter could have been liquefied due to the decomposition process. Estimated gestational age of this baby was twenty weeks.

The remains of one baby, which for some unstated reason was not shown to the jury, was described as missing both feet severed above the ankle and a right hand severed above the wrist. The inference of that baby's disfigurement was clear. This was a child whose limbs were harvested for Gosnell's grisly private collection.

***

Pennsylvania law requires that a death certificate be filed for fetuses sixteen weeks' gestation and beyond. If a baby is "live born," both birth and death certificates must be filed. Gulino told the court that he filed death certificates for those babies who were estimated to be sixteen weeks and older. In two cases, Babies 1B and 1C, reports were made to the Department of Health notifying them that viable babies had been aborted. Because testing was inconclusive, no "live birth" certificates were issued for any of the babies found at Gosnell's Women's Medical Society.

Of the forty-seven babies examined, 95 percent were determined to be under twenty weeks' gestation. Forty-three had no discernible "neck defect," meaning the "snipping" slit to the back of the neck. Gulino explained, "Some of the fetal remains were fragmented so there was not necessarily a neck for me to examine."

***

The subject of viability was a touchy one that was revisited by McMahon during his aggressive cross-examination of Dr. Gulino. Shockingly, McMahon marched to the jury box and dramatically asked Dr. Gulino, "If the baby is dead, it can't be viable, can it?"

McMahon suggested that any movements by a baby after birth were simply a condition known as cadaveric spasm, which was described as movement of muscle groups as the result of the rapid onset of rigor mortis. The medical examiner indicated that was unlikely due to the under-developed nature of muscles at the gestational ages being discussed.

Testimony ended when a shouting match broke out between McMahon and prosecutor Edward Cameron over whether the babies were born alive. Cameron was conducting questioning on re-direct when McMahon angrily blurted out a question out of turn. The two men began shouting at each other, but both were quickly shouted down by Judge Jeffery Minehart, who rebuked McMahon and told him to "act like a lawyer."

The argument ended questioning for the day.

CHAPTER 29

KARNAMAYA MONGAR

The following morning, court resumed with more deeply emotional testimony. It was time for two members of Karnamaya Mongar's family to take the stand and testify about events that lead to the death of their loved one, a slight forty-one-year-old immigrant from Bhutan.

Yashoda Gurung, Mongar's adult daughter, testified the Nepali language through an interpreter. Gurung testified that she was born in Bhutan, a small nation near India on the eastern edge of the Himalaya Mountains. Her family fled from dangerous political upheaval in Bhutan when she was a baby and came to live in a refugee camp in Nepal. The family lived there for nearly 20 years in crude thatched huts constructed of wood and corrugated tin. In 2009, they came to the United States under a refugee relocation program. They were assisted by the program for three months, then Karnamaya, her husband, daughter, son, and several members of their extended family were on their own to build new lives for themselves in America.

Within a couple of months of their arrival in Virginia, Yashoda had landed a job at a nearby McDonalds, and her father became employed in a turkey processing plant. They were a hard-working family that all pitched in to make their new life a success. About seven months after settling in Virginia, Mongar suspected she might be pregnant. Her suspicions were confirmed by a home pregnancy test. The family was poor and barely made ends meet. Mongar worried that she could not afford to raise a baby in this new country. Yashoda urged her mom to keep the baby, but Mongar made the fatal decision to have an abortion.

Mongar spoke no English, except for a very few words like, "thank you." At the time of Mongar's abortion Yashoda spoke a little more English than her mother, but had difficulty understanding the spoken language. It is doubtful that anyone in the family was aware of the availability of assistance programs for pregnant women who struggle with similar challenges as those faced by Mongar.

Fifteen days before her death, Mongar went to a "family planning" clinic just fifteen minutes from her home. However, Mongar was turned away for an abortion because, at somewhere between sixteen to nineteen weeks, she was too far along in her pregnancy. Mongar was referred to an abortion clinic in Fredericksburg, Virginia, which also refused to conduct her abortion due to her advanced pregnancy. That facility referred her to yet another abortion clinic in Washington, DC. This time, Mongar never even saw a doctor. Instead, the receptionist handed her a paper with the Women's Medical Society address and phone number. Not knowing what she was about to face, she made an appointment.

Most women might have given up or considered the roadblocks a sign from God not to abort, but most women have not lived the kind of life the Mongar family had endured. She was used to overcoming hardship, but this time, her determination to overcome obstacles, which had served her well during nearly two decades as a refugee, cost her her life.

***

It was November 19, 2009. Mongar made the 5 to 5 1/2 hour trip to Philadelphia in the passenger seat of a car driven by her relative by marriage, Damber Ghalley. Mongar viewed Ghalley as a brother. Mongar's daughter explained that he was a bit more acclimated to America, having first arrived in 1999. Yashoda said that her mother was taken into the clinic and had "medicine put inside her." It was only after Mongar's abortion had been started that they were told it was a two-day procedure, and that they would have to come back the next day. The family got in the car and made the long trek back to Virginia that night.

At several points during her emotional testimony, Yashoda wept as she spoke. At one point, the young woman broke down sobbing and needed time to compose herself before she could continue.

Mongar began feeling strong abdominal pain that night and took ibuprofen for relief. The next day, Ghalley drove Mongar, Yashoda, and other family members back to Philadelphia to finish the procedure.

Mongar, who was only five feet two inches short and weighed about 135 pounds, was taken back to a room full of grungy, worn recliners where she would stay for the next five hours. She was given some white pills by a woman.

After that, Mongar's pain increased. She told her daughter, "It hurts all over the place." Yashoda went to get help. No one at the clinic was qualified to give IV medication, yet one of the female workers gave her mother an IV. After that, Mongar dozed in the recliner.

She identified at least two of Gosnell's employees, a white woman named "Sherry" and a black woman, who she saw medicate her mother. Sherry gave Mongar pills. Yashoda remembered the other woman putting additional drugs in her mother's IV bag.

At around 8:00 pm that night, Yashoda was told the doctor was there and she would have to return to the main waiting room. Before leaving Mongar's side, she tried to wake her mother, but could not.

After "waiting a long time," about an hour and a half, Yashoda said she heard ambulance sirens. She and all family members of other patients were ushered to a second-floor waiting room where she sat anxiously for fifteen to twenty minutes.

Her name was called, and she was rushed by a clinic worker downstairs where she caught a glimpse of her mother in a tiny room laying on a bed with her head back as if she was in pain. Yashoda tipped her head back to demonstrate to the court. She tried to enter the room and get to her mother, but Sherry pushed her back. Instead, she was taken into the parking lot where she began to sob with fright amid the confusion of the ambulance lights and people running about. She stood by, helplessly afraid of what was happening, while she watched paramedics lift her mom into the ambulance.

It was Sherry West that rode with the family in Ghalley's car to help guide them to the hospital where the family held anxious vigil throughout the night. Ghalley had managed to get a glimpse of Mongar and reported to Yashoda that her mom was being given oxygen. Someone kept telling the family that Mongar was going to be fine. Yashoda's dad also arrived at the hospital the next day, but by then, it was too late.

Some doctors from the hospital came to inform the family that Karnamaya Mongar was dead. "We tried our best," they said. "Her heart just stopped working."

Yashoda was taken to see her mother's body.

At the prosecution's behest, a smiling photo of Mongar and her husband, Ash, taken shortly after their arrival in America sadly flashed across the courtroom's view screen, eliciting another flood of emotions from Yashoda, who broke down sobbing. This prompted Judge Minehart to allow a much-needed break.

McMahon's cross-examination of an understandably emotional Yashoda Gurung was a delicate task. He went to great effort to treat her as kindly as he could, and not to appear mean or adversarial as he had through much of the trial. McMahon asked her to once again explain the number of clinics Mongar had gone to before being referred to Gosnell for an abortion and the events once they arrived at the Women's Medical Society.

McMahon showed Yashoda a photo of the front waiting room at Gosnell's clinic and questioned her about its condition.

"When we were there it was dirty. In the picture it looks cleaner," she said. Earlier testimony stated Gosnell had ordered the clinic cleaned and painted after Mongar's death and again after the initial police raid in February 2010.

Yashoda testified that she never saw Gosnell the entire time she was at the clinic.

McMahon presented Yashoda with a copy of a letter from Gosnell to her dated November 27, 2009. She told him she didn't recognize it. That ended Yashoda's testimony and she was dismissed, but we would hear more about that letter when her "uncle," Damber Ghalley, took the stand.

***

Like Karnamaya Mongar, Damber Ghalley was also a native of Bhutan who lived for a time as a refugee before coming to America in 1999. He described his relationship with the Mongar family as a complicated one in which he considered them a part of his own family.

At the time of Mongar's death, Ghalley "took them everywhere" and seemed to be their primary means of transportation. Ghalley took her to the two Virginia clinics and to the one in Washington, DC. The women were not completely forthcoming about all the trips and didn't want him to know that Mongar was seeking an abortion.

It was Ghalley who drove Mongar and her daughter, Yashoda Gurung, to Gosnell's West Philadelphia abortion business in November, 2009. Once there, he went inside with the women, but didn't stay there long. He chose instead to wait for them outside. During that first visit, he waited two to three hours, and was anxious to be headed home. It was during the return trip that the women first told him they needed to go back to the clinic the next day.

Ghalley really did not want to make the trip again, but he was a fast and loyal friend. He finally agreed after the women told him Mongar had taken medication and it was important for her to return as scheduled. They spoke no more of it during the long car ride back to Virginia.

He took Mongar, and some other family members back to Philadelphia the next day as requested. Again, he accompanied them into the office, then left to wait in his car. It seemed like he had to wait a long time. He passed the time watching people come and go from the clinic. He had no indication anything was wrong until he heard the sirens and saw the ambulance.

"People came outside running around," Ghalley said. Among them was Yashoda, and he noticed she was crying.

He then saw firemen with bolt cutters headed for the back door. They cut the chain off the door and removed Mongar on a gurney.

From the sidewalk, Ghalley saw Gosnell just inside the now-opened back door, and asked him what happened.

"The procedure was done. Your sister's heart stopped," Gosnell replied, but did not elaborate.

Ghalley testified that Sherry West rode to the hospital with the rest of the weeping family. She tried to calm them down, and stayed with them through the night as they waited for word on Mongar's condition. At one point, a doctor from the hospital stopped by the waiting room to inform the family that doctors were able to bring back a heartbeat and pulse, which gave them a glimmer of hope. But that hope was dashed when a group of doctors arrived to tell the family that Karnamaya had passed away.

The defense posed the possibility that Mongar had taken medications on her own to help her lose the baby before she reported to Gosnell's clinic for an abortion. It was a reaction with those drugs that caused Mongar's death. But Ghalley did not believe it. He testified that Mongar never could have told them she took any medicine because she spoke no English.

In the morning, Gosnell arrived to get West from the hospital in a "big truck," identified as a newer model Ford F-150 extended cab pickup. Distraught, Ghalley went to speak to Gosnell, who calmly insisted that he had done everything right, and would answer any questions at any time. Ghalley was adamant during his testimony that Gosnell expressed no sympathy to them for the loss of their loved one.

Defense attorney Jack McMahon questioned Ghalley about a "sympathy" letter sent to Yashoda by Gosnell. Ghalley testified he did not remember ever calling it that. It remained clear that he saw no expression of sympathy in it.

***

Mongar's husband, Ash, was not in court during Yashoda Gurung and Damber Ghalley's testimony. He took his wife's death hard. To cope with his grief, Ash dove into his job, working six days per week at the turkey processing plant.

The family filed a civil suit against Gosnell for wrongful death, and the City of Philadelphia for not shutting down the clinic earlier. While the state's lack of action to protect the public certainly made it at least partially responsible for Mongar's death, the state was sadly immune from prosecution.

Even though the State of Pennsylvania had enacted laws to protect women prior to Mongar's death, it never bothered to enforce them. When laws are not enforced, there is nothing to stop people like Gosnell from violating them. This lack of enforcement stemmed from the abortion-friendly political climate in Pennsylvania, which created conditions where there was simply no incentive for State agencies to fulfill their duty to enforce even the most basic of health and safety regulations at abortion businesses.

If they had, Karnamaya Monger might still be alive today.

CHAPTER 30

"HOUSE OF HORRORS"

James "Jimmy" Johnson was employed by Gosnell as a handyman who was responsible for maintenance at all Gosnell's properties, which included his homes in Mantua and at the shore, a four-unit row-house that Gosnell rented to college students, the house where Gosnell's son lived, and the abortion clinic at 3801 Lancaster. For his work, Gosnell paid Johnson $300 to $400, and sometimes $500 per week, depending on his tasks.

Johnson testified about the horrendous conditions at the Women's Medical Society. The roof of the ramshackle brick building chronically leaked. He had attempted to fix it "quite a few times," but no matter what he did, he could never repair the leak.

The clinic was infested with rats, as evidenced by rat feces found regularly throughout the clinic. A pest control company supposedly came by once a month, but the problem persisted. Johnson tried to get rid of them with poison bait, but that didn't work either. Gosnell brought in a cat and Johnson installed a pet door so the cat could get to the rats in the basement, but the rats were never under control. Apparently, all the cat did was urinate on the rugs and defecate in the plants that were plentifully scattered throughout the clinic.

Perhaps predictably, the clinic also had a flea problem.

Each morning at 9 am, Johnson would report to the clinic and perform his regular duties such as sweeping up, cleaning the cat litter, and caring for the fish and turtle tanks.

He would also go to each procedure room and remove the "medical waste," which consisted of aborted baby remains, and take them to the basement where he would store them in the freezer. Once a week, Johnson would go to the clinic and take the remains out of the freezer and box them up for Stericycle.

However, at some point, Stericycle stopped picking up the boxes due to an apparent billing dispute, so the bags just piled up in the basement, which appeared to Johnson to be the primary source of the rat infestation. At one time, he had twenty-seven bags full of aborted baby remains piled up in the basement with nowhere to send them.

Johnson testified of the gruesome pumbing issues that plagued Gosnell's facility. The toilets in the clinic would back up once or twice a week. Once, when Johnson opened the clean out drain on the outside of the building, out gushed material from the sewer line in which he observed tiny arms and other body parts. He went inside and told Gosnell what had happened. Gosnell told him to clean it up. Johnson took a shovel and scooped up the human remains into a plastic bag, and put it in the freezer. He testified he had to conduct this drain unclogging process over and over.

In December, 2009, right after the death of Karnamaya Mongar, Gosnell told Johnson they had "an inspection coming" and he needed to get the clinic cleaned up. Gosnell hired another man named LeRoy to help, but Johnson said he really didn't do much. During that time, Gosnell replaced the waiting room chairs and ordered some of the walls to be painted.

Johnson also testified to installing four security cameras, all of which were mounted inside the abortion facility and positioned to monitor employees, especially in areas where cash was handled. Apparently, Gosnell didn't trust his employees, especially with cash.

***

Della Mann was a retired military nurse who once worked for Gosnell for three to four years in the 1980s prior to her military deployment. She was also a patient at his clinic until 2008. Mann's testimony was bizarre, to say the least. Mann testified that she heard in 2009, that Gosnell was looking to hire a nurse, so she sought him out and applied for the job. He agreed to pay her $31 per hour, six hours per week to observe staff and review charts.

"It was awful," Mann testified when asked about the clinic conditions she found at Gosnell's clinic. She described floors as filthy and equipment as outdated and dirty. She said Gosnell had the same equipment that he was using in the 1980s when she previously worked for him.

She saw used, dirty speculums that were apparently being reused without cleaning. She also testified to observing suspiciously "woozy" patients that appeared to have been overmedicated.

Mann only worked for Gosnell for two days before quitting out of fear of losing her nursing license. She cited the unorthodox way she was paid and the dirty conditions. She explained how Gosnell would write her a check then have her sign it back to him in exchange for cash. While it wasn't fully explained in court, this behavior has been documented at other abortion facilities by Mark Crutcher of Life Dynamics, Inc. as a method of evading the payment of taxes through keeping double books on clinic finances.

From Mann's testimony, it soon became clear that she had been hired because she was a registered nurse, which Gosnell needed only temporarily to deceive an NAF representative who was scheduled to conduct a membership inspection. Mann testified that she was never interviewed by the NAF representative.

Mann was also a patient at the Lancaster clinic from 1990 until 2008, which seemed odd since, as a registered nurse, she was well acquainted with substandard conditions and practices there. She did not see Gosnell, but was instead treated by Gosnell's unlicensed "doctors," Eileen O'Neill and Steven Massof.

Mann was routinely treated for back pain by "Dr." O'Neill. She said she had no idea O'Neill wasn't licensed because she acted like a doctor, diagnosed conditions, and wrote prescriptions. While she saw Massof for hypertension and allergies, it was O'Neill who wrote the prescriptions for all drugs Mann received there. Mann said she was not aware if Gosnell was in the clinic or consulted at the time O'Neill wrote the prescriptions, but records showed he was not present.

Mann recalled that O'Neill once gave her an injection, but that treatment was never recorded in her chart.

Mann stopped visiting the Women's Medical Society in 2008, supposedly because Gosnell's business did not make the switch to electronic medical records and due to billing irregularities. She admitted she paid no insurance co-payments for visits to the Women's Medical Society, as she would be required to do at any other clinic, but understood her Blue Cross insurance was billed for her visits. She also testified to an unorthodox insurance billing practice that seemed slightly shady, implying that insurance was billed for days she was not seen.

O'Neill's defense argued that Gosnell allowed Mann to be treated at his clinic for free, as he generously did for other patients that would have struggled to pay.

Prosecutor Ed Cameron prompted Mann to confirm that the clinic billed her insurance, asking, "Do you think you got all that treatment for free?"

To the surprise of everyone in the courtroom, O'Neill, from the defendant's table, blurted out, "Yes!" She was quickly rebuked by Judge Minehart, who told her she was not allowed to speak then cautioned the jury to disregard her comment. O'Neill was allowed to apologize to the court for her outburst.

***

Finishing up the day of testimony was Lorriane Matikjiw, who provided quality assurance for a federally funded children's vaccine program in which Gosnell was enrolled. She testified that every twelve to eighteen months participating sites would be visited for a chart review to ensure that children were receiving their vaccines on schedule, and to check to make sure the vaccines were being stored properly. When Matikjiw first visited the Women's Medical Society for the routine review in July 2008, she didn't know it was an abortion clinic until she got there. Things she encountered at the clinic raised red flags.

Gosnell was not present for their appointment. The woman at the reception desk, Tina Baldwin, wasn't prepared for her visit. No charts were made available. She observed generally filthy conditions throughout the parts of the clinic she visited along with the smell of cat urine. Two large fish tanks were in desperate need of cleaning. There was junk, clutter, and an overabundance of plants in various stages of brown and green throughout.

Matikjiw noticed a price list for abortions and papers taped to the counter and wall that stated if a patient changed her mind about having an abortion procedure, she would not get her money back.

She was taken to the two refrigerators where the vaccines were supposed to be stored. One was a "dorm-style" refrigerator where she found that some of the vaccines had expired. The larger two-door refrigerator had incomplete records for temperature checks that were supposed to take place twice a day.

She inspected a freezer where aborted baby remains were stored along with the vaccines. She found blood frozen to the bottom.

Matikjiw reported Gosnell to her supervisor, Lisa Morgan, and sent a note to the director of the vaccine program, but nothing seemed to happen. She was sent back to Gosnell's clinic the following year when he reapplied for program participation. When Matikjiw returned, Gosnell shook her hand, then left the building. She met with Eileen O'Neill for about forty-five minutes, during which she asked to review charts of children in the vaccine program. O'Neill told her that the clinic had no children as patients, yet Matikjiw's records showed that nineteen to twenty children were enrolled.

Matikjiw testified that O'Neill did not seem to understand her explanation of the program or that it was for children. O'Neill thought the vaccines were for all patients. She found it odd when O'Neill told her that Gosnell needed to be in the program so his granddaughter could get the free vaccines. Matikjiw asked for O'Neill's medical license number for her records, and O'Neill told her she had a license that lapsed in Delaware but hadn't bothered to get a license in Pennsylvania because Gosnell "doesn't pay me enough."

Because the expired vaccines needed to be taken by Matikjiw for disposal, she needed Gosnell to sign a form noting what was being taken. She left a form for him to fax to her office because Gosnell was absent from the clinic.

Matikjiw was confused as to why a clinic that never saw children would be so adamant about enrolling in a children's vaccine program. The obvious conclusion was that Gosnell was bilking money from this children's vaccine program by reporting non-existing children as patients. She reported Gosnell again to her supervisor, but nothing was ever done.

CHAPTER 31

FILES

t was Wednesday, April 17, 2013. We were halfway through the fifth week of Gosnell's trial, during which we had heard such shocking testimony that the jurors long stopped flinching at each new grisly revelation. The men and women of the jury, who were now familiar to me by face, if not by name, sat intently listening to the testimony and viewing the evidence as one dreadful fact after another was paraded before them.

This day, two witnesses provided their unique perspectives as a patient and an employee of Gosnell's Women's Medical Society.

Mary Kincade had been referred by a friend to Gosnell's Women's Medical Society and was a patient for about 10 years. She was last seen as a patient there sometime in 2009. Kincade testified that she was never seen by Gosnell, but only by Eileen O'Neill for yearly well-woman exams. Kincade thought O'Neill was a licensed physician and noted that certificates hung on the wall of her office, which led her to believe they allowed her to practice medicine. The other workers at the clinic always referred to O'Neill as "Doctor."

There was a discrepancy in Kincade's patient file concerning co-payments for office visits. Kincade testified that she remitted a co-pay of $30 to $40 each time she saw O'Neill. However, in her file, there was only one receipt for $40 to indicate she ever paid any money.

This seemed to be an odd bit of testimony, considering everything else that was being talked about over the past four weeks. I assumed that the prosecution was trying to prove that there were irregularities in the billing and record-keeping practices at Gosnell's clinic. The prosecutors did not fully detail their theory concerning what appeared to be evidence of financial malfeasance. That would come during closing arguments when the prosecution would take all the elements of evidence and testimony and systematically connect all the dots for the jury.

***

The longest testimony of the day came from Latosha Lewis, 31, a medical assistant who worked for Gosnell for almost ten years from May 2000 to February 2010, when the clinic was shut down. Lewis was not arrested with Gosnell and his eight co-workers in January 2011. Instead, she was arrested and charged by the federal government related to apparent drug activities at Gosnell's clinic. Like the other Gosnell co-defendants, with the exception of Eileen O'Neill, she entered a guilty plea agreement and agreed to testify against Gosnell in return for leniency at the time of her sentencing.

While on the witness stand, Lewis told the court that she graduated from an eight-month training program with a Medical Assisting Diploma. During her training, she was not taught how to conduct ultrasounds or give anesthesia. Once hired by Gosnell, her duties at Women's Medical Society grew until she was not only conducting those tasks, but also assisting with surgical abortion procedures.

Lewis gave anesthesia in standard dosages according to a chart she was provided. Sometimes she changed the amounts that were recommended. In 2007, she overdosed a woman and was worried about whether she would ever come out of anesthesia. Because of that scare, she stopped assisting with the surgical abortions. She also said she stopped administering Cytotec, a drug that caused powerful and often unpredictable contractions around the same time.

"I saw women deliver too quickly and didn't want to deal with that," she explained.

Lewis testified that Gosnell was well aware of why she refused to continue to drug women. He reassigned her to work at the front desk, but she continued to conduct ultrasound examinations. According to Lewis, Gosnell's equipment was outdated and never inspected. She said that Gosnell's brother-in-law used to inspect the equipment, but after he died, the inspections just never resumed.

Gosnell often reused disposable curettes in order to cut costs. The curettes were washed, dried, and placed in an antiseptic solution, then reused. Lewis noticed that women who had abortions using the reused curettes began returning to the clinic suffering from sexually transmitted diseases.

Lewis was on duty when Karnamaya Mongar came for her first appointment, and through the use of a relative as a translator, she helped fill out Mongar's medical history forms and took her vitals. Lewis remembered asking her if she had any medical issues and was told there were none. She went over the forms then escorted Mongar to another room for an ultrasound.

Mongar's original chart that was seized from Gosnell's clinic was examined in court. Those who touched it were instructed to don purple latex gloves because the file was stained with blood and other bodily fluids and emitted an unpleasant odor. As Lewis examined Mongar's contaminated medical records, she noted that there was no notation of Mongar's weight on the chart, which is necessary information for women undergoing anesthesia. Lewis testified that the scale in the clinic had been broken for a month and she had no way to weigh patients.

Lewis said that Mongar started her abortion on the first day she arrived at the clinic, which violated a law that requires information be given twenty-four hours prior to an abortion. Nevertheless, Lewis admitted she inserted a consent form into Mongar's chart and signed it, falsely affirming that the twenty-four-hour waiting period had been observed.

The next day, Mongar returned to complete her abortion. According to Mongar's medical record, she arrived at 2:00 pm and at 3:30 pm. Tina Baldwin gave Mongar one Cytotec pill and three Restorils, a drug approved for the treatment of insomnia. Another Cytotec pill was administered at an unknown time by an unknown person. At 6:30 pm, Elizabeth Hampton gave Mongar yet another dose of Cytotec. Just sixty-six minutes later, another dose was given by an unknown worker.

It was Lewis' testimony that Mongar's record did not accurately reflect the drugs she was given. Record keeping at the Women's Medical Society was unreliable because many of the workers were sloppy and failed to make accurate notations in the medical charts and in a narcotics log book. She tried to encourage the others to properly document, but they just wouldn't change. In truth, no one really knew exactly what drugs were administered to patients or when. Dosages were also not reported or were inaccurate.

Lewis left the clinic at 5:00 pm that day at the end of her shift and was not present when Mongar died.

***

In one of the more dramatic moments of the day, Prosecutor Ed Cameron brought Lewis to a square white rolling table that had been seized from

Gosnell's clinic and brought into the courtroom along with other pieces of outdated and filthy furniture and equipment. The metal legs of the table were rusted and dirty. Lewis agreed that Gosnell would pull out a flat shelf from that table and there he would use a "protractor-kind of thing" to measure fetal feet that were placed in glass trays, just as Cameron demonstrated for the jury.

Cameron then began the tedious process of reviewing one patient file after the other, confirming the amounts of drugs given as well as the size of the baby's heads on the multiple ultrasound images and the fetal ages as recorded in the charts.

In reviewing the thirty or so charts, a pattern began to emerge. Ultrasound measurements showing the biparietal diameter, or BPD, which is the measurement across the baby's head at the widest point, varied from 53–75.8 mm. This measurement was used to determine fetal age. According to a measurement chart found on the Internet, 53 mm BPD equates roughly to 22 weeks gestation. A 75.8 mm BPD would represent 29–30 weeks gestation. However, recorded in the charts almost uniformly was the fetal age of 24.5 weeks, no matter what BPD number was recorded.

Included in the charts was that of ShayQuana Abrams, the twenty-one-year-old mother of Baby Boy A, who Gosnell joked was so big he could have walked him to the bus stop. Her three ultrasounds put her baby's BPD at 61.8, 75.8, and 74.8. Even though those measurements would have put her baby in the 28–30 week range, her chart showed her baby, like the others, was only 24.5 weeks.

Many charts had notations concerning the cost of the second trimester procedures. Prices ranged from $830–$1,665. Many women who did not have the full amount were aided by an abortion fund that raises money to pay for portions of an abortion bill that patients cannot cover. However, more women signed promissory notes and were put on a payment plan for the balance. Lewis testified it was not unusual for women to disappear and never pay their balances.

Defense Attorney Jack McMahon also reviewed each of the files with Lewis. He noted that there were signed consent forms in most of that charts that included a 24-hour consent for abortion, a consent to be given Cytotec, and a consent form for the use of digoxin for the purpose of bringing about "fetal demise" prior to the abortion.

Another digoxin form in some of the charts contained a diagram of a pregnant abdomen with intersecting lines defining four quadrants. That was where a notation was to be made to indicate the location of the digoxin injection.

On cross-examination, McMahon went back though each file, pointing out the consent forms in each. One by one, each file was re-examined to the point that those of us in the gallery were bleary-eyed with tedium.

McMahon made much of the paperwork for the sake of the jury and emphasized how it showed that Gosnell did indeed obtain the necessary consent. Attention to the digoxin forms was meant to bolster his argument that all the babies aborted at Gosnell's clinic were already dead before being expelled from the womb.

On re-direct, Cameron powerfully nullified McMahon's afternoon of work by pointing out that each and every file contained information about abortions done at 24.5 weeks. The last day an abortion can legally be done in Pennsylvania is twenty-three weeks six days.

"He got consent to do illegal abortions?" Cameron forcefully asked.

McMahon erupted with objections, but Cameron had made his point.

CHAPTER 32

PATIENT TESTIMONY

Lisa Dungee testified that she was a patient at Gosnell's Women's Medical Society in 2009. She saw Eileen O'Neill for an early medication abortion. Dungee testified that she never received counseling prior to her abortion. She admitted that she signed a form indicating that she had been given informed consent twenty-four hours prior to the abortion, but was adamant that she signed the forms on the same day her abortion began.

"When I came in to the facility, I already had my mind made up about what I wanted to do, so yes, I signed it," she testified.

Gosnell was certainly not alone in playing fast and loose with waiting periods and other regulations. Lack of adherence to waiting periods and informed consent laws are not uncommon at abortion facilities throughout the US, according to the vast amount of documentation collected by Operation Rescue on this topic.

I couldn't help but think of my friend, Jennifer, who had been tricked into an abortion against her will by the notorious Michigan abortionist Alberto Hodari, even though she had signed no consent forms.[1]

Hodari was involved in another forced abortion case in 2009. Caitlin Bruce filed a suit against Hodari and his assistant, "Victor," over an incident that took place at his Flint, Michigan, abortion clinic in April 2008. In her suit, Ms. Bruce alleged that she went to Hodari's clinic seeking an abortion, but before the procedure began, she changed her mind and decided against it. She notified Hodari that she no longer wanted the abortion.

However, Bruce claimed Hodari and his assistant, Victor, forcibly restrained Ms. Bruce, holding her down. Ms. Bruce screamed, "Stop, stop, I don't want this," but her mouth was covered to muffle her pleas while Hodari forced the abortion upon her.[2]

That case was settled out of court for an undisclosed, but reportedly substantial, sum of money.

It's hard to imagine a greater betrayal than to have a "doctor" use deception to forcefully abort a child against its mother's will.

In ignoring waiting periods and informed consent laws, Gosnell's clinic acted no differently than hundreds of other abortion clinics around the country. Authorities rarely discipline or prosecute on violations of informed consent laws, so abortionists have no incentive to abide by them. This is a problem that is rampant throughout the abortion cartel.

***

Dungee testified that she thought O'Neill was a licensed physician because she wore a white coat and had certificates on the wall of her office. No one ever told her that O'Neill held no valid medical license.

According to Dungee, O'Neill gave her one abortion pill to take at the clinic and another pill to take later at home, along with a prescription for antibiotics. She said she never saw Gosnell, who should have been consulted before drugs were prescribed, at the clinic.

Dungee never returned to O'Neill for her follow-up appointment due to the filthy conditions at the clinic. Instead, she saw her own physician for follow-up care. Dungee insisted under oath that neither O'Neill or anyone else from the clinic ever called to see how she was doing, even though O'Neill noted in the records that such a follow-up call had been placed.

The unlicensed practice of medicine, unqualified staff, failure to provide follow-up care, and falsification of medical records are accusations that are certainly not new to the abortion industry.

For example, in 2009, Bertha Bugarin, owner of a chain of abortion clinics in Southern California, pled guilty to illegal abortions and practicing medicine without a license. She was doing abortions with no medical background whatsoever. The licensed abortionists she did hire almost all at some point had their medical licenses revoked. At least two of her abortionists had no medical license at all. Another was a convicted sex offender with a history of raping and molesting abortion patients.

Bugarin's back-alley-style abortion business was so appalling that even Planned Parenthood, which had its own problems complying with patient safety standards, denounced her. At the time of Bugarin's arrest, Blanka Rubio of Planned Parenthood in San Diego said, "We think that this really indicates the need for safe, legal abortions. I think that there's a lot of vulnerable women out there that may be desperate, may be scared . . . we're 100 percent behind the prosecution of this case."

Yet, despite the likes of Gosnell, Hodari, Bugarin, and a host of others, Planned Parenthood and other abortion clinics balk at regulations that would hold abortion clinics accountable to minimum medical standards.

In Kansas, where abortion abuses have been recorded that reach Gosnell-like proportions, laws that would require abortion clinics to meet safety standards have languished in court for years, with no end in sight, while unsafe conditions continue. In Virginia, protests broke out when clinic safety standards were under consideration, even though clinics in Virginia regularly endangered women's lives with their substandard conditions, as evidenced by reams of violations cited in deficiency reports.[3]

Another point of interest in Dungee's testimony was introduced by O'Neill's defense attorney, James Berardinelli, who up until that point had few, if any, questions for prosecution witnesses. Berardinelli's legal theory was unique, but that was about all that could be said for it. He insisted that since Dungee did not actually expel her four-week baby until twenty-four hours after she took the first abortion pill, then the twenty-four-hour waiting period had been observed.

This bizarre theory turned the intent of such laws on its head and showed gross ignorance, intentional or otherwise, about how medication abortions work. The first round of pills actually block hormones to trick the body into thinking it is no longer pregnant, and the second round of pills induces contractions that expel the baby. There is absolutely no doubt that the abortion begins when the first pill is taken. It appeared that misdirection and redefinition were the only defenses O'Neill's attorney had.

***

Next came a witness for Eileen O'Neill's defense. Normally, defense witnesses would wait until the prosecution had rested its case, but this was an unusual and unavoidable situation. The witness was scheduled for back surgery the following day and would not be available to testify afterwards for medical reasons, so Judge Minehart allowed her to testify out of order.

Natalie Tursi had been a good friend of Eileen O'Neill's for six or seven years and was also the on-and-off live-in girlfriend of O'Neill's brother, Paul. She testified about events that took place during a visit to O'Neill's house while she was being interviewed by law enforcement personnel.

Tursi testified that she arrived at O'Neill's home on March 9, 2010, to drop off a pair of dog grooming shears for her friend. When she got there, she greeted Connie, O'Neill's mother, who was sitting in the living room, then walked into the kitchen. There, she found four men who appeared to be with law enforcement sitting at the kitchen table with O'Neill.

She immediately felt unwelcome, so she retreated to the living room, and later the bathroom due to the "confrontational" nature of the conversation. She testified that she overheard only bits and pieces of the kitchen conversation, but described it as a soft, conversational exchange that she found "agitated, confrontational, and brash." The tension seemed to escalate.

Tursi thought that one of the men, FBI Agent Jason Huff, sounded aggressive while O'Neill appeared to be apprehensive.

"Am I under investigation?" she heard O'Neill say.

Huff responded, "You're a witness in this case."

Huff continued to question O'Neill about her typical week at Gosnell's clinic, and about prescriptions, co pays, and insurance. Tursi said she heard O'Neill tell Huff that Gosnell didn't charge insurance companies or ask for co-pays. He just saw who needed to be seen.

Again, Tursi testified that Agent Huff became sterner as the questioning progressed until O'Neill asked again if she had anything to worry about. Huff responded by telling O'Neill that if she ever wanted to practice medicine or obtain a medical license, "You will be a witness."

However, upon cross-examination by Assistant District Attorney Ed Cameron, Tursi admitted she conveniently did not hear other statements reportedly made by O'Neill to the men, including the admission that she ducked out the back door during the police raid on the clinic in 2010, fearing she would be in trouble since she did not have a license to practice medicine.

Cameron also indicated that O'Neill made the statement to law enforcement interviewers that about seventy-five percent of what she did at Gosnell's clinic was done in Gosnell's absence, indicating that she had no physician oversight as she conducted the duties of a licensed physician.

The conclusion was that Tursi's memory was selective, at best.

In a surprising moment, Cameron asked if O'Neill had an attorney present during questioning. Tursi indicated that O'Neill did not. She offered that while O'Neill is very book smart, "common-sense wise, I don't think she has it."

"You are saying she doesn't have common sense?" Cameron asked almost incredulously.

"No. I'm sorry to say it," she replied.

**

Speculation about tactics that might be used by the defense to counter the overwhelming evidence presented so far was a subject of conversation among the reporters present in court as week five wrapped up. How could anyone defend the indefensible conduct that had been so far presented in court?

Some speculated that Gosnell would testify while others thought that unlikely, given the severity of the charges and Gosnell's own over-exuberance during several interviews prior to his arrest in 2011. Others wondered who might take the stand in his defense.

I thought it could be of great interest to see if any abortionist would come forward as an expert witness to support Gosnell's horrific abortion practices. While it was hard to imagine any abortionist sticking his neck out that to defend Gosnell, it was not out of the realm of possibility.

However, most of the abortion industry had already backed away from Gosnell, and some publicly condemned his actions. I knew that so many abortion clinics shared some aspects of Gosnell's conduct that they would not want the spotlight to shine any further than the walls of Gosnell's West Philadelphia "House of Horrors." To do so would be to put the entire abortion cartel on trial in the court of public opinion, where they were acutely aware they simply could not win.

CHAPTER 33

KAREEMA CROSS

I f there was a crescendo to the prosecution's case, it was surely the testimony of Kareema Cross. Cross, a young and attractive African-American woman, worked for Kermit Gosnell for a harrowing four years from 2005 through December 2009. During that time, she helped with abortion procedures amid conditions so frightful that she snapped personal photos to document them in 2008, a year before the death of Karnamaya Mongar.

So disturbed was she by what she saw, she reported her boss to the authorities. She was worried enough about reprisals from Gosnell that she filed the complaint under the name of her sister. But no one listened. Two years later, authorities raided Gosnell's clinic, thinking it was a pill mill only to discover that it was frightfully so much more.

Cross was not arrested with Gosnell and his other co-defendants. She was arrested instead by federal agents on February 7, 2013 and charged with one count of conspiracy to distribute controlled substances. In exchange for her cooperation and testimony, Cross believed that she would receive a probationary term with no jail time.

Cross testified that that she was paid $10 per hour for full-time work. At first, she began just taking vital signs and working the front desk, duties that, as a medical assistant, she was qualified to do. But after about two weeks, Cross said she began doing ultrasounds, injecting drugs when Gosnell was not in the building, and assisting in the grungy, bloodstained procedure rooms.

Her "training" in sonography at Gosnell's clinic consisted of observing one ultrasound procedure. After that she was on her own. When Cross got a measurement that was beyond twenty-four weeks, she would have one of the other women who were a little better at using the relic from the 1980s to verify her findings. Gosnell would always redo those ultrasounds, which would all suddenly measure precisely 24.5 weeks gestation, which Gosnell mistakenly thought was just under the legal limit in Pennsylvania.

While she worked for Gosnell, Cross testified that at least twice a day, six days a week, at least two babies would "precipitate" (Gosnell's term for childbirth) before Gosnell ever arrived. She said "Dr. Steve" would be there to snip the babies' necks. She saw him do it around fifty times. When babies "precipitated" in Gosnell's presence, he would do the dirty deed himself.

Cross sometimes worked from 8:00 am until 3:00 am the next day helping with procedures.

She described the clinic as poorly equipped. No one at the clinic ever tried to use the ancient defibrillator machine that sat before her in court. Cross knew of only two blood pressure cuffs in the entire building, and neither of them were in the procedure rooms. Women who were sedated were not monitored during the surgical abortions.

As a matter of routine, second-trimester abortion patients came in around 2:00 pm. They were sedated, given Cytotec to induce uterine contractions, then taken upstairs where no one monitored them. Only occasionally would anyone go up to check on them, even though the workers all knew that as the Cytotec kicked in, so would the women's pain.

Cross said she didn't know much about Cytotec. Doses were put into paper envelopes clipped to the patients' charts. One or two pills were given to abortion patients every hour. Some workers soon realized that the more Cytotec women were given, the faster they would "precipitate." This led to women being dosed more than recommended.

Gosnell was never in the building when she administered drugs to pregnant women prior to their procedures. Cross knew how much to give by referring to one of two charts that hung on the wall in the office. She knew that other workers gave other drugs to women that were not on the chart, but she refrained from doing so.

During her employment with Gosnell, she routinely saw babies born alive, moving, breathing, and moaning.

Once, in Gosnell's absence, Cross saw a large baby delivered into the toilet. She saw his little arms and legs moving in a swimming motion as he struggled to get out of the toilet bowl. Cross held her hands twelve to sixteen inches apart to demonstrate to the jury how big the baby was. Cross saw Adrienne Moton, who was the first worker to testify for the prosecution, snip the baby's neck in front of the mother while she sat bleeding into the toilet. Moton then took the body away and put it into a container.

Sometime in 2009, Cross said that another co-worker, Lynda Williams, called her over to see a baby that had just been born. Cross saw the baby's chest heaving up and down in steady breathing motions. Lynda reached down and lifted the baby's hand up, but the newborn pulled it away on its own strength. Cross said she saw the baby breathing for about twenty minutes before Williams murdered the child by severing its spinal cord with scissors. Cross demonstrated again with her hands that the baby was about a foot long.

***

Earlier in the trial, the subject of digoxin use was explored. The prosecution presented testimony from a medical examiner that there were no puncture wounds in the fetal remains he examined. A toxicologist testified that there was no trace of digoxin in any of the babies' bodies.

However, despite being present at the clinic six days per week, Cross testified that she only saw Gosnell perform a digoxin injection twice, and both times, it failed to stop the babies' hearts.

She told the court that she routinely assisted with the abortion procedures by identifying the baby's heart on ultrasound. Gosnell told her that digoxin was meant to slow the baby's heartbeat. When the women returned for the second day to complete the abortion, Cross would use the ultrasound to identify the heartbeat just moments before Gosnell finished the procedure. Gosnell would ask Cross if the heartbeat had slowed. Cross testified that she would always tell Gosnell it had, even though the babies' their heartbeats actually remained normal.

Cross remained composed as she testified about observing breathing babies on more than ten occasions. She had a three-year old daughter, and knew when a baby was breathing and when it wasn't. She didn't really buy Gosnell's claim that even though the chest may rise and fall, it wasn't really breathing, just reflexes, because the baby was already dead.

Once while working, she heard a soft, whimpering cry. Ashley Baldwin, the fifteen-year-old high school student that also helped out with the procedures, was working in the larger Monet abortion room, where the crying sound originated. Ashley sought out Cross' help, but when Cross saw the baby, she simply turned and left the room.

***

Pretty much everyone who worked for Gosnell administered medications without supervision, even though none were qualified to do so. Several of the ladies tried to follow the sedation charts when mixing and administering sedation, but Cross noticed that Williams and another woman, Sherry West, never referred to the dosage charts while mixing drugs or when giving them to women. On occasion, some who received injections from Williams and West showed Cross their swollen arms and complained that their injections were not done properly.

Cross complained to Williams and West about the way they handled the drugs, but nothing changed. She discussed it with Gosnell, who noticed there were missing drugs and consulted the notoriously unreliable narcotics log book. That was never much help since Williams and West did not accurately record times or dosages in the log. There was no indication that anything changed after Gosnell became aware of the dangerous situation.

***

Fed up with the conditions and the appalling way women were treated at Gosnell's clinic, Cross began to document the clinic's horrific conditions with her personal camera. Ten of the full-color photos taken on October 22, 2008, were shown to a darkened courtroom on the large viewing screen as Cross referred to hard copies of the pictures provided to her by the prosecution.

The first photo elicited gasps from the gallery, then frantic scribbling on notepads as those of us reporting on the trial rushed to record descriptions of what we were seeing. Cross had photographed the blood-caked procedure table in the Monet room that had rips in the vinyl where the women laid during their abortions. There were large amounts of blood visible on the stirrups. That same table had been seized from Gosnell's clinic and was present in the courtroom throughout the prosecution's case. Some of what appeared to be rust was actually described as dried blood.

The ultrasound machine that appeared in the same photo was the same ancient unit that was displayed in court, complete with its brownish-yellow vaginal transducer probe that had been used on women for years without a protective disposable cover. That alone was enough to send shudders through any woman that saw it.

Cross' second photo showed two shelves located above the same sink where Liz Hampton washed aborted baby remains down a drain and into the garbage disposal. Crammed and stacked onto the shelves were about fifty jars containing severed fetal feet floating in liquid. Each jar was labeled with patient information, which the prosecution had rendered unreadable.

The sheer number of jars was alarming. When Officer Taggart testified about the five collection jars he seized in which were floating severed baby feet and other parts, I was left with the impression that those jars were all there were. I suspected that when Gosnell ordered the clean-up of the Women's Medical Society after the death of Karnamaya Mongar, he must have disposed of this grisly collection to keep it from being discovered by the National Abortion Federation inspector.

The third photo showed a harrowing close-up of Gosnell's gruesome collection. Perfectly formed little feet with the familiar creases in the sole, complete with toes and toenails, floated in the ghastly jars. When workers asked Gosnell about the display, he told them he was saving them in case their DNA was needed. However, that appeared to be Gosnell's thin cover story since the limbs were submersed in formaldehyde, which ruined them for DNA collection.

The thought of fifty jars with limbs from fifty once living, breathing babies was hard to process from an emotional standpoint. Again, I found no time to dwell on the thought as the parade of horrors continued to flash on the screen, one after the other.

The fourth picture showed obvious blood near the malfunctioning autoclave, which was supposedly used to sterilize instruments. The cross-contamination and risk of infection was obvious.

The fifth photo showed six syringes containing pre-drawn medications laying on the counter in one of the procedure rooms, unlabeled, and unsecured.

Photo six appeared to show an incredibly rusty leg rest that had been removed from the procedure table, apparently for whatever cleaning Gosnell's staff felt like giving it. But Cross informed the court that the leg rest wasn't rusty at all. It was heavily streaked with blood from some poor woman who had the misfortune of enduring an abortion at Gosnell's clinic.

The seventh of Cross' pictures depicted a display from a procedure room that featured a blood-stained ultrasound machine, syringes, and various other obviously dirty clutter. This was followed by a photo of the defibrillator kept in the larger Monet procedure room. It was never used, probably because it didn't work. Later, the crime investigation forensics team found what was likely the same machine stuffed under Gosnell's bed at his Mantua home.

Next came a picture of Gosnell's cat sleeping in a chair on the second floor. The cat was kept at the clinic in an attempt to control the rat population that infested the basement, but, like everyone else in Gosnell's employment, it wasn't very good at its job. Cross testified that the cat freely wandered throughout the clinic, even into procedure rooms, and made a habit of relieving itself just about wherever it wanted.

The final photo came from the sterilization room. It looked like a scene from a butcher shop. There was an indescribably filthy stainless steel sink where used plastic speculums and curettes were washed for reuse. It was piled with bloody equipment and caked in a thick layer of grime. There was a cluttered shelf over the sink where the washed (but not clean) plastic speculums and curettes were stored.

It seemed inconceivable that regulators could ignore photos like that, but after Cross submitted them anonymously, that is exactly what they did.

The lights came on and those of us observing the trial collectively leaned back and sucked in deep breaths. The horror show was over for now (or so I thought) as Assistant District Attorney Ed Cameron resumed the questioning of Kareema Cross.

***

One patient was particularly memorable to Cross. Her name was ShayQuana Abrams. Cross had a friend that worked with Abrams, so the two women made a friendly connection. After Abram's abortion, they stayed in touch. Abrams was far advanced into her pregnancy when she came to Gosnell for a two-day procedure. Why she decided to end the life of her baby so late into her pregnancy was not discussed in court. At that point, it seemed irrelevant.

Abrams had been heavily sedated. As she lay sleeping on that filthy, torn table in the Monet room, the biggest baby Cross had ever seen in her years with Gosnell "just came out." Cross again indicated with her hands that the baby was twelve to eighteen inches long.

Gosnell picked up the little boy and placed him in a plastic shoe box lined with a blue chux pad. The baby was so big that he didn't actually fit. His arms and leg were splayed out and draping over the edges of the plastic rim. Suddenly, on his own accord, the breathing baby drew in his arms and legs in an effort to fit himself in the box. Gosnell took the box over near the antiquated ultrasound machine and snipped the baby's neck, but never suctioned the cranial contents, as he sometimes did after babies had completely entered the room.

Cross called young Ashley Baldwin and Adrienne Moton into the room and both took pictures on their cell phones. It was Moton's gut-wrenching photo that was displayed in court and included in the grand jury report.

His courtroom designation was Baby Boy A. The horrendous photo taken by Cross seemed to overwhelm the courtroom. His corpse was supposed to be taken to the freezer that night, but when Jimmy Johnson came in the next morning to take out the "trash," which included removing the abortion remains from the procedure rooms, he found the large, dark-haired baby still lying in that box in the Monet room next to the ultrasound machine where he had been left. Jimmy complained loudly about his gruesome discovery, then took the baby to the basement with the rest of the human remains.

His body was not among the forty-seven bodies recovered by police from Gosnell's clinic two years later. Perhaps he was collected for disposal by Stericycle when Gosnell was still paying his bill, but what actually became of him remains unknown.

***

Somewhere between 2007 and 2008, Cross became pregnant and decided to have what she called "a procedure," but she just could not stand the thought of having an abortion at the clinic where she worked. Instead, she made an appointment at the Philadelphia Women's Clinic, a competing abortion business located on Appletree Street. When Gosnell found out that she had obtained an abortion elsewhere, he "addressed her" about it and was very clear he was not happy that she had not allowed him to do her abortion.

"I just couldn't do it there because it was filthy and he was my boss," she testified. "I just couldn't do it."

In 2009, Cross again became pregnant. This time she decided to keep her baby. Again, Gosnell was not pleased. He confronted her and attempted to pressure her into an abortion. He wrote letters to her that continued to question her decision. "How can you work here being pregnant?" he asked. He offered her a discount on an abortion.

Gosnell's attitude toward her pregnancy offended Cross. Wasn't it supposed to be her choice?

***

Sometimes Cross worked at the front desk where she would often observe Eileen O'Neill seeing patients when Gosnell was not present at the clinic. She testified that she sometimes fielded calls from insurance companies complaining about O'Neill billing for services. Cross often saw the unlicensed O'Neill issue prescriptions on pre-signed prescription pads, just as Steven Massof did, without Gosnell being present for consultation.

At one point, Cameron asked about why certain paperwork was not filled out. Cross replied, "Dr. Gosnell did not pay taxes."

The two defense attorneys roared objections. After a sidebar discussion, Judge Jeffery Minehart instructed the jury to strike Cross' answer from their memories and not consider it during deliberations.

It is more than likely the rest of Cross' testimony will remain emblazoned in their minds in such a way that no judge's order could ever erase it.

With that, the prosecution rested.

CHAPTER 34

JUDICIAL SHOCKER

Once the prosecution's case concluded, the defense was given the routine opportunity to make motions. If a defense attorney believes that the State did not prove their case, the defense can move for the dismissal of all or part of the charges.

When Gosnell was charged with hundreds of criminal counts, the state almost literally threw the book at him. He was charged with violating thirty-nine different laws, everything from illegal abortions, to drug charges, to murder. But it was the eight murder charges that garnered the most interest. If convicted of committing first degree murder for killing babies during abortions, that would be historic.

Then came the most shocking development in the trial so far.

After heated arguments made on April 23, 2013, by Defense Attorney Jack McMahon and Assistant District Attorney Ed Cameron, Judge Minehart dismissed the following charges without explanation:

- Three counts of first degree murder in the deaths of Babies Boy B, Baby G, and Baby F (after correction by the judge).

- Five counts of Abuse of Corpse related to the discovery of five jars containing the severed feet of large aborted babies.

- One count of Infanticide in the case of Baby Boy B

- However, according to court records, Conspiracy and Solicitation to Commit Murder charges for Baby G remained active and were not dismissed with the murder charges.

Dismissal of nine criminal charges against accused murderer Kermit Gosnell stunned many who followed the macabre case, including me. The testimony had been compelling, in my opinion. The medical examiner and toxicologist indicated that there was no evidence the babies were injected with digoxin to ensure the babies were dead prior to the abortion, as the defense has claimed. I began to wonder if the prosecution's case would completely fall apart.

As the initial surprise of this significant development wore off, I realized that the dismissals were likely to have little effect on the trial's outcome. Gosnell still faced over 380 criminal counts, including five murder charges. A conviction on any of the first degree murder counts would mean he could still receive the death penalty or life in prison without parole.

I hoped that would be the case.

The prospect of Gosnell released to return to his grisly practice was simply unthinkable. If Gosnell were to get off scot-free, that would send a message that murdering live babies and abortion patients is now acceptable behavior in America and that abortionists who engage in such depraved practices are above the law. This would put women and babies in grave danger (more than they already face) at abortion clinics throughout the nation.

Judge Minehart also dismissed six counts of Theft by Deception against defendant Eileen O'Neill, leaving only three remaining counts, including perjury, to be considered by the jury.

The following day, Judge Minehart attempted to straighten out some confusion that resulted from a simple mistake in the reading of the dismissed charges. Initially, Minehart announced first degree murder charges related to Baby C had been dropped. Witnesses had testified that Baby C was breathing for twenty minutes before her was stabbed in the neck by Lynda Williams in Gosnell's presence. Considered one of the strongest of murder charges, the dismissal raised a bit of an uproar with the prosecution team.

Judge Minehart quelled concerns by clarifying he never meant to dismiss the murder charge related to Baby C. Instead, murder charges should have been dismissed in the death of Baby F, for which there was less compelling evidence. Because of the volume of baby remains that were discussed during the trial, it was easy to understand how Judge Minehart got his wires crossed.

Following are descriptions of the dismissed cases that would never have made it to the jury.

- Baby Boy B was discovered during the original 2010 law enforcement raid of Gosnell's abortion clinic frozen in a red biohazard bag along with the remains of forty-six other aborted babies. The medical examiner told the grand jury that he estimated gestational age of Baby Boy B to be twenty-eight weeks. This baby was intact and bore the now-familiar neck wound that indicated his spinal cord had been severed. However, there was no testimony presented during the trial that this baby ever moved or breathed. Gosnell had been charged with infanticide related to the death of Baby Boy B.

- Baby G was of an unknown gestational age. An unlicensed abortionist who worked with Gosnell testified before the grand jury that he helped Gosnell deliver Baby G and observed a "respiratory excursion," or a breath. He said Gosnell then turned the baby over and severed his spinal cord with scissors.

- Baby F was estimated to be twenty-five to twenty-seven weeks' gestation when Steven Massof, an unlicensed abortionist employed by Gosnell, assisted his boss in the abortion and delivery of the intact baby. Massof testified that he saw a leg "jerk and move" after which he saw Gosnell sever its spine.

Also dismissed was an infanticide charge related to Baby B.

The five Abuse of Corpse charges dismissed by Judge Minehart were related to the five jars of severed feet seized from Gosnell's clinic. While Gosnell's defense argued that they were kept for possible DNA sampling and as proof of gestational age, medical professionals who testified all said that there was no known medical reason or precedent for such behavior.

The murder counts that were about to be considered by the jury included:

- Baby Boy A, the biggest baby that Kareema Cross had ever seen delivered at Gosnell's abortion "House of Horrors" clinic in the four years she worked there. He was delivered to seventeen-year-old ShayQuana Abrams at 29.4 weeks' gestation, according to an ultrasound record. Baby Boy A was so large, he did not fit into the plastic shoe box that Gosnell tossed him in. Cross said she saw the baby pull in his arms and legs while Gosnell explained the movements as "reflexes," telling her the baby really didn't move prior to cutting the baby's neck. Baby Boy A was so large, Gosnell joked that "this baby is big enough to walk around with me or walk me to the bus stop." Cross and fellow employees Adrienne Moton and 15-year old Ashley Baldwin were all so "startled" by the size of the baby that they all took photos of the baby with their cell phones.

- Baby C was an intact baby of over twenty-five-weeks' gestation. Kareema Cross testified that she saw Baby C breathing and described the up and down chest movements she observed for twenty minutes. She told the court she saw Lynda Williams lift the baby's arm and watched as the newborn drew it back on its own power. Afterwards, Williams inserted surgical scissors into the baby's neck and "snipped" the spinal cord. Gosnell was said to be in the room at the time.

- Baby D was described by witnesses as twelve to fifteen inches long, with the head the size of a "big pancake" when he was delivered into a toilet. Kareema Cross testified that she saw the baby struggling, using swimming motions in an attempt to get out of the bowl. Adrienne Moton pulled the baby out and "snipped" the neck, as Gosnell had taught her to do, while the mother watched. Gosnell has also been charged with criminal solicitation of Moton to commit murder of Baby D.

- Baby E was estimated to be at least twenty-three weeks' gestation, and maybe more. After Baby E was delivered, teen Ashley Baldwin heard the baby cry and called Kareema Cross for help. Cross described the baby's cry as a "whine." Baldwin said that Gosnell went into the room, then came out with the baby (which now had an incision in its neck) and tossed it into the waste bin.

The third-degree murder charge in the drug overdose death Karnamaya Mongar was also still active. Witnesses testified that Mongar was not breathing right but Gosnell completed the abortion before attempting to revive Mongar. A defibrillator present in the room at the time was broken and unusable. Gosnell also faces several other charges related to the death of Mongar, including murder by drug delivery resulting in death.

It was important to also understand that Gosnell still faced numerous federal drug charges for the illegal distribution of narcotics that ended up on the streets of Philadelphia. He would be tried separately for those crimes in federal court.

The prospect of Gosnell being completely exonerated began to appear highly unlikely. A conviction was critical for the pro-life movement. For the first time, the national spotlight on this case sparked a dialogue about conditions at other abortion facilities. I was acutely aware that abortion clinics across America were operating in Gosnell-like conditions, committing violations that Gosnell also committed. It was hoped that a conviction on the more serious charges would prompt lasting change in the way abortion facilities were regulated and perhaps eventually lead to the end of abortion in America for good.

***

Once Minehart finished clarifying the nine charges that had been dismissed, it fell to the defense to present their case. There was great anticipation in the courtroom. Who would testify in Gosnell's defense? Would Gosnell himself take the stand?

In yet another bombshell move, the defense in the Kermit Gosnell murder trial rested without calling a single witness.

CHAPTER 35

DEFENSE'S
CLOSING ARGUMENTS

Closing arguments were set for Tuesday, April 29. By this time, interest in the case had peaked within the pro-life community. While before the trial my invitation to pro-life leaders to join me in Philadelphia to observe the trial went largely ignored, on the day of closing arguments, the Gosnell courtroom was *the* place to be.

In fact, the courtroom was completely packed with news reporters and pro-life leaders who sensed the historic nature of the moment. Many members of the public were even turned away because, for the first time, every possible seat was occupied.

When there were only a handful of us in the gallery, we were granted the freedom to come and go from the courtroom during proceedings as necessary. Now, with so many observers in court, there was a concern that if people were coming and going during the proceedings it would lead to disruptions and distractions. Therefore, once Judge Minehart called the court to order, the courtroom door was locked and no one was allowed to leave until the next recess.

Meanwhile, on the street in front of the courthouse, Rev. Patrick Mahoney, Director of the Washington, DC-based Christian Defense Coalition, led a group of pro-life supporters in prayer, including those who were denied access to the crowded courtroom. It was great to know that praying Christians were seeking justice from the Supreme Judge of All.

Gosnell was brought into the courtroom at 10:07 am. As was his custom, he scanned the gallery and seemed almost pleasantly surprised to see it completely full. Once he was seated at the defense table next to his attorney,

Jack McMahon, the jury and alternates consisting of eight women and seven men (eight blacks and seven whites) were brought in.

The witnesses had been heard. The evidence had been presented. All the players were present and accounted for. Now, the final push for conviction or exoneration in the most important abortion trial in history was about to begin.

***

Judge Minehart addressed the jury members about how to process information that they were about to hear in closing arguments. He instructed them, "Depend on your own memory of the evidence, not on the lawyer's."

With that, Judge Minehart nodded at Mr. Berardinelli, Eileen O'Neill's attorney, to begin.

Defense attorney James Berardinelli started by thanking the jury for their service and sacrifice over the past weeks of often trying testimony. Then he launched into a rehearsal of the evidence against his client. He reminded the jurors that they must find Eileen O'Neill guilty of the charges against her "beyond a reasonable doubt." It is the government's burden to prove each element of their case. The defendant has no burden to prove anything.

Reasonable doubt is a high burden to reach, he reminded them. It is greater than in civil court where the preponderance of the evidence is sufficient, and much more difficult than family court, where a case must simply be clear and convincing.

The government, Berardinelli claimed, did not meet the burden of proof in their case against his client. He admitted that O'Neill had no valid medical license, but noted she was never charged with the specific crime of "practicing medicine without a license."

One crime with which she was charged was theft by deception. He explained that like the Bernie Madoff case, it required a scam in which a falsehood is used. That falsehood must involve something of monetary or pecuniary value.

For example, if someone takes their car to a mechanic who isn't licensed, that isn't fraud because you get what you pay for. In the same way, argued Berardinelli, patients got what they paid for, which was O'Neill's education, background, and experience. No one paid for a license.

Because O'Neill was a medical school graduate, completed a residency, and has the same training and knowledge as a licensed physician, there was no fraud.

He noted that FBI Agent Jason Huff testified that if a doctor is overseen by another doctor, that can be a gray area in the law where sometimes licensing for supervised doctor is waived.

The attorney as giving it his all, but he wasn't doing much to convince me, and I doubted this spin on the licensing requirement for physicians would make much impact on the jury, either.

Berardinelli moved on. He noted that O'Neill had nothing to do with Gosnell's abortion business. Every worker on the night shift, when abortions took place, had agreed that O'Neill consulted with patients in their 60s and didn't see patients when Gosnell was not present in the clinic.

Then Berardinelli's topic shifted to the death of Karnamaya Mongar. He reminded the jury that Mongar's chart indicated that she was given three doses of Restoril along with other drugs noted in the chart. Mongar's ensuing coma was due to multiple doses of that drug.

O'Neill's attorney noted that Sherry West had testified that Gosnell was in the building on the night Mongar died. Even though West testified that she never administered drugs to Mongar, yet she and Lynda Williams were still charged with murder.

O'Neill only took Mongar's blood pressure and vitals, he said. It was Tina Baldwin who admitted to giving three doses of Restoril to Mongar, yet she was not charged with murder.

Berardinelli then proceeded to cast doubt on Baldwin's motives and shift the blame for what happened to Mongar onto her alone. Baldwin testified that O'Neill saw patients when Gosnell was not at the facility but told the grand jury that O'Neill only wrote prescriptions when Gosnell was in the building. Ashley Baldwin, Tina's daughter, testified O'Neill wrote the prescription but then took it to Gosnell for his signature.

Pointing out other inconsistencies in her testimony, Berardinelli noted that Tina Baldwin testified that Eileen O'Neill slipped out the back door leaving her belongings behind during the initial raid on Gosnell's clinic. She was contradicted by another witness who said he drove home after the raid. Agent Huff had testified that there had been no property of O'Neill's recovered during the raid.

Baldwin entered into a plea agreement for the purpose of resolving murder charges against her. Baldwin would say anything to save herself because the quality of her testimony would be repaid with leniency during sentencing. Therefore, Baldwin had a tremendous motive to lie. Berardinelli urged the jury to consider Tina Baldwin a corrupt and polluted source.

When it came to the testimony of Della Mann, a registered nurse who was seen at Gosnell's facility as a patient, Berardinelli did his best to make her a liar, too. Mann lacked credibility because she acted like she didn't know O'Neill wasn't licensed, when according to Berardinelli, she did. Inconsistencies in Mann's testimony were also pointed out. Mann told the grand jury she got an injection from O'Neill, but her chart had no mention of an injection. Mann testified that O'Neill diagnosed her dermatitis, but the records show it was Massof who made the diagnosis.

Mann paid no money out of pocket to be treated at Gosnell's Women's Medical Society. The prosecution said that her Blue Cross insurance was billed, but no Blue Cross witness was produced to testify that money was ever paid. Mann said she stopped going to Gosnell's facility in February 2007, but by then Blue Cross had already stopped paying Gosnell's claims.

Berardinelli argued that former patient Mary Kincade testified that the treatment she received from O'Neill was "just fine." He noted that the only "prescription" ever given to Kincade by his client was actually just a referral. There was no record that insurance ever paid for Kincade's visits.

Next, the attorney attacked the credibility of former patient Lisa Dungee, who testified that O'Neill had given her medication to induce a chemical abortion.

"Ms. Dungee paid for an abortion. She got what she paid for," he said.

He went on to say that Dungee had to wait three hours for Gosnell to come in from his home in New Jersey. He noted contradictions in her testimony and accused her of "embellishing." Dungee testified that the second floor of the facility was filthy while all others said it was "clean." She said O'Neill wore a white coat while others indicated O'Neill always dressed in business casual clothing.

Berardinelli addressed the charge O'Neill faced related to corrupt organizations. He explained that an organization that engages in criminal conduct would fall under that crime, however, O'Neill never worked on the "abortion side" of Gosnell's business. She only worked on the "family medicine" side.

In order to be convicted under the corrupt organizations charge, one had to commit two actions that related to each other. One act must facilitate the other. However, Berardinelli defended his client, noting that her actions just didn't add up to the corrupt organizations charge.

He then attacked the credibility of Agent Huff, who, according to Berardinelli, couldn't even say if the walls were clean inside Gosnell's facility.

Agent Huff testified that O'Neill told him that Gosnell wasn't in the room 75 percent of the time while she saw patients when she actually said that 75 percent of her duties were administrative.

Another agent said O'Neill saw patients on the first floor of the clinic when she actually saw them on the second floor.

Berardinelli's message was clear to the jury. Out of the witnesses from the FBI, former patients, and O'Neill's own co-workers, none could be taken at their word. Eileen O'Neill was a person of good character, Berardinelli concluded. She was decent, honest, and law abiding. With his voice rising as in anger, Berardinelli told the jury that when the allegations against her came to light, it was only "because of a firestorm that got out of control."

"[District Attorney] Seth Williams had a big press conference," he accused, and because of that, Williams was forced to file charges to save face. That was the only reason his client had been charged.

Berardinelli ended by asking the jury to find his client not guilty.

O'Neill's defense attorney took his seat. It was time for the first recess of the day.

***

Jack McMahon was an imposing figure in the courtroom who commanded attention. Tall, lean, tastefully bald, and well-dressed, McMahon was an articulate and convincing advocate. He spoke with passion and authority when making his final case before the jury.

McMahon leaned on the jury box to address the men and women who held the fate of his client in their hands. He reminded them of their solemn oath to judge the case on the evidence. A jury, he said, relies on common sense, human experience, and honesty to reach a verdict.

"This is a case with emotions in it," McMahon said. "When you see a picture of a fetus with a hole, it affects you. But you promised you will transcend that."

Like Mr. Berardinelli, McMahon took a moment to speak about reasonable doubt.

"If your mind tells you that you are not quite sure, you have a reasonable doubt," he said.

He explained how much we all value freedom above everything else. We value it more than money. The government cannot take that away from someone without meeting a high burden of proof.

"There is no 'innocent' verdict," McMahon argued. "This is all about whether the prosecution removed all doubt."

He explained that a "not guilty" verdict did not mean "innocent." Instead, it meant "not proven." Even McMahon knew the word "innocent" could never apply to his client.

"If you say, 'That baby could have been alive,' that's reasonable doubt," he said.

Then McMahon tried to distance his client's case from the highly charged issue of abortion.

"This case is not about abortion," he said, then admitted that abortion was how this case came to exist in the first place. "You are not here to decide if abortion is okay. You are here to decide if Gosnell is a murderer."

No surgery is pretty, he explained. But the issue isn't that abortion is ugly and bloody. That was a notion that McMahon urged the jury to rise above.

"Never in my career have I seen the presumption of innocence stomped on as in this case," McMahon state, growing indignant. He described the prosecution as a "rush to judgment" based on "knee-jerk assumptions" without evidence.

"If it can happen to Dr. Gosnell, it can happen to us all," he warned.

The jury was urged not to "roll with the tsunami of press rhetoric," but to act with independence and character. They must face the facts of the case and "show courage and rage against the irresponsible use of rhetoric."

McMahon insisted that the government tried to manipulate the jury by bringing items from Gosnell's clinic, which sat in storage for two years, into the courtroom. Those items sat in court for two months in order to influence the jury's emotions, he opined. He accused the prosecution of taking only the oldest equipment that was in the worst shape in order to sway them and prey on their fears.

In addition, the witnesses were manipulated by the prosecution in a further effort to take advantage of their fears. He used Sherry West, who pled guilty to the murder of Karnamaya Mongar, as his first example.

"She was framed!" McMahon roared. He told the jury that the prosecution used fear to manipulate her into pleading guilty.

Lynda Williams also pled guilty to "snipping" the neck of a baby she thought was already dead, while Adrienne Moton, who never said she "snipped" a living, moving baby, also pled guilty to murder.

"They pled out of fear of the tsunami swallowing them," he said with a dramatic flair.

McMahon shifted gears to discuss his client's supposed altruism. Gosnell provided the community a service, he explained. Some patients never paid for the services he rendered. He never turned anyone way because they didn't have money. These were desperate young ladies, McMahon surmised.

"Who comes to help them?" he asked. "Kermit Gosnell. He provided young, desperate girls with relief, with a solution to their problems."

Gosnell was known to help those without health insurance. He gave access to health care to those who didn't have it. Life becomes a desperate and difficult situation "when you don't have that card," McMahon said attempting a bit of manipulation of his own.

"You are not here to issue a report of deficiencies you may see at 3801 Lancaster," he noted sarcastically. "This is not about the rip in the table or the fish tank that wasn't clean. Dirt is a red herring to distract attention from the lack of evidence!

"Mongar didn't die from bacteria or germs. Filth had nothing to do with it. I'm not here to tell you it's the premiere clinic or that everything was done right. That would cost too much."

McMahon then went on to attack the quality of the prosecution's case. He pointed out that out of the thousands of abortion patients visited Gosnell's clinic, yet only two testified: Shay Abrams and Shanice Manning. Both said they got digoxin to terminate the baby while still in the womb. Manning's baby was stillborn, he stated as if it was undisputable fact.

"No one said they didn't get the digoxin shot," McMahon argued. Out of the thousands of abortions, the prosecution's case came down to a few anecdotal stories.

"The quality of the case isn't there," he concluded.

Latosha Lewis, a damaging witness for the prosecution, worked with Gosnell for ten years. She never said anything about "snipping" or "live babies" during her testimony, McMahon stated. "The one there the longest gave the least!"

This was nothing but an "elitist, racist prosecution," McMahon accused.

He slammed Dr. Benjamin, an abortionist who testified against Gosnell, as a doctor who doesn't know what it was like to serve a poor urban area since "he works out of a big hospital."

"This isn't a perfect place by any stretch of the imagination," McMahon admitted, but for those who never ran an urban clinic, it was wrong for them to "pontificate."

Then, McMahon once again played the race card, an argument that did not sit well with my friend who sat next to me, Day Gardner, who is a leader of a Black pro-life organization.

"An African American was signaled out for prosecution," he said.

He discussed the fact that the District Attorney is also black, but noted it was the grand jury, not District Attorney Seth Williams, who charged Gosnell.

"To say this is black–on–black crime is racist," McMahon said, referring to William's public support of Gosnell's prosecution. "If you don't see that reality, you are either checking out of reality or live in La-La-Land."

McMahon strenuously objected lead prosecutor Joanne Pescatore' use of the term "House of Horrors" during her opening arguments, "as if it was some kind of TV show."

"This has been the greatest hype and exaggeration in the history of the criminal justice system!" McMahon emoted, while Pescatore scowled and Ed Cameron sat at the prosecution table with his head in his hands.

McMahon accused the prosecution of pigeon-holing the case.

"They *want* this case to be a house of horrors!" he said, telling the jury not to pre-judge but to think only about the facts.

He emphasized that the condition of the clinic was irrelevant to the criminal charges.

So what was the condition of 3801 Lancaster, according to McMahon?

He flashed some of the photos previously shown by the prosecution onto the big viewing screen and explained how they depicted a typical "urban community clinic situation," and not a "house of horrors."

However, the photos chosen by McMahon were those taken after Jimmy Johnson and some of the rest of the staff painted and cleaned the facility as they had been ordered to do by Gosnell after the FBI raid. Once that cleaning took place, the clinic never again opened for business.

McMahon showed pictures of a clean hall, a file room that was organized and neat, and the O'Keefe abortion room with newly painted walls that had not a spot of blood.

"The pictures don't lie," McMahon said, hoping that the jury forgot exactly when those photos were taken.

McMahon continued to show photos of a clean counter, an ordinary-looking nurse's station, a stainless-steel scrub sink, and the upstairs procedure room that had been "beautifully painted."

"There's not a spot of blood," the defense attorney argued, "And this is a bloody environment."

McMahon then went down the list of witnesses and discussed their testimony that related to the clinic's conditions from the defense's perspective.

Ashley Baldwin had said that the facility was cleaned daily, and that her mom wouldn't have let her work there if it was really a "house of horrors." Lynda Williams had testified that the cleaning was always done and Adrienne Moton said that the clinic was sterilized and clean.

"The House of Horrors was a political press fabrication," McMahon insisted with a tone of indignation.

He then moved to the topic of ShayQuana Abrams' testimony and her infant, Baby A.

McMahon argued that the fact that digoxin, when injected into a pre-born baby causes fetal demise, was not disputed in the case. Abrams signed a consent form for the use of digoxin during her abortion.

"The intent was to kill the baby intra-utero to prevent live birth, and that's what was done," McMahon concluded.

Abrams, he said, testified that she received the digoxin shot. He then read a portion of the trial transcript where Abrams testified that she received the digoxin injection into the abdomen, not the cervix.

"If the digoxin was administered, the baby would be dead," he stated.

Moton testified she saw one arm move, but Gosnell had told her it was a "last reflex." Other testimony noted that Baby A's "appearance was like he was sleeping." There was no movement.

Once again falling back on his conspiracy theory, McMahon argued that some witnesses had been manipulated by the government. For example, Ashley Baldwin never saw Baby A. She only saw a photo of him.

"She went out then came back in and changed her testimony!" McMahon alleged, earning a grunt of disbelief from Cameron loud enough for everyone to hear.

McMahon told the jury that after the Partial Birth Abortion Ban Act was enacted, prohibiting the killing of live babies as they were partly birthed during abortions, Gosnell changed his methodology to comply with the law and began using digoxin.

"If you're a cold-blooded murderer, you don't change your methodology to comply with the law," he said.

Next, McMahon attacked the credibility of Kareema Cross, the prosecution's star witness in an attempt to plant the seed of doubt into the minds of the jurors. He argued that she testified the baby moved after his neck was cut. However, Medical Examiner Sam Gulino said that the cutting would have caused "instantaneous death."

McMahon began to discuss information Cross told police when interviewed after the initial raid, but Cameron immediately objected because that conversation was not in the trial record. Cameron asked for a sidebar conference with Judge Minehart.

Cameron could be seen intensely arguing his point that was apparently related to Cross' conversation with police, then returned to the prosecution table shaking his head in disagreement, having apparently lost the argument.

McMahon briefly referenced discrepancies in her story, then moved on.

Dr. Daniel H. Conway, the specialist in fetal development, had testified that he couldn't look at the photo of Baby A and determine whether he had been born alive. In fact, of all testing that had been done on the forty-seven fetal bodies found at Gosnell's Women's Medical Society, of which Baby A was not included, showed no conclusive evidence of aeration or any other conclusive signs that any of the babies had been born being alive.

"How could that be if he's killing live babies?" McMahon asked rhetorically.

The matter of another baby that Gosnell was charged with murdering, Baby C, came up next. McMahon focused first on the testimony of Lynda Williams, who said she saw Baby C move only once as a "last reflex," before she snipped its neck at Gosnell's direction. Lynda had testified that she thought she was snipping a baby that was already dead. Left unanswered was the question of why Gosnell would bother to order the baby's neck to be snipped if he had previously died in the womb.

McMahon recited William's testimony, that the movement of Baby C was like a "quick spasm" and that she never meant to hurt anyone.

"I'm sorry, I help people. I wouldn't hurt no one," McMahon read from the transcript of William's testimony. He then recounted a note that Williams had written on the police report that read, "Just want this all to end. He's done nothing wrong!!!"

McMahon discussed how Williams had testified that she personally witnessed Gosnell snipping the necks of about thirty babies, none of which were seen moving, breathing, or crying.

In the same regard, Kareema Cross testified she saw Steven Massof snip the necks of fifty to seventy-five babies, however the defense claimed that all of those babies were already dead.

"Did she ever see Steve snip a neck after movement? No," McMahon recounted.

Digoxin was meant to produce a dead baby and that is exactly what it did, he said, noting that twenty-one patient files numbered 228 to 240 all had consent forms for digoxin, proving that all those babies were already dead at the time of birth.

McMahon insisted that Williams only pled guilty to murdering Baby C after the prosecution used fear to cause her to plead to something she didn't do.

"The government should be ashamed of themselves to be involved in that," he chided.

Despite what the defense described as a lack of evidence of digoxin's failure, there was evidence of its success, McMahon continued.

Shanice Manning, was a fifteen-year-old girl who was taken by her mother for an abortion at twenty-nine weeks. McMahon used the fact that her baby was stillborn at a hospital (where she had gone after suffering complications) to argue that the digoxin shot worked. He reminded the jury that there was no evidence that the lungs were aerated, implying that there was no evidence the baby took a breath.

"Cross saw an arm drop when picked up. That doesn't prove live birth," McMahon argued, stating again that Gosnell had changed his methods to comply with the law.

"Why go through that process if he is a cold-blooded murderer?" he asked.

Then McMahon floated a new theory before the jury. If the digoxin hadn't taken 100 percent, then Gosnell used the snipping to alleviate pain in the event that the brain could somehow feel it after being "digoxinized."

This argument left me scratching my head. *If someone is dead, then they can't feel pain*, I thought. The sensation of pain would indicate life, in my opinion.

McMahon argued that there were thousands of abortions going through 3801 Lancaster. Did some babies move? Probably yes. But one twitching movement is not an indicator of life, according to the defense, which noted the neonatologist that testified said twitching after death is rare. Out of the thousands of abortions, movement was only seen in four cases. These four cases could have been the "rare" twitching after death spoken of by the neonatologist, the attorney opined.

Out of those seen moving was Baby D, who Adrienne Moton saw swimming in the toilet. "I think it was making a voluntary movement,"

Moton had said. However, McMahon pointed out that the prosecution never asked Moton if the baby was alive and she never testified to that.

And as for Kareema Cross, she never said a word to Moton or Williams about moving babies. Cross also had testified that she only heard a baby whine one time. She never mentioned anything about a swimming baby in her original March 5, 2010, statement. That only came later, he noted, implying she made it up to gain leniency.

Referring to the baby that was seen swimming in the toilet, McMahon told the jury, "It was dead and if you don't know that, you're not listening!"

But through it all, Cross never left Gosnell. If babies were really being murdered, McMahon questions why she would stay. He mockingly called Cross "Forrest Gump" because she seemed to be everywhere in the clinic and see everything that went on.

"She got the best deal of anyone," said McMahon, who portrayed Cross as filled with anger, bias, and resentment toward Gosnell, so therefore, lacked credibility.

McMahon again shifted gears to discuss the evidence in the forty-seven babies whose bodies were seized from Gosnell's clinic.

Of those forty-seven babies, forty-five, or 96 percent, were under twenty-four weeks, the legal limit for abortions in Pennsylvania, McMahon reminded the jury. Twenty-seven had their eyes fused, which was an indicator that they were less than twenty-four weeks.

"In every single case, there was no evidence of being born alive," McMahon stated with authority.

He referred to a chart that referenced different stages of maceration, which is the breaking down of the skin after long exposure to water. When babies die in utero, the babies will show signs of maceration, he explained.

McMahon discussed Baby 3F, a twenty-one-week baby with a "neck defect" that showed signs of maceration, proving that the baby died in the womb.

"The Commonwealth only has anecdotal evidence," he told the jury.

Gosnell's defense attorney then turned his attention to the death of Karnamaya Mongar. He postulated that Mongar's death was a tragic accident; a complete aberration. He went through the witnesses and tried to explain away their testimony as mistaken or inaccurate.

First, he attacked the evidence that Mongar had been overdosed on Demerol. McMahon noted that Mongar's chart showed she only received 75 mg of Demerol and that her complication was an unusual one. But from the testimony, I knew that the medical records from the Women's Medical Society were notoriously unreliable. Several witnesses had indicated that drug dosages were not always recorded.

McMahon again lapsed into his conspiracy theory that some of the witnesses changed their testimony concerning Mongar's death after they signed a plea deal with the prosecution "out of fear." Lynda Williams' testimony before the plea bargain, according to McMahon, was that Mongar stopped breathing after the abortion procedure was complete. After the plea deal, she said Mongar stopped breathing during the procedure.

McMahon told the jury that Sherry West gave Mongar no drugs, was not in the procedure room during Mongar's abortion, and even tried to help the family at the hospital after Mongar was transported.

"She pled to murder out of fear!" McMahon accused.

As for the damaging testimony of Kareema Cross, McMahon noted that she testified that she never saw anyone given too much medication. The rest of her testimony was unreliable. Some of the workers who gave drugs may have been unqualified, but there were no adverse reactions to medications at Gosnell's facility, he explained.

But McMahon told the jury that the testimony of Mongar's adult daughter, Yashoda Gurung, was the most reliable. Perhaps he understood that attacking Gurung's credibility would not play well with the jury, which appeared sympathetic to her grief over her mother's death. Gurung testified, according to McMahon, that Mongar was given three Cytotec pills in the waiting room and one prior to the procedure, an amount that was not considered excessive.

Cameron's reaction to McMahon's arguments was priceless. He sat at the prosecution table once again with his head in his hands, openly displaying his incredulity. Cameron seemed upset and even angry as McMahon introduced testimony that Cameron believed had not been entered into evidence during the seven-week trial. At times, he interrupted McMahon and later asking for a sidebar conference over what he saw as objectionable. But despite Cameron's interruptions, McMahon continued on down the witness list, explaining why the jury should disregard nearly all the testimony presented by the prosecution's witnesses.

Dr. Timothy Rohrig was the Wichita, Kansas, toxicologist who testified that Mongar's toxicology results showed that she had been given 400 times the suggested dosage of Demerol for a woman of Mongar's height and weight. But McMahon explained that away by saying Rohrig's analysis was largely invalid with a high degree of error.

Dr. Gary Collins of the medical examiner's office took nine months to determine that Mongar's cause of death as an accidental, unintentional poisoning. Then the grand jury happened. The publicity around the case created what McMahon described as a "tsunami and firestorm." After a meeting with the District Attorney, Seth Williams, Collins was manipulated to change the accidental death determination to one of homicide. McMahon mocked Collins, reminding them that while on the stand, he had jumped down and began ripping down a chart that he did not agree with.

"He was more of a court jester than a court medical examiner," he said.

All this happened because of the government agenda "to transform this into what they want it to be, not what it is."

McMahon emphasized that in the medical examiner's determination, there was no mention of anything improper about the abortion procedure itself, "Nothing was wrong with how he did the abortion. He did it well."

***

Gosnell's able defense attorney moved on to the charges themselves as his lengthy arguments on behalf of Kermit Gosnell drew to a close. Of the 227 counts of informed consent violations, the prosecution did not bring in anyone as a witness. Instead, the government relied on forms to make their case on those counts.

There were twenty-three counts of abortion after twenty-four weeks, the legal gestational limit where abortions are allowed in Pennsylvania. McMahon did not even try to dispute these charges, admitting that there were some abortions done past twenty-four weeks. However, the counts with which Gosnell was charged were all based on gestational age "estimates" and "guesswork."

Only two of the babies said to have been aborted after the legal limit, Baby 1B and Baby 1C, were the only ones for which there was evidence to substantiate Gulino's fetal age determinations.

As for the charges related to the death of Karnamaya Mongar, the jury had only two choices: third-degree murder or involuntary manslaughter. This was unfair, according to McMahon, since he considered Mongar's death accidental.

"All Dr. Gosnell and I can do is ask you to be fair," McMahon explained in a lowered and cracking emotion-laden voice.

He referred to President John F. Kennedy's *Profiles in Courage* as he ended his closing remarks. This book, he said, was about people who defy public opinion.

"Have the courage to say no. Embrace the true facts, not the hype they want it to be," McMahon pled, pointing toward the prosecution table. "If you demonstrate this courage, you will demonstrate to the world personal integrity. If you vote for acquittal, you are a profile in courage."

McMahon sat down. It was time for lunch.

CHAPTER 36

"ARE YOU HUMAN?"

I joined a few pro-life supporters for lunch at the Marriott across the street from the courthouse. The conversation, at first, was grim.

"How do you think that went?" asked Day Gardner.

I could see she was troubled by some of McMahon's arguments, as was I. Could the jury really fall for the argument that Karnamaya's death was an accident or that the babies were already dead when they were so brutally stabbed in the neck with scissors? Would they be swayed by the defense's assertion that Gosnell was a victim, caught up in a "tsunami" of negative publicity that prosecutors contrived for political gain?

"I don't know. We need to wait and see the prosecution's closing arguments," I suggested. But the truth is, I was worried too. Yet, I couldn't imagine any one letting him off the hook after all the damning evidence and testimony presented by the prosecution. What a travesty of justice that would be!

McMahon was considered one of the best criminal defense attorneys in Philadelphia for good reason. He was masterful at attempting to seed doubt into the minds of the jurors. Yet, it is often true that when one side of an argument is presented, it can seem very compelling until the other side is heard. I hoped that the prosecution would be just a bit more convincing than Mr. McMahon.

***

Back in the courtroom, we settled into our seats as court was about to resume. It was finally time for the prosecution to address the jury with its closing arguments. I assumed that lead prosecutor Joanne Pescatore would make the final presentation, and was a bit surprised to see Ed Cameron rise to the podium and face the men and women of the jury.

In the end, I'm glad he did. Cameron was the more experienced prosecutor. It is hard to know how many trials he handled over the course of his thirty-two years with the District Attorney's office. Besides, Cameron's was the more forceful personality and the perfect counterpoint to McMahon's own assertive nature.

Cameron told the jury he would be summarizing the testimony of the fifty-four witnesses who testified in this sensational capital murder case.

"It is important to go over all the facts in this case, every single one," he began.

"This is going to be a long afternoon," I thought to myself. It had been a long seven weeks, and as fatigued as I was, I was also excited as well. This was the big moment for which I had been waiting, when the prosecution would tie up all the testimony and evidence with a bow and present it to the jury.

"Viability or survivability is irrelevant," Cameron began, explaining that whether the babies were born alive is the standard the law asks them to consider.

"Outside the mother, all things change. It is a human being and has to be treated as such," Cameron continued. "To accelerate the death process is to commit murder."

Cameron addressed the defense argument that all the babies were dead before birth because Gosnell always used the drug digoxin to bring about fetal demise. Crime Scene Unit Officer John Taggart testified that he had collected and cataloged all the drugs found inside Gosnell's clinic. He found no digoxin in that inventory.

Cameron reminded the jury that they had heard testimony from expert witnesses who said there were no puncture wounds in any of the babies nor was there any trace of digoxin in their systems. On the contrary, witnesses had said that Gosnell tried using digoxin for a while, but that it rarely worked. He even tried increasing the dosages to as much as 400 times the recommended amount, only to eventually give up. It was then he began "snipping" the necks of babies, according to testimony.

"This was someone going through the motions, taking the easy way out," he said.

Cameron slipped on a glove and picked up one of the warped and filthy reused plastic cannulas utilized in surgical abortions at Gosnell's business and with a flourish, displayed it for the jury. The plastic cannulas were meant to be used only once then thrown away because they could not be sanitized. But that didn't stop Gosnell from using them over and over even though he was aware they were spreading infections and sexually transmitted diseases between his patients.

"He reuses something that costs a dollar!" Cameron said, to illustrate how he valued profit over the lives and health of women.

McMahon seemed to make a critical misstep when he explained that the neck snipping was to alleviate any pain that the brain might detect, indicating that there may have been brain function and the sensation of pain in these babies before their spinal cords were cut, an important sign of life. Cameron seized on that misstep, giving an agonizing account of how the newborn babies must have felt as they struggled to be born, finally "entering the light" only to be stabbed by Gosnell and doomed to slowly suffocate to death.

"This case is not about 'us,' the prosecution. It's not about Ed or Joanne or Jack or Jim," Cameron explained. "It is about Karnamaya Mongar and the babies that died."

Abortion is legal as long as it's done before twenty-four weeks in sterile conditions, he said. The babies that died, they were black, they were white, and they were Asian. This is not about race or elitism.

"This case was brought by a grand jury, a large group of people like you," he said, countering the argument that the prosecution of Gosnell was done for political gain.

McMahon described how there had been an unprecedented "rush to judgment" in this case, with "knee-jerk assumptions without evidence," while no reporters wrote about the presumption of innocence.

"Never in my career have I seen the presumption of innocence so stomped on," McMahon had said.

But Cameron indicated that the only "rush to judgment" had been by Gosnell, for whom profit outweighed any considerations for a woman's health.

Cameron lambasted Eileen O'Neill for sharing culpability in the atrocities that took place at Gosnell's clinic, and accused her of hiding in her office and looking the other way when women suffered and babies were murdered.

Everyone is taught to trust and show respect for doctors. All of Gosnell's patients trusted him and he took advantage of that.

"Being a doctor isn't a right. It's a responsibility that both Gosnell and O'Neill abused," Cameron continued. "The Hippocratic Oath is about honoring tenets of that oath. What he did was a violation of that oath."

Cameron described how private medical charts were found lying all over the clinic where just about anyone could see them. This further violated his patient's privacy rights, further betraying their sacred trust.

The arguments shifted from trust to credibility. Cameron described accomplices as those who were part of the crime. When they later turn to point the finger, they can be viewed as reliable witnesses. It is possible to convict based on accomplice testimonies. He brought up Gosnell's accomplices Sherry West, Lynda Williams, Steven Massof, and Adrienne Moton, and urged the jury to consider these witnesses as credible because they each participated in the crimes and understood exactly what happened.

Cameron then launched into his summary of witness testimonies as if they were bullet points in an essay. While it sometimes seemed plodding, each point was important to counter defense arguments. Officer Taggart had sketched a layout of the clinic. The place was such a maze that firemen had a difficult time finding their way inside as Karnamaya lay dying.

FBI Agent Jason Huff obtained the initial search warrant on February 18, 2010. When he arrived at the Gosnell facility at 8:30 pm, women were drugged into stupors.

Inside, they found clinic workers who were not only incompetent, but had mental disorders. Williams, who had only an eighth-grade education, was taking three drugs a day for bipolar disorder and anxiety. West was on Prozac for anxiety after having a "nervous breakdown," Cameron explained.

Ashley Baldwin, who was a fifteen-year-old high schooler at the time she was employed by Gosnell, designed a color-coded drug chart to keep her from overdosing women. Gosnell showed her how to administer the powerful sedation drugs that women were given in Gosnell's absence. Ashley also gave ultrasound examinations and examined tissue through a microscope for disease, all while a junior in high school.

Adrienne Moton had lived with the Gosnells and worked for Kermit Gosnell for three years, often administering sedation to patients even though she was not qualified to do so. She testified that she saw Gosnell manipulating ultrasounds to obtain the gestational age reading he wanted.

When Baby A was born at 29.4 weeks gestation, he had an 80 percent chance of survival. But then, Moton testified that Gosnell rushed in and the baby disappeared. It was standard practice at Gosnell's clinic to cut the neck of any baby that moved. In fact, Moton testified that the digoxin did not work all the time, and the necks were only cut if the baby was moving.

ShayQuana Abrams was the mother of Baby A. She came into the clinic, signed forms, and got laminaria all on the same day in violation of the state mandated twenty-four-hour waiting period. Shay testified that a needle was inserted into her belly by a "nurse" but not under ultrasound guidance. This virtually insured that the shot, presumably of digoxin, would not work.

Shay had been unsure of her baby's age because of history of irregular periods. She did not realize that her child was nearly thirty weeks' gestation, and Gosnell never told her, yet she was charged $2,400 above the twenty-four-week fee scale. Cameron emphasized that according to testimony, her baby had been born alive. After her abortion, Shay developed serious complications that required two weeks of hospitalization to treat serious abscesses and blood clots.

"That baby would be four and a half years old if he had survived," Cameron noted. "Instead, scissors were stabbed into his neck and the baby slowly suffocated to death."

Dr. Daniel Conway was a neonatologist who testified about the behavior of newborns. He testified that "movement is indicative of life." The babies born alive at Gosnell's clinic were doing more than "twitching" reflexively. Their arms were moving. They were purposefully drawing their arms in. These were obvious signs of life.

A doctor has the obligation to make a baby comfortable if he happens to be born alive. The babies that Gosnell is accused of murdering were old enough to live outside the womb. Baby Boy Manning was twenty-seven to thirty weeks' gestation. Baby Boy A was twenty-seven to thirty weeks. Baby B was twenty-eight weeks, with hair on her back and smooth skin.

"At minimum, the he had an obligation to make the baby comfortable, which didn't happen to any of them," Cameron accused with growing indignity. Instead, they were born in a metal pan using plastic instruments that should never be reused because they can, and did, spread disease.

"Cutting the neck is not a means of instantaneous death. It causes the baby to suffocate over minutes," said Cameron, explaining the suffering the babies were forced to endure.

He then turned to the testimony of Dr. Andrew Herlich, an anesthesiologist who testified about the way drugs were administered at the Women's Medical Society. Herlich described the standard of patient care, which included adequate equipment and a well-stocked and functioning crash cart. Those things did not exist at Gosnell's facility. Disposable instruments were reused. The defibrillator on the crash cart didn't work, and the emergency medications that were found on it expired in 2007.

"He doesn't deserve the honor of being called 'doctor,'" Cameron said concerning Gosnell.

Dr. Herlich testified that patient care standards require the use of an interpreter when a patient cannot understand English. Gosnell and his staff relied on Karnamaya Mongar's daughter, who spoke only a bit more English than her mom, to interpret, which Cameron described as "pure recklessness" on Gosnell's part.

In anesthesiology, one size does not fit all. For example, Cameron noted Dr. Herlich's testimony that Asians are typically more sensitive to anesthesia than whites or blacks. Nevertheless, Gosnell never took differences in race, weight, or height into consideration during an abortion process.

Demerol is a drug that is rarely in use today due to the dangers, according to Herlich. It is a drug that hurts the heart. But Cameron told the jury that Gosnell would cut corners for profit and Demerol was cheaper than safer drugs.

In an emergency, time is of the essence, yet Gosnell waited twenty long minutes before calling 911 while and oxygen-deprived Mongar was never intubated or given oxygen by Gosnell or his staff.

Mongar's breathing was shallow, which should have been a warning sign. But instead, Gosnell administered extra Demerol and another drug, and put her into a coma, Cameron explained.

"Mongar would be alive today if he had acted like a doctor!" argued Cameron with disgust.

***

Eleanor Barsony was what Cameron described as an "uninspector" with the Department of Health. She never inspected the Women's Medical Society and didn't seem to care whether it was ever inspected. The consequences of Barsony's unwillingness to do her job were catastrophic.

On the night of the initial raid on Gosnell's abortion mill, two patients were transported to the hospital. Others were in the midst of same-day abortions that violated Pennsylvania's law that requires a mandatory twenty-four-hour informed consent waiting period prior to abortions.

Equipment found at the scene was outdated, dirty, and never inspected or maintained. The gauge on the suction machine was so dirty it couldn't be read. For effect, Cameron picked up the loose-fitting glass cover on the suction machine gauge with a gloved hand and waved it at the jury. It was clouded not just with dirt, but with dried blood.

***

Lt. Don Burgess of the Philadelphia Fire Department responded to the 911 call on the night Karnamaya Mongar died. He testified that when he arrived, Gosnell looked "discombobulated and confused." Yet, he still continued to do abortions on other women even after Mongar died.

Cameron reminded the jury that Dr. Timothy Rohrig came to Philadelphia from Wichita, Kansas, testify at no pay. He described Rohrig as an honest man who is considered a national expert in meperidine (Demerol) levels and what exceeds them. It was Rohrig's testimony that Mongar was overdosed on meperidine, the effects of which were only enhanced by an antihistamine drug given her called promethazine, also known as Phenergan.

"It was meperidine that killed her!" Cameron exclaimed. "Promethazine had a multiplier effect."

Dr. Raina Merchant was an emergency room physician that treated Karnamaya Mongar at the hospital. She testified concerning proper procedures, which were almost completely absent at Gosnell's establishment. Merchant explained that she was able to get a heartbeat one hour after Gosnell had given up on her after her abortion. She testified that if Mongar had received proper treatment, she would be alive today.

Cameron took a moment to point out that Sherry West lied when she said that Mongar was in the recovery area watching television when she died. In fact, Mongar never made it off the tattered and filthy abortion table until emergency responders came to her aid.

***

Dr. Gary Collins served as the Chief Medical Examiner. There was some controversy regarding his changing Mongar's cause of death, but his determination was always a medical one, not a legal one, Cameron explained. The cause of death has always been due to an overdose of meperidine, or Demerol. Cameron used a Grand Canyon analogy to push his point home. When someone falls off a cliff into the Grand Canyon and dies, it is always ruled an accident—that is, until a witness comes forward to say he was pushed. Then it becomes a murder.

Cameron discussed the minor lung condition suffered by Mongar that the defense had attempted to blame as a contributing factor in her death. While living for years in refugee camps, Mongar was deprived of modern conveniences we take for granted. She was forced to cook for her family over an open fire that subjected her to frequent smoke inhalation. She developed a minor lung condition as a result, but it was doubtful that she even was aware of it. It was only discovered during her autopsy. However, Cameron emphasized that her condition had absolutely no effect on her death, contrary to defense claims.

Cameron pivoted to conditions at Gosnell's "House of Horrors." He worked his way around the furnishings and equipment that had occupied the courtroom during the entire trial, pointing out problems to the jury. One could smell the recovery room recliner, which still bore a putrid stench. The ultrasound machine was ancient. The defibrillator didn't work. In fact, Ashley Baldwin received a shock when she tried to turn it on. The atrocious conditions were only exacerbated by Gosnell's unqualified and improperly supervised staff.

***

Dr. Karen Feisullin was an abortion provider that did procedures only in a hospital setting. She testified that twenty-four-hour consent is required prior to abortions, a law frequently ignored by Gosnell and his staff. Feisullin stressed the importance of accurate ultrasound examinations and the necessity of using ultrasound during abdominal injections of digoxin. However, Gosnell routinely logged false ultrasound findings and whether or not he actually used digoxin was a matter of debate. According to Feisullin's testimony, the digoxin injections were necessary to prevent late-term babies from being aborted alive in violation of the Partial-Birth Abortion Ban Act of 2003, but Gosnell would conduct late-term abortions even when he knew the baby's heart was still beating. She further described the final stages of abortions done on babies in the later stages of pregnancy. After the cervix has been adequately dilated, the fetus is manually extracted. The extraction occurs one dismembered body part at a time, or the baby can be born intact.

But the process takes time, usually two to four days, depending on the gestation of the baby. But Gosnell didn't want to wait that long. He rushed the process by administering large doses of Cytotec to women in order to induce strong contractions that would open the cervix faster. This had the effect of forcing women into long, extremely painful labors. Gosnell made women suffer for hours, Cameron explained. Then when it was time for women to deliver, it would, in the words of Steven Massof, "rain fetuses."

Medical standards as well as laws mattered little to Gosnell. The upper gestational limit for legal abortions in Pennsylvania was twenty-three weeks, six days, but he went well beyond that limit, like he did in Karnamaya Mongar's case.

"He could have stopped the procedure if there was a problem, but he didn't in Mongar's case," Cameron said, emphasizing how Gosnell was more concerned about getting an abortion done quickly than he was for the mother's life.

***

Cameron moved on to the testimony of Officer John Taggart, the investigator with the Crime Scene Unit who photographed Gosnell's clinic and gathered the forensic evidence. Taggart had combed through every nook and cranny and knew the inside of that office almost better than Gosnell himself. Taggart recovered and cataloged all the drugs that were in the facility. There was no digoxin.

Cameron informed the jury that conditions at the clinic had only deteriorated with time, and the reason they were not taken there to see the facility for themselves was because it was no longer safe. There was no need to bring in the rest of the furnishings and equipment from the clinic because what was left was in the same shape as the items already in court with few exceptions. Among those exceptions was a newer ultrasound machine in the slightly cleaner upstairs abortion room where white women received their abortions. Even though Gosnell is a black man, he made sure white women got special treatment.

***

Cameron pivoted briefly to the testimony of Chris Smith, a paramedic that responded to the emergency dispatch on the night Karnamaya Mongar died. He testified that when he arrived, Gosnell was doing nothing for Mongar. He had already moved on to other patients.

Elizabeth Hampton was a Gosnell family member, in addition to being an employee at his Women's Medical Society. She testified of Gosnell's wealthy lifestyle, his many properties, and his elaborate vacations to Rio de Janeiro and Jamacia. Despite Gosnell's personal wealth, he cut corners and costs down to the bone at his abortion business. The roof chronically leaked. Fetal remains were put down the garbage disposal.

Hampton had testified that Gosnell once had a contract with Stericycle, which is a medical waste disposal company that many abortion facilities contract with for the legal disposal of aborted baby remains. But Stericycle had stopped coming and the aborted baby remains had started to pile up.

Gosnell had told everyone that Stericycle stopped coming to pick up the aborted babies at the Women's Medical Society due to a "billing dispute," yet there was no evidence such a dispute ever occurred.

"Gosnell was too cheap to pay Stericycle," Cameron accused.

Hampton testified about her struggles with addiction and her efforts clean up and get her life together. But something happened at Gosnell's mill that was so bad that she "fell off the wagon" because of something she saw. That only reignited my curiosity about what could have been so bad that it drove Hampton back to the bottle. There was no doubt that Cameron and Pescatore knew Hampton's terrible secret and were content to allow her to keep it.

***

Steven Massof had worked for Gosnell for five years between 2003 and 2008. While he held a medical degree from a little-known medical school in the Caribbean, he was never licensed to practice in the United States. Massof passed himself off as a real doctor and conducted abortions, even though it was illegal for him to do so. He quit his job after Ashley Baldwin's father threatened to beat him up for reasons that still remain unclear.

Cameron rattled off a list of abuses to which Massof had testified.

- Massof said he thought he was in a residency program when he worked for Gosnell, only to discover later that Gosnell had deceived him.

- Massof explained how Gosnell would manipulate the ultrasound transducer to make the baby look smaller if it was past the legal cut-off time for abortions.

- Massof insisted that insurance companies were indeed billed for abortions, contradicting the defense's claim that they weren't.

- Massof also said that not all the drugs at the Women's Medical Society "went into the book," so there was no accurate record of what was going in and out of the facility.

During his time with Gosnell, things at the clinic started going downhill. Gosnell would talk on his Bluetooth telephone device and eat cereal during abortion procedures.

In 2007, Gosnell stopped doing partial-birth abortions. He sometimes tried to use digoxin, but it never really worked. Massof said he could still see the babies' heartbeats on the ultrasound before Gosnell aborted them.

He had some doubts about the abortion practices at the Women's Medical Society, but took Gosnell at his word when he said the "snipping" was an acceptable part of the abortion procedure that was in the medical books. Massof asked on four occasions to see the medical book that talked about snipping the necks of babies, but Gosnell never produced it.

Massof also testified that it was more dangerous to put women into labor prior to their abortions than it was to "do it manually." meaning to abort the baby through dismemberment. Gosnell instead put women into painfully strong labor and forced them to deliver their sometimes still living babies.

Cameron jumped to the matter of Sherry West, another one of Gosnell's workers who testified against him. West had hepatitis-C, a serious infectious disease, yet Gosnell still allowed her to give patients shots. She also had psychiatric issues and didn't seem to remember a lot, but she was loyal to Gosnell, and that meant more than anything to him.

West testified, like Massof, that the narcotics log book was not accurate. She heard Gosnell tell Lynda Williams to lie about it and other offenses at his clinic.

West heard one baby, which she referred to as a "specimen," making noise. She described the infant as eighteen to twenty-four inches long, which is compatible with a full-term baby. She said she heard the baby "scream like an alien," and when she heard that, she ran away.

But Sherry West had a credibility issue. McMahon had said that the prosecutions' witnesses, including West, pled guilty when they weren't. Cameron explained to the jury that West and all other witness who were offered plea deals each had attorneys who all agreed their clients were guilty. Each witness was questioned extensively by a judge, who was also convinced of their guilt, or else he would not have allowed them to enter into a plea agreement with the government.

Cameron noted that West was convicted of conspiracy. He explained the charge of conspiracy as "In for a penny, in for a pound." In other words, because West conspired to commit murder, she was just as guilty as if she wielded the stabbing scissors herself.

***

The next witness discussed in Cameron's methodical and sometimes tedious recitation of the evidence was Det. James Wood, who participated in the initial raid on the Women's Medical Society in 2010, and recovered evidence. Of the "fetuses" that were recovered, 24 percent of them were over twenty-four weeks' gestation, making their abortions illegal.

Wood photographed the red biohazard bags piled high in the clinic's basement that contained contaminated refuse and aborted baby remains. That photo was one of just a few that appeared in the grand jury report.

According to Wood, Gosnell had curiously kept Karnamaya Mongar's cash payment for her fatal abortion. It was still there at the clinic months later. Cameron left the jury to reach their own conclusions about what that signified, but to me, it seemed that somewhere in the darkness of Gosnell's twisted mind, it may not have seemed right to spend her money. Yet, he did not refund it to the Mongar family. Whatever his moral struggles might have been over taking money from a woman he killed, if any existed, greed won out.

Wood said Gosnell lied when he told investigators that he had been present at the clinic the whole time Mongar was there, and again when he said the drugs given to Monger was done intra-muscularly, when they were actually pumped through her IV. After awhile, Gosnell refused to answer any more questions, but Wood noticed that his "complexion changed" when he was asked about Mongar's ultrasound.

***

While Cameron continued to recount testimony to the jury, I sat back a moment from my furious note-taking and tried to absorb the moment. I glanced around the packed courtroom where reporters, pro-life supporters, and other interested or curious folks sat with rapt attention on Cameron. The members of the jury listened intently, as they had throughout the weeks-long trial, giving no hint to their feelings or proclivities concerning the arguments they were hearing or Gosnell's guilt or innocence.

This was a historic moment when, for the first time, an abortionist was on trial for murdering babies. All the horrendous conditions and abuses he inflicted on women and their babies were testified to under oath and on the record. No one could say it didn't happen.

Over the years, I had worked to expose similar conditions and practices that my research had uncovered at abortion facilities around the nation, but that information had been generally dismissed and ignored. The abortion cartel insisted we made it all up even though we carefully documented every claim. But now, as I sat in that Philadelphia courtroom, I hoped that would all change.

***

As I tuned back in to Cameron's closing arguments, he was discussing the testimony of Lynda Williams. She was another of Gosnell's unqualified, undereducated employees. In fact, she only had an eighth-grade education, yet was involved in patient care duties that should have been reserved for a registered nurse.

Cameron recounted testimony that Williams, like West, had a history of mental health issues. She had met Gosnell while they both worked together at an abortion facility in Delaware. She had moved down to Philadelphia after the death of her husband left her struggling mentally and financially.

"Williams is as much an exhibit as a witness in this case," Cameron told the jury, referring to her bizarre behavior on the stand as she stared ahead at nothing and answered questions with uncomfortable pauses and an emotionless voice.

Cameron explained that while Gosnell was out of the office in Delaware, or swimming, or running, Williams was afraid to call him because he would become angry at the interruption of his leisure activities. So instead, Williams gave medications. All patients got the same doses, according to Williams.

Williams had testified that half way through Mongar's abortion, the petite refugee began to turn gray, but Gosnell continued with the procedure another twenty minutes without stopping to stabilize his overdosed patient.

At times, women like Mongar were so drugged with Cytotec and Demerol that they would "precipitate," Gosnell's word for giving birth, before Gosnell arrived at the abortion mill. When this happened, staff members, including Williams, would follow Gosnell's standing instructions to snip the baby's spinal cord with surgical scissors through the back of the neck. When Williams would inform him that a woman had "precipitated" in his absence, his reply was, "That's great! Less for me to do."

Cameron looked straight at the jury and declared, "Every killer has his first victim. He's not entitled to a 'do over' or a 'freebie.'"

The seasoned prosecutor was becoming more forceful with his arguments. He mocked the fact that since Gosnell showed the grossly unqualified Williams how to give IVs and meds that somehow that made it okay. He displayed disgust at the squalid conditions women were forced to endure. For emphasis, Cameron walked over to the dirty, outdated ultrasound machine that sat before the jury, picked up the filthy, yellowed vaginal probe, and began waving it at the jury.

"This is one of the most disgusting things in this case!" he exclaimed, then dropped it as if he feared the contaminants might somehow crawl up his arm.

Returning his attention to William's testimony, Cameron told the jury that she admitted that statements she initially gave the police weren't true. When Williams referred to the up and down movement of a baby's arm that she had witnessed as a "spasm," that wasn't true either.

"It was more than a spasm, more than a twitch," he said, his indignation growing. Yet Williams had acted like she had done nothing wrong in the years she depended on Gosnell for employment.

"I'd rather live in a box on the street than work for this guy!" he said with obvious disgust.

Cameron then turned to evidence provided by Dr. Frederick Hellman, a medical examiner in Delaware County, Pennsylvania, located in the outskirts of Philadelphia. Hellman had received the body of a stillborn baby that had been delivered at a hospital in Chester. The mother had been a recent abortion patient of Gosnell's.

Hellman's examination of the infant's body revealed several disturbing facts. The baby showed no sign of needle marks, which might indicate the use of digoxin. There was no sign of digoxin in the baby's system. All organs and physical features were normal, with no indication of any "fetal anomaly." He carefully measured the baby and was disturbed by what he found. He determined that the baby was thirty to thirty-two weeks' gestation, far beyond the Pennsylvania limit of twenty-four weeks.

Hellman sent a letter and subpoena seeking additional information about the woman's abortion. Gosnell wrote back. In his letter to Hellman, Gosnell said the baby was 24.5 weeks gestation (just like all the other late-term babies he aborted). He indicated that he had injected 5 grams of digoxin into the baby prior to preparing the patient for an abortion that was to take place the following day, had not the patient ended up in the hospital emergency room.

But Hellman was unconvinced. Five grams was an extremely high dose of digoxin. Other things about the chart he was provided didn't look right. Hellman suspected that Gosnell had mishandled an illegal abortion and lodged a complaint with the state along with his report, but the state took no action. Cameron used this as an example to the jury of another documented incident of Gosnell attempting an abortion beyond the legal limit.

He described one of the babies that Gosnell was accused of murdering as a "full-term" baby that cried and was bleeding from the head, something that would indicate a live birth.

"You can't have a bleeding head injury unless you are alive," Cameron said.

Cameron then referred to what happened to Shanice Manning, the mother of Baby Boy Manning. Gosnell was not charged with her baby's death that took place years before. Her baby died from an infection, probably due to the laminaria dilator that was inserted into her cervix.

According to Cameron, there was no counseling. Manning signed the forms, then the procedure started without the mandatory twenty-four-hour waiting period.

"To this day, she regrets what happened," said the prosecutor.

On the second day of her abortion, Manning was brought into the Women's Medical Society through a side door because she was too big with her pregnancy for others to see. After the abortion, Manning inquired about the sex of her now dead baby.

"What sex? If you're a good girl, maybe I'll tell you," Gosnell responded.

Gosnell had committed an illegal abortion on Manning's living, viable baby, Cameron accused. "He would be six years old if he had lived. I wish he could walk into this courtroom today and do the things that six-year olds do. Gosnell may not have been charged with his murder, but he killed him just the same."

***

As a reminder that the jury would also be deciding the fate of Gosnell's co-defendant, Eileen O'Neill, Cameron briefly touched on the testimony of Detective Jack McDermott, who was present at the initial 2010 raid on the Women's Medical Society. McDermott said that O'Neill fled the night of the raid, afraid she would be in trouble. She denied having pre-signed prescriptions but admitted she broke the law by practicing medicine without a license.

Cameron returned to his summary of witnesses against Gosnell by turning to the testimony of Ashley Baldwin, who worked for Gosnell when she was a teenaged high school student. He characterized her testimony as an 'unpolluted' source. Ashley started working for Gosnell when she was in just the eighth grade. Over her time at his clinic, she worked her way up to the job as an ultrasound technician after training by Gosnell that took five minutes. She was taught to handle "precipitations" by taking women to the bathroom and having them deliver their babies into the toilet.

Ashley was present on the night of Karnamaya Mongars' fatal abortion. In the chaos of the emergency, she had tried to use the defibrillator on Mongar, but was shocked by the malfunctioning machine.

She remembered one really big baby. After delivery, the baby whined, made other noises, and moved its shoulders. When she returned to the room later, the baby had disappeared.

It was Ashley's testimony that babies would "precipitate" two to three times per week. She saw Lynda Williams, Steve Massof, and others snip the necks of babies after they were born. She saw one particularly large baby, known as Baby A, laying in a box by the autoclave where surgical instruments were sterilized.

I knew from reading dozens of abortion facility deficiency reports that there was no way an aborted baby's remains should be that close to the "clean" instruments due to cross-contamination. Other facilities have been cited for this violation because women can become sick or infected from this type of cross-contamination.

Yet, this was only a minor offense considering the scope of Gosnell's offenses. However, the faulty attempts at instrument sterilization, when anyone bothered with it, were ineffective, resulting in the spread of infections and sexually transmitted diseases to his patients.

***

After the police raid, Baldwin testified that Eileen O'Neill called her and asked her to lie to the police about where O'Neill had gone. O'Neill had slipped out of the clinic during the raid, telling Baldwin that she had "fled."

***

Cameron began to move more quickly through the witness testimony. He mentioned Planned Parenthood abortionist Charles David Benjamin, who had thirty-five years of abortion experience and had conducted about 40,000 abortions during that time. Benjamin testified that it is a medical standard for abortions to be done using sterile equipment and qualified nurses.

Dr. Sam Gulino was the medical examiner who examined the aborted baby bodies recovered from Gosnell's facility and addressed several important issues related to them. This was the first time anyone had to take fetuses from the freezer and determine if they were at the time of death. Babies he examined had been sloppily stored in limeade and cat food containers. Neck "defects" were found in all babies twenty-one weeks or older that he examined. That included four out of forty-seven bodies.

Gulino indicated he could not make a determination on whether the babies had been alive after birth. However, he found no maceration (decomposition) or digoxin present in the bodies. When he used the float test to determine if there was air in the lungs, that test was not valid due to the breakdown of tissue during the freezing and thawing process.

The medical examiner had also explained cadaveric spasms to the jury, which the defense argued accounted for the movement of the babies that Gosnell's workers observed. He said that such spasms don't happen in babies because their muscles are too weak. If they moved, it was because they were alive.

Gulino also testified that there was no medical reason to keep the severed feet of aborted babies that were found in jars at Gosnell's clinic. He had no explanation for that morbid discovery.

***

Yashoda Gurung was Karnamaya Mongar's adult daughter who accompanied her mother to Gosnell's clinic for her abortion. "That place was dirty," she testified. She also said that the laminaria was given to her mom on the first day without regard to any waiting period. On the second day, she left her mother at 8:00 pm, and didn't know what happened to her mom between 8:00 pm and 11:00 pm on the night she died.

Damber Ghalley was a close friend of Mongar's family who was considered like a brother. He drove Mongar to Gosnell's West Philadelphia clinic and waited outside most of the time she was inside. He testified that Sherry West rode with Mongar's daughter and him to the hospital. The next morning when Gosnell came by the hospital to pick up West, he told Ghalley that he had done nothing wrong. Gosnell later sent a letter to the family again denying wrongdoing.

***

Jimmy Johnson worked as a maintenance man at a number of Gosnell's properties, including the clinic. He testified that mice and the cat's fleas plagued the abortion facility. Exterminators didn't seem to solve the problem. He said that the toilets at the Women's Medical Society were constantly backing up because babies were being flushed down them. He told of opening the clean-out drain only to have arms and legs flood out. Gosnell had Johnson install security cameras at the abortion clinic to watch the employees, because Gosnell didn't trust them completely with his mostly-cash business.

***

Della Mann was a registered nurse that worked for Gosnell in the 1980s, then returned later and worked two days for the benefit of the inspector from the National Abortion Federation who was considering Gosnell's application for membership. Cameron summarized the salient points of Mann's testimony. She said Gosnell engaged in an unusual payment process that involved her signing over her paychecks to him after which he gave her money in return. Mann was fooled into thinking that O'Neill was a licensed physician because she portrayed herself as such. According to Mann, records were not properly kept at the clinic, and that the charts and insurance billing documents were all inaccurate.

***

Lori Matijkiw was from a children's vaccine program in which Gosnell's facility participated. She said that the clinic was dirty and the vaccines were out of date. She thought Eileen O'Neill was a doctor. She was surprised to learn that the clinic didn't see children.

Cameron made the obvious conclusion for the jury, saying, "He tried to scam the city's vaccine program!"

Speaking of scams, Cameron recounted how patient Mary Kincaid testified that she saw O'Neill bill her insurance for doctor's visits, even though O'Neill wasn't actually a licensed doctor qualified to bill for such services.

***

Latosha Lewis was not arrested with Gosnell or the other workers, but was later charged and pled guilty to federal drug crimes. Lewis said she was concerned by the amount of drugs being given to women and cut dosages on her own. She tried to warn Gosnell about this and various other problems, such as the scales not working. Lynda and Sherry gave out too much medication to patients. The reused curettes were increasing the number of STD cases among their patients. The twenty-four-hour waiting period was being ignored. However, no matter how much she tried to improve things, nothing ever seemed to change. Lewis said she finally stopped monitoring the log book because neither it or the charts were accurate anyway.

***

Lisa Dungee was a patient who received the abortion pill from Eileen O'Neill on her first visit and without a twenty-four-hour waiting period. Dungee said the place was dirty and she saw blood on the floor. She never went back. Dungee testified that files that noted the facility had followed up with her were wrong.

Natalie Tursi was a friend of Eileen O'Neill's who testified for the defense. Cameron politely described her memory as "selective." Her main testimony was that the police raised their voices as they questioned O'Neill at her home on an evening Tursi stopped by for a visit. She couldn't remember many other important details of what happened.

***

Cameron spent a bit more time on the testimony of Kareema Cross. She said she saw a baby in the toilet that was twelve to fifteen inches long with a head as big as a pancake. The baby moved in the toilet and almost appeared to be swimming. Cross heard the audible whine of another baby. She saw hearts beating after digoxin was ineptly administered, and said that ShayQuana Abram's baby moved after his neck was cut.

"That means they missed the spinal column," Cameron clarified.

Cross knew that the clinic's records were inaccurate, but didn't know that O'Neill and Massof weren't real doctors.

Cross took photos to document what she understood to be appalling conditions at Gosnell's "House of Horrors" before Mongar's death and the ensuing attempts to "clean" it. Those photos backed up her testimony in grotesque fashion.

Sure, Cross had problems with Gosnell. He resented the fact that while in his employment, Cross obtained an abortion at another facility instead of allowing him to do it. When she became pregnant again and decided to keep her baby, Gosnell retaliated by opposing her unemployment benefits.

Nevertheless, Kareema Cross was a credible, believable witness. Cameron urged the jury to give weight to her testimony.

***

Cameron breezed through the list of O'Neill character witnesses. He wasn't impressed with any of them. He emphasized that FBI agent Jason Huff said O'Neill saw patients 70 percent of the time without Gosnell present, and that she had a pre-signed prescription pad that she used at her discretion.

***

As he neared the end of his closing arguments, Cameron explained the applications of the law to the jury. He discussed concept of "prior bad acts," and that he was prohibited from bringing them up in this case.

"The defense said they never had problems before, but don't think for a minute that there weren't prior bad acts," said Cameron, planting a seed in the jurors' minds. He reminded them that they must judge this case on its facts, and nothing else.

The Assistant District Attorney then took a moment to explain the difference between a baby that is viable verses one that may be born alive.

"Viability or survivability are irrelevant," he reiterated. "'Born alive' is the standard you must use. Outside the mother, all things change. It is a human being and has to be treated as such. At that point, one cannot speed up the death process."

Next Cameron discussed the statute related to illegal abortions. He explained that in Pennsylvania, abortion cannot be done after twenty-four weeks. He showed the stack of patient charts from which they were able to determine contained evidence of abortions done at twenty-four weeks or later.

"We don't have to put each woman on the stand and make her go through that. The charts are sufficient," Cameron said.

Cameron then discussed the importance of the twenty-four -hour consent laws that Gosnell was accused of breaking.

"Abortion is one of the most important decisions a woman can make," he said. "There are no do-overs."

For example, Shanice Manning was young when she had her abortion without being allowed the waiting period to think things over. She still has regrets. Lisa Dungee got the abortion pill on the same day without the benefit of the waiting period.

Cameron emphasized that even the defense stipulated that the charts showed 227 women all signed forms and received abortions on the same day. That represents 227 violations of the twenty-four -hour waiting period law.

"The only rush to judgment was by Gosnell, who was more interested in making a buck than about the health and safety of women," Cameron said, referencing the defense's accusation that the prosecution and rushed to judgment in charging Gosnell.

Cameron went on to explain that the murder of Baby Abrams qualified for a conviction on the charge of infanticide because of his advanced gestation. He said that instead of killing that infant, it was the doctor's obligation to provide care, keep him warm, and out of the harsh bright lights until other medical assistance could arrive.

The murder charges were perhaps the most serious faced by Gosnell. Cameron explained the two kinds of murder that the jury would have to consider. The intentional killing of Babies A, C, D, and E qualified for murder in the first degree.

However, in the case of Karnamaya Mongar, her death was the result of a reckless killing. Gosnell did not intend to kill Mongar when he began her abortion, but she died due to his reckless conduct and conscious disregard for her life. Therefore, Gosnell should be convicted of murder in the third degree. Three experts testified that Mongar died of a drug overdose, but the drug Narcan, which was present at the clinic but was expired and never used, could have saved her life.

When Mongar's breathing became shallow, Gosnell chose to give her more medications. When she turned gray, he continued her abortion for an additional 20 minutes rather than stopping to treat her. It was the reckless manner in which Gosnell conducted her abortion that resulted in Mongar's death, in addition to employing two women with mental health issues and a 15-year old, to whom he entrusted Mongar's care prior to the abortion.

Cameron next addressed the matter of using a deadly weapon on a vital part of the body. He went through each case of a baby killed by Gosnell explained the signs of life that made their killing murder.

Adrienne Moton testified that she believed Baby Abrams could make it. She saw him breath and move, until Gosnell killed him.

Lynda Williams picked up Baby C's arm and the baby pulled his hand back.

Kareema Cross said that Baby D was making swimming motions in the water after he was delivered into the toilet.

Baby E was heard whining. Sherry West said the baby was eighteen to twenty-four inches long and off the charts. That means Baby E was a full-term baby.

Next came the charges of theft by deception and conspiracy as they applied to defendant Eileen O'Neill.

"She knew what was going on" inside Gosnell's mill, said Cameron with a tinge of disgust. "She hid upstairs with her head in the sand. She's not fit to be a doctor. She's just as culpable because she failed to report what was happening."

Cameron related an incident when he once had a dog that got sick and had to be put down. The dog was given two injections; the first to put it to sleep and the second to kill it.

"My dog was treated better than he treated women and children," Cameron said.

He described Gosnell's "Henry Ford Model" of medicine, which consisted of an assembly line that allowed Gosnell to make vast amounts of money while cutting back on expenses. Such cutbacks included the reuse of one-dollar disposable curettes, a practice that endangered the health of women and spread sexually transmitted diseases among his patients.

At one point, for emphasis, Cameron donned another set of purple latex gloves and held up the filthy brownish-yellow curettes that were slightly warped from reuse. He then held up once more the disgustingly filthy vaginal probe and waved it for all to see. Cameron gestured toward the dirty, outdated suction machine and picked up the glass that covered the pressure gage and showed it again to the jury before tossing it back in an open display of revulsion.

"Courage is the moral strength to withstand pressure," Cameron continued. "It means we go out of the way to protect and save the lives of others."

Then Cameron dramatically turned to Gosnell and thundered the most stunning question of the trial, "Are you human?"

He then turned to the jury while pointing to Gosnell and said, "He's the one in this case that doesn't deserve to be called human."

I noticed that Joanne Pescatore was sitting at the prosecution table wiping away tears. So moving were Cameron's arguments that she sat there sobbing for the loss of innocent life. It was such a powerfully emotional moment that I had to choke back tears of my own.

As Pescatore cried quietly at her seat, Ed Cameron launched into an impassioned plea for justice in the final moments of his closing arguments.

He described how Gosnell "doesn't even have the basic humanity" to treat the remains of his victims properly.

"We know what happened to them," he said, then reminded the jury how the remains of innocent babies were placed in limeade containers and cat food cans, ground in a garbage disposal, or flushed down the toilet until the plumbing clogged. He reminded them of the testimony of Jimmy Johnson, who described how he opened up a clean-out drain at the abortion facility and out pored recognizable fetal remains, such as arms and other body parts.

Gosnell once had a promising career, but at some point, Cameron said, it stopped being about career and became about him.

Of Karnamaya Mongar, Cameron concluded that she epitomized the American Dream, coming to America seeking a better life after twenty hard years in a primitive Bhutanese refugee camp in Nepal. But Mongar went to Gosnell and "laid on that rusty table and he killed her. She should be alive and those babies should be alive," he said.

"Those babies didn't have a chance," he continued, his voice expressing a blend of sorrow and disgust. "They couldn't say 'Let me live,' except for one baby that whined."

Cameron recalled that McMahon talked in his closing arguments about a firestorm created by this case, characterizing it as a political tsunami that was racist and elitist in nature, threatening to swallow up all those involved. McMahon told the jury that District Attorney Seth Williams had "a big press conference, and things got out of control from there."

But once again, Cameron turned McMahon's words against him, telling the jury that there was indeed a firestorm, but it was the one described by Steven Massof, the unlicensed abortionist who worked for Gosnell, when he testified, "I felt like a fireman in hell."

"That hell was 3801 Lancaster and Gosnell was the captain of that hell," said Cameron. "It was raining fetuses," he proclaimed, referring again to Massof's testimony.

"It's time to extinguish that fire, that hell he created."

It was over. Ed Cameron gathered his notes and took his seat next to his tearful co-counsel. A somber jury was escorted away, and court was dismissed for the day.

CHAPTER 37

IN THE HANDS OF THE JURY

As the courtroom emptied, I decided to hang around for a few minutes. For weeks, I had sat in the gallery of that courtroom with furnishings and equipment brought in from Gosnell's abortion facility just out of range for a close inspection. This equipment was the most convincing evidence of the squalid conditions that existed at the Women's Medical Society. It also provided a context for the testimony about practices that deteriorated to the point where murdering living babies in cold blood was a daily occurrence, hardly worth a second thought for those who worked there. Gosnell's "House of Horrors" was indeed aptly-named.

I sought out a bailiff and asked if I could enter the front part of the courtroom to get a closer look, now that the closing arguments were over. The bailiff asked Judge Minehart if he would permit that, and thankfully, after a stern glace in my direction, he nodded that it was okay.

"Just make sure you don't touch anything," the bailiff warned.

Really? I thought sarcastically. Given the frightening testimony I had heard over the weeks of the trial, which was just superbly summarized by Ed Cameron in graphic detail, there was certainly no danger of that.

I slowly browsed through the equipment, pausing often to remember various bits of testimony or get a better look at some particular piece. I clasped my hands behind my back to avoid inadvertently brushing against something as I leaned over for a closer inspection.

The photos of the abortion table and other objects simply did not relate the full extent of the ancient equipment and the filth that encrusted it. The blood-caked glass cover on the suction machine gage sat askew on the machine just where Cameron had tossed it in disgust. I winced at the thought what one rusty rolling table was used for—measuring the dismembered feet of aborted babies. I shuddered as I inspected the plastic box full of those brownish, warped suction cannulas. I tried hard to commit as much to memory as possible, since photographs were not allowed. Finally satisfied that I had seen all there was to see, I left the court and hurried back to my hotel room. I had one heck of a story to write.

***

The following morning, I was back in court to hear Judge Minehart's instructions to the jury. I watched as Gosnell entered the courtroom looking tired and pale, as if he did not sleep well. Or maybe he just wore the downcast look of defeated resignation after hearing Cameron's powerful closing arguments.

As I made myself comfortable in my favorite seat in the second row behind the prosecution table, I could not help but notice that the courtroom, which had been packed to maximum capacity the day before, was more than half empty. I guessed that jury instructions were not as sexy as the drama of closing arguments, although they were of great interest to me.

Instructions are a very important part of a trial because how they are worded can make all the difference in how a jury votes. With hundreds of counts to be considered, helping the jurors understand all the legal terms and exactly what was expected of them was crucial to the process of justice.

Once the jury was finally seated, Judge Minehart began to read his prepared instructions to the jury. The jury is a fact finder, the judge explained. The judge cannot answer questions of fact. Minehart warned the jury than emotional statements made by the defense or prosecution could not be considered as fact. For example, Cameron's question of whether Gosnell was human, or McMahon's accusation that the prosecution was racist were emotional statements.

"Such emotional statements shouldn't be given any consideration at all," Minehart read. "They are not part of the evidence."

He reminded the jurors that they were considering two separate cases. One was related to Kermit Gosnell and the second was related to Eileen O'Neill. He explained that evidence that applied only to Gosnell could not be held against O'Neill. For example, evidence of ultrasound manipulation and the delivery of babies born alive did not apply to O'Neill, and the jury was not allowed to consider it as evidence against her.

It was the jury's duty to determine a verdict using the high standard that guilt was beyond a reasonable doubt. The prosecution does not have to prove their case beyond all mathematical possibility. If there are doubts, those must be real and not imaginary or manufactured to avoid making an uncomfortable decision.

Minehart urged the jury to judge the credibility of the witnesses.

Neither Gosnell nor O'Neill testified in their own defense, but the jury was warned to make no inferences from that.

They were reminded that the expert witnesses in the case were stipulated, or in other words, both sides agreed to them being presented as experts. The only exception was the Planned Parenthood abortionist Charles David Benjamin. McMahon had objected to his designation as an "expert," but Minehart reminded the jury that he had ruled that Benjamin should be accepted as such.

Any statements made by any of the witnesses that were attributed to the defendants should not be considered unless it could be determined that they were actually made by the defendants. For example, when O'Neill was interviewed by agents at her home, those statements were voluntary. She was not in custody, so no reading of her Miranda rights was necessary.

Evidence of good character can present a reasonable doubt, Minehart explained. O'Neill presented several witnesses that testified of her character, but there was also testimony that O'Neill fled when the police first raided the Women's Medical Society. Such flight can be evidence of consciousness of guilt, however, that also may not be the case. The jury was instructed not to find guilt based solely on evidence of flight or concealment.

Inconsistent statements made to the grand jury speaks to the witnesses' credibility and should be carefully considered.

The jury was cautioned that it was not necessary to understand a motive in order to find guilt. The state was not mandated to show motive, but if a motive was presented, it can be considered.

Minehart then moved on to the subject of accomplice accountability. Some of the witnesses, such as Sherry West, Steven Massof, Lynda Williams, and Adrienne Moton, were considered accomplices because they aided or helped in planned the crimes that were committed. But the jury was cautioned that some accomplices who testify may try to place blame on others in order to get favorable treatment, and that should be considered when reviewing accomplice testimony.

When considering testimony, the jury was urged to determine whether the witness was a corrupt and polluted source, and look for supporting evidence to back up their claims. However, if the jury determines that a witness' testimony was true, then it is acceptable to rely solely on that testimony when determining the facts and guilt.

While Minehart continued reading from his list of written jury instructions, I scribbled a quick comment in the margin of my notebook, remarking that I was surprised at how the judge's thoughts seemed so unorganized; however, I realized that the instructions were complex because of the nature of the case, which involved hundreds of counts. I also understood that some of the instructions were submitted by the defense and some by the prosecution, so that likely contributed to the disjointed presentation, which I had expected to flow in a logical progression.

As much as the judge jumped from one instruction to another, each point was necessary to help the jury understand exactly what was expected of them and to clarify legal definitions so that all the jurors understood and were on the same page when considering various crimes.

For example, Minehart explained that a defendant can be held criminally responsible for another person's conduct even if it was done outside of the defendant's presence. He defined a member of a conspiracy as when "two or more people agree to commit a crime and one person acts on that agreement." Those actions had to happen while the conspiracy existed and must further the goals of the conspiracy.

An accomplice, on the other hand, was slightly different. A person was considered an accomplice if he or she, on their own, helped commit the crime. Just knowing the crime was committed is not enough to be considered an accomplice, but it is enough to be a conspirator.

Minehart then walked the jury through some of the crimes for which Gosnell and O'Neill stood accused and defined them.

First Degree Murder: "An unlawful killing done with malice." Malice was defined as "intent to kill or intent to inflict serious bodily harm."

Gosnell faced first degree murder for the killings of Babies A, C, D, and E. If Gosnell had the "intent to kill," that qualified as first degree murder.

"Intent to use a deadly weapon is circumstantial evidence of intent to kill," Minehart explained. In Gosnell's case, homicide was further defined to the jury as, "if, after fully expelled from the uterus, there was a heartbeat, pulsing of the umbilical cord, voluntary movement, or any brain wave activity," that would indicate that the baby was still "alive at the time of the act alleged to cause death."

Third Degree Murder: "An unlawful killing with malice, but without specific intent to kill." If the jury decided the murders of Babies A, C, D, and

E did not reach the standard for conviction on first degree murder, they were allowed to consider the option of Third degree murder for the deaths of the four babies.

Involuntary Manslaughter: "Reckless or grossly negligent conduct that displays indifference to the value of human life." For the death of Karnamaya Mongar, the jury had the options of third degree murder, or the lesser charge of involuntary manslaughter.

In order to qualify as involuntary manslaughter, the jury had to find that Mongar's death was caused by the defendant's conduct, and that his conduct was reckless or grossly negligent.

Violations of the Abortion Act (illegal late-term abortions): "To knowingly induce an abortion at twenty-four or more weeks."

Gosnell was charged with twenty-four counts of violating the ban on abortions after twenty-four weeks. He could be found guilty if the jury determined that he "did not reasonably believe that the baby was under twenty-four weeks."

Racketeering as a Corrupt Organization or Enterprise: "Acts of racketeering committed comprised by two or more actions." The jury was instructed to determine whether the Women's Medical Society met the legal definition of an "enterprise." In order to qualify, they had to find that the medical practice engaged in commerce.

"If you determine it is an enterprise, the pattern of racketeering activity must be directly related to the enterprise," Minehart explained.

He emphasized that a pattern of racketeering had to be established, not just random criminal events. The acts must be related. Minehart used the example of illegal gambling with the use of bribery to cover it up to illustrate related criminal acts that would qualify for the Corrupt Enterprise charge.

Minehart elaborated further to dispel any confusion. In Gosnell's case, if the jury found him guilty of at least two criminal acts, such as murder, theft by deception, or violation of the Abortion Act, then he could be found guilty of running a corrupt enterprise. In O'Neill's case, the jury also had to agree that she committed two or more acts in order to be convicted of participation in a corrupt enterprise.

Infanticide: "Intentional killing of an attended child born alive during an abortion."

This charge applied only to Baby A, the large baby that Gosnell joked was so big he could walk Gosnell to the bus stop. The jury was told to find guilt on this charge only if they determined that Gosnell failed to provide care and treatment, and did so intentionally, recklessly, or knowingly.

***

There was a discussion of the witnesses who had entered guilty pleas as part of an agreement with the prosecution. Lynda Williams, Steven Massof, and Adrienne Moton each pled guilty to murder. Tina Baldwin had pled guilty to participating in a corrupt organization.

Minehart cautioned the jury not to consider their guilty pleas as evidence against Gosnell or O'Neill during deliberations. Just because they each pled guilty to crimes did not necessarily prove guilt on anyone else's part and could not be used to convict others. However, the jury was allowed to consider the pleas in order to evaluate the witnesses' testimony.

During deliberations, the jurors were encouraged to rely on common sense and everyday knowledge of practical life. Because this case involved capital crimes, there were concerns that the jury may have a difficult time convicting anyone if they knew that the punishment might include the death penalty. To make it easier to reach their verdicts, Judge Minehart told the jurors, "You should concern yourself only with the verdict on the charges before you, not on any possible consequences."

Minehart instructed them to elect a foreperson who would keep things going and send out questions to the judge, if they had any. Each question should include a date, time, and signature of the foreperson.

Minehart ended his instructions with an important reminder: "The verdict must be unanimous."

After receiving final instructions, the jury of seven women and five men were escorted from the courtroom to begin deliberations. There was much discussion among the courtroom observers as we straggled out of the courtroom about how long it might take to return a verdict and what that verdict might be.

Outside, I accompanied a group of pro-life ladies down the street to the Reading Terminal Market, a famous farmer's market just a couple of blocks from the courthouse. As we walked down the street, I noticed that for the first time there were satellite news trucks crowded onto the street and in a corner parking lot, apparently set up to await the verdict. *If only there had been this much attention at the beginning of the trial*, I thought!

After a wonderful deli lunch and great fellowship, I hopped a taxi to the train station. I was scheduled to give a presentation about the trial to a group of pro-life leaders who were meeting in Washington, DC.

Having lived most of my life in the Midwest or in Southern California, I had never taken a commuter train before, and found the experience enjoyable, much more so than flying, which I find arduous and stressful. My travel agent was thoughtful enough to book me into business class where the seats were comfortably large and the leg-room was plentiful. It was a relaxing ride and I found myself wishing I could travel by rail more often. As the train clattered down the tracks, I dropped the adjustable tray in front of me and began to tap out my final story from Philadelphia on my iPad.

The train eventually delivered me to Union Station in Washington, DC, with its welcome familiarity. I had been there many, many times on other pro-life excursions to the nation's capital. From there, is was a quick taxi ride to my hotel. I took note of news reports that the jury had retired for the day without having reached a verdict, and would reconvene the following day to continue deliberations.

***

My reception at the meeting was completely unexpected. When I was introduced, I was stunned to receive a standing ovation from my peers! I guess someone had been reading my reports after all! I had not realized the extent that other pro-life leaders had relied on my daily reports for news about the Gosnell trial. As the head of Operation Rescue, Troy Newman was the one who usually got the accolades while I worked quietly in the background. It was an honor to be recognized for my work, especially since I had been the first to recognize the significance of the Gosnell case even as I heard news of the initial raid on the Women's Medical Society.

If Gosnell was convicted, I understood it would send shock waves through the abortion cartel where so many Gosnell-like crimes were rampant. It would send a clear message to other shoddy abortionists that there were consequences for their sloppy and dangerous practices.

On the other hand, if Gosnell was acquitted, it would signal abortionists that they never had to worry about being caught, because if Gosnell couldn't be convicted for his egregious conduct, no one could be. There would be no incentive to comply with the law or patient care standards. I was concerned that an acquittal would only create a climate that would further endanger the lives of women and their babies and leave them unprotected from exploitation and abuse.

***

Local journalists and a few reporters from national news organizations staked out seats during what was expected to be a long and tedious jury watch, while the rest of us left for home or other assignments. I had come to know most of them. Sean G. O'Sullivan was an intelligent and friendly reporter from *The News Journal* in Delaware who reported the news with a decidedly liberal bent. He headed up organizing an email list comprised of reporters who would be notified by the court when the jury returned with the highly anticipated verdicts. It was also used to update reporters on various courtroom developments. I was glad to be included in that list.

From reports coming out of the courtroom, it became clear that the jury had made the decision first to focus on Eileen O'Neill's fate before tackling the more complex charges against Gosnell, probably because O'Neill's charges were the first ones listed on a thirty-page jury form.

The jury had asked the court for definitions of some of O'Neill's charges, and to review other testimony and evidence, including the floor chart depicting the maze of cramped rooms and hallways that comprised Gosnell's squalid office space at 3801 Lancaster Avenue.

On the third day of jury deliberations in the trial that was now in its seventh week, the focus of the jury remained on O'Neill. The jury asked to review testimony from one of O'Neill's abortion patients, Lisa Dungee, who testified that she received an abortion by pill at Gosnell's Women's Medical Society from O'Neill in 2009, without the state mandated twenty-four-hour informed consent waiting period. Dungee said she never saw Gosnell at the clinic at the time she received her abortion pills, an important point, since O'Neill could not legally practice in his absence. She indicated that she never returned to the clinic for a follow-up appointment due to the filthy conditions she observed, choosing instead to seek follow-up care with her own physician.

As the jury watch continued, more news outlets became attracted to the case, and O'Sullivan's media list grew ever longer.

CHAPTER 38

DELIBERATIONS AND FOX NEWS

As jury deliberations continued the following Monday morning, Judge Jefferey P. Minehart surprised court watchers by calling the jury into the courtroom. He questioned them about the Fox News Special that ran over the weekend called "See No Evil" and asked if any of them had seen the show, which Gosnell's defense attorney, Jack McMahon, believed was meant to sway the jury.[1]

"It was irresponsible to put on that show," McMahon said, according to tweets from J. D. Mullane of PhillyBurbs.com.

Sean G. O'Sullivan, of *The News Journal* in Delaware, tweeted that McMahon said, "They [Fox News] should be ashamed, but shame and Fox News are not mutually exclusive."

Under Minehart's careful questioning, all of the jurors responded that they had not seen the Fox News special. The jurors appeared to me, as they had throughout the proceedings, to be taking their responsibilities very seriously. They had been repeatedly warned not to look at new reports related to the trial, and there was no evidence to suggest that they were not complying with that order. In the end, the Fox News special had no impact on the case. The jury returned to their deliberations, as the rest of us continued our anxious vigil awaiting a verdict.

***

By Friday, the fourth day of deliberations, the focus of the questions seemed to have finally shifted to Gosnell. The jury asked for information to help them differentiate between the four babies for which Gosnell stands accused of first degree murder. With Gosnell facing a possible death penalty if convicted on any of these charges, it was crucial for the jury to get it right.

The jury requested clarification on the specifics for each baby. Given the volume of information the jury received over the weeks of testimony and the number of babies referenced, it was understandable if there was some confusion over which baby was which. The judge sent in information to help the jury distinguish between them.

Was this line of questioning an indication that the jury would soon reach a verdict? I didn't really care how long the process would take, as long as in the end, justice was served. I continued to pray for that result.

***

For the next few days of deliberations, there was little indication of what was happening behind the closed door of the jury room. At the end of each tense day, there was still no verdict.

On Day 8 of deliberations there was a request for more witness testimony to be read back to the jury.

They had specifically asked for the testimony of Adrienne Moton, the first of Gosnell's former employees to testify. It was presumed that the jury was considering the First Degree Murder charge related to Baby D, who had been seen "swimming" in a toilet bowl.

Up until this point, the jury requested to re-hear testimony related to Baby C and Baby D, both of which were directly murdered by Gosnell staff, indicating they may be trying to zero in on Gosnell's role in the deaths.

It appeared that the jury may have been struggling with some of the other charges as well. They asked for files related to two of the twenty-four felony counts of illegal abortions past the twenty-four-week limit.

In perhaps a glimpse into the emotional state of the jury, they questioned Judge Minehart about the 227 counts of violating the twenty-four-hour informed consent law. The Defense stipulated that the forms in all 227 files were signed on the same day as the abortion procedure was done. The jury asked if the files were the only evidence of those misdemeanor counts and whether they could issue one verdict for the entire lot of charges. *The News Journal's* Sean O'Sullivan reported that some of the jurors appeared somewhat downcast when told they had to reach 227 separate verdicts on those counts. They still had a lot of work to do.

Not surprisingly, Day 8 ended once again without a verdict.

After four and a half hours of deliberations on Day 9, the jury sent out a note to Judge Minehart informing him that they were "drained," but still had not yet reached a verdict. After weeks of very emotional and disturbing testimony and nine days of deliberations, it was easy to see why the jury was tired. They desperately needed a break. While Minehart was a down-to-business, no-nonsense kind of judge, he was not cruel. He released them for the weekend, instructing them that deliberations were to resume Monday morning.

***

While the jury deliberated, Priests for Life, headed by Fr. Frank Pavone, conducted a naming ceremony for all forty-seven of the babies whose remains were recovered from Gosnell's abortion clinic. Each baby received a name, and prayers were said for each of their souls. By doing this, Fr. Pavone hoped to restore dignity and humanity that was denied them during their brief lives.[2]

Fr. Frank had a special burden for the Gosnell babies. He had attended a few days of the trial and heard some of the gruesome testimony first hand. He had also been present during the closing arguments. For decades, Fr. Frank, has shepherded Priests for Life, a large, multi-million dollar organization that serves as an umbrella group for several other pro-life groups, including Rachel's Vineyard, a post-abortion healing organization, and the youth outreach Stand True. His dedication to ending abortion was an inspiration to thousands of pro-life activists around the nation.

It was interesting for me, being a Protestant, to see the incredible respect the Catholic community of Philadelphia had for this priest. While we were standing together in the security line before court one morning, one person after another acknowledged Fr. Frank's presence. One gentleman approached us and asked for Fr. Frank's blessing on his own legal issues, which he was about to face later that morning. Without hesitancy, Fr. Frank gave his blessing and ministered to him. I doubt that anyone actually understood that he was a celebrity priest in pro-life circles. They respected the collar and what it stood for, even if they weren't the most devout of practicing Catholics.

In the courtroom, it was no different. In fact, on one of the breaks, Judge Minehart came down into the gallery to show his respects to Fr. Frank and allowed him into the front of the courtroom for a closer look at the furnishings and equipment that had been brought in from Gosnell's decaying Women's Medical Society.

Fr. Frank, along with Rev. Patrick J. Mahoney, director of the Washington, DC-based Christian Defense Coalition, had spear-headed efforts to claim the remains of the forty-seven babies from the Coroner's office where they had been stored for three years. It was their intention to respectfully lay them to rest with the dignity of a proper Christian burial.

Other groups also began to hold events to draw attention to the reports of abortion atrocities that had come out of Gosnell's courtroom. The Center for Urban Renewal and Education (C.U.R.E.) and several ministry partners hosted a press conference and legislative briefing at the National Press Club in Washington, DC titled, "Abortion and the Impact on Black America . . . Is there a Gosnell in your community?"[3]

It was gratifying to hear such news. It was evidence that the events in that Philadelphia courtroom were already inspiring educational outreaches and political action. I hoped that once a favorable verdict came in that those efforts would multiply. But in the meantime, we waited for any word from the jury, which continued to painstakingly consider the fate of Kermit Gosnell and his associate, Eileen O'Neill.

CHAPTER 39

WAITING FOR JUSTICE

Monday, May 13, 2013, represented Day 10 of deliberations, but instead of another tedious day of waiting, it turned out to be a day full of surprises. First, I heard reports that the jury had sent out yet another message to Judge Minehart. But this time, it was to inform him that it was hung on two unspecified counts. I couldn't think of worse news, except for perhaps a full acquittal. My mind began to race. What did this mean for the case? Would there have to be a new trial? What would happen next?

The jury did have some encouraging news to share, however. It indicated that it had reached verdicts on 261 other counts. Apparently, they were very close to completing their task, but just could not come to an agreement on two of the charges.

Judge Minehart took less than five minutes to instruct the jury to go back and reconsider the two hung charges and attempt to come to a consensus without violating anyone's conscience. He tried to encourage them by telling them that their disagreement is a sign that they are taking the case seriously. I can only imagine how the jurors must have felt as they were once again escorted out of the courtroom for further deliberations. I was sure this had been a long and trying process for them and their families.

There was a possibility that if the jury could not agree on the two hung charges, Judge Minehart could accept the verdicts already reached and declare a mistrial on the two hung counts. A mistrial even on two counts was unthinkable to me. After ten long weeks of trial and deliberations, this case needed to be decided once and for all. The family of Karnamaya Mongar needed closure. The family of Semika Shaw needed closure. The mothers of the dead babies murdered amid squalor by Gosnell and his unqualified staff needed closure. Heck, *I* needed closure!

With the possibility of the death penalty looming over the case, it was worth an extra effort on the part of the jury to try to resolve the final two counts. I prayed they would. I supposed the likelihood that the jury could reach an agreement that day was slim, so I resigned myself to another long day of waiting. *Maybe we'd see verdicts tomorrow*, I thought, and turned my attention onto the rest of my workday.

***

When the email I had been waiting for came in, I was surprised. About three hours after news broke that the jury was hung on two counts, I was notified through the O'Sullivan media list that the verdicts were in. Reporters who were not already waiting in the courtroom dropped everything and rushed to get there. I carefully monitored the Twitter feeds of several reporters that I knew were in the courtroom for more news.

Soon, it was time for the verdicts. The courtroom was once again locked down, as it had been during closing arguments. The bailiff ordered all electronic devices turned off. There would be no more news until after the verdicts were read.

It was a tough few minutes of waiting for me, but finally the news came flooding out of the Philadelphia Court: Gosnell had been found guilty!

According to in-court reporters, the courtroom fell silent as one guilty plea after another was read. A reporter I had met from CNN, Sarah Hoye, said that one of the prosecutors wept as the verdicts were read. I was pretty sure she was referring to lead prosecutor Joanne Pescatore, since I had witnessed her emotion in this case first hand. I remembered how she sat at the prosecution desk sobbing during closing arguments made just days earlier by her assistant prosecutor Ed Cameron. After the verdicts had been read, there were more tears and hugs.[1]

The jury had returned guilty verdicts on three counts of first degree murder for the neck-snipping deaths of three babies born alive after abortions. Gosnell was also found guilty of one count of involuntary manslaughter in the death of late-term abortion patient Karnamaya Mongar, who died from a drug overdose administered by Gosnell's unqualified and incompetent staff.

Those convictions qualified Gosnell for the death penalty, but today there would be no decision on whether that option would be pursued. That question would have to wait until the penalty phase of the trial, which was initially set for May 21.

The lengthy list of guilty verdicts continued. Gosnell was found guilty of twenty-one out of twenty-four felony counts of illegal abortions beyond the twenty-four -week limit. Out of the 227 misdemeanor counts of violating the twenty-four -hour informed consent law with which Gosnell had been charged, the jury found him guilty of all but sixteen.

He was also convicted on multiple conspiracy and corrupt organization charges. After the verdicts were read, the jury was dismissed and Gosnell was returned to his holding cell to await transport back to prison.

On the sidewalk outside the courthouse, defense attorney Jack McMahon addressed a large crowd of reporters. He described Gosnell as "disappointed and upset."[2]

In the confusion of the immediate aftermath of the day's stunning developments, news of verdicts against Gosnell's co-defendant, Eileen O'Neill, was spotty. Soon, I learned that she had been found guilty of conspiracy, participation in a corrupt organization, and two counts of theft by deception.

Overwhelmed by emotions and excitement, I struggled to focus enough to compose Operation Rescue's press release in response to the verdicts, including Troy Newman's quote for the media. I quickly posted the following brief statement:

> *We are ecstatic about these verdicts. Justice was done. This could spell the end of Roe v. Wade. For the first time, America has gotten a long hard look at the horrors that go on inside abortion clinics. We see documentation of similar shoddy practices in other abortion clinics across our country. Gosnell is not alone by any means. Now it is time for America to do some real soul searching and decide whether the abortion cartel's unaccountable and out-of-control abuses of vulnerable women are really how we want to treat each other. There are better ways to help women than to subject them to the kind of horrors found at abortion clinics in our nation. It's time to end the inhumane and barbaric practice of abortion for good.*[3]

Following the verdicts, Gosnell was photographed by a reporter as he was taken out through the parking bay under the courthouse in shackles and clad in an olive prison jumpsuit—much different attire than the expensive suits he had been allowed to wear during his trial. He was carrying a few papers wrapped in a towel, the only belongings the once wealthy and respected doctor was allowed to keep. Despite his reversal of fortunes and public disgrace, Gosnell pleasantly smiled for the cameraman, as if none of the nightmarish revelations of gruesome murder had ever happened.

CHAPTER 40

THE SENTENCE

The same jury that found Gosnell guilty of murder was expected to hear more arguments on May 21 from prosecutors Joanne Pescatore and Ed Cameron, as well as Gosnell's defense attorney Jack McMahon. But this trial, which had been chock-full of the unexpected, still had some surprises left.

McMahon had met with Pescatore and Cameron in the prosecutor's office and come to an agreement that Gosnell would give up all his rights to appeal in exchange for the prosecution dropping their case for the death penalty. It was a good move on Gosnell's part, since it probably saved his life.

On May 15, 2013, Gosnell was sentenced to three consecutive life sentences for the murders of Baby A, Baby C, and Baby D, ensuring that he would be incarcerated for the rest of his life with no chance for parole.

District Attorney Seth Williams issued the following press release on the sentencing of Kermit Gosnell:

Kermit Gosnell Sentenced to Life In Prison

May 15, 2013: "I have seen a lot of senseless and cruel acts as the District Attorney of Philadelphia, but this case is arguably the most gruesome," said District Attorney Seth Williams. "I will not mince words, Kermit Gosnell is a monster. Any doctor who cuts into the necks severing the spinal cords of living, breathing babies, who would survive with proper medical attention, is a murderer and a monster. He knowingly and systematically mistreated female patients for years, which ultimately resulted in the tragic death of Karnamaya Mongar."

At age 72, Kermit Gosnell was sentenced to three consecutive life sentences for the deaths of three babies, known as Baby A, C and D, who were born alive but were killed when their spinal cords were severed with a pair of scissors. Gosnell also received an additional two and a half to five consecutive years for manslaughter charges relating to the death of Mrs. Mongar. Gosnell was also sentenced to concurrent sentences for the remaining charges against him. A jury of seven women and five men on Monday convicted Kermit Gosnell of First Degree Murder, Involuntary Manslaughter, Conspiracy, Performing Abortions at 24 or more weeks, and other related charges.

I would like to thank the jurors for their hard work," continued the District Attorney. "This was an exhausting and often times morbid ten week trial, and I applaud you for tremendous fortitude. I would like to give my heartfelt respect and gratitude to Ann Ponterio, Joanne Pescatore, Edward Cameron, Suzan Willcox, Mariana Sorensen, Christine Wechsler, Officer John Taggart , Officer James Woods, Officer Bob Flade, Officer Terry Lewis, Detective Jack McDermott, Officer Carlos Cruz, Detective Aaron Booker, Detective Tim Bass, Sgt. Bob Kuhlmeier and Lt. Mark Deegan. You all have worked every day on this case since the Women's Medical Clinic was raided in 2010. I hope that the family and friends of Kermit Gosnell's victims will be able to feel a small sense of justice with the resolution of this case.

This was a groundbreaking criminal prosecution, where this office, these prosecutors and most importantly these 12 jurors found these heinous acts to be willful, intentional, deliberate, premeditated murders. This doctor's illegal purposeful actions against the smallest and most vulnerable human beings born alive were properly called murder by our citizens, and we have acted to seal and preserve those verdicts for all time. The defendant was also found guilty of dozens of other charges which demonstrated his pattern of endangering the lives of his patients, mostly poor women. It is our highest priority that these important verdicts are protected forever, not vulnerable to being disturbed by other lawyers or other courts. By our decision, we have ensured and secured these landmark verdicts forever.

Jurors also found Gosnell's co-defendant, 56-year-old Eileen O'Neill, guilty of conspiracy and theft charges. Eileen O'Neill will be sentenced on July 15, 2013 in courtroom 304. She was placed on house arrest after posting a $30,000 bail.

After the sentencing was finished, three of the twelve jurors stepped out onto the sidewalk in front of the Juanita Kidd Stout Center for Criminal Justice and, for the first time, addressed the press. A video recording of highlights of their remarks was aired by NBC-10 News out of Philadelphia, which had embedded a reporter in the courtroom throughout the trial.

It was then that we learned the identities of Jurors, 4, 5, and 6. Juror 5 was 27-year old David Misko, who had served as foreman of the jury. He was a slender man of medium height with a close-cropped beard and short brown hair that he attempted to tame into submission with hair gel. He struck me as an average citizen doing an extraordinary job. Misko was the first to address the media.

"Obviously, it was emotionally tolling for everyone involved," Misko said as a throng of reporters and television cameras pressed in tightly. "The premeditation idea was just business as usual, and he snipped the necks no matter what happened."[1]

Juror 4, Joe Carrol, a tall, partially graying athletic-looking man who often appeared in court in sports attire and sweat shirts, described the "evolution" of the jury's perception of Gosnell.

"Most of us thought that the doctor, he probably started out good and helping the community. But for most of us, it came down to a greed factor," Carrol said. Several jurors were said to have believed Gosnell's practice was a "killing and money machine."[2]

It was obvious that Carrol didn't think much of late-term abortions, and thought the women who had gone to Gosnell for abortions so late into their pregnancies needed to accept some responsibility.

"Women know when they're pregnant and if they didn't know after twenty-five weeks they were pregnant . . . they should have taken appropriate action before that," Carrol said.[3]

Misko said that since the prosecution put on no witnesses and Gosnell himself did not testify, they tried to get a sense of the man by observing his reactions in court.

"He gave me nothing to give me an impression on," Misko said. "He just sat there for the past eight weeks smirking."

When a reporter asked what he thought of Gosnell's smirk, Misko responded, "I didn't care for it. . . The guy fights for his life and he sits back and smirks. It doesn't rub you the right way."[4]

Juror 6 was a twenty-three-year old Department of Defense worker named Sarah Glinski, who sported a pleasant smile and two-toned hair that swept over one eye. She was just another average young woman one might expect to see at the mall or the perhaps the local Starbucks sipping a latte and chatting with her friends. But what she was asked to do as a juror would forever change her.

"Seeing those photos and having to say to myself 'This happened to those kids. There were children that died at the hands of this man.' That was hard for me to admit that this kind of evil exists in this world," Glinski said.[5]

She continued, "I think somewhere, something went wrong in his mind perhaps that made him do these things to these children that were born alive."

Glinski noted that the fact that she had no children helped her "detach" emotionally from the victims and look at the case solely on the evidence.

After hearing the perspective of the jury, it was disappointing to hear Jack McMahon's comments when it was his turn to answer questions from the press.

"[Gosnell] believes that what he did was not homicide," McMahon stated. "He believes he never killed a live baby. That was our defense. We respect the jury's verdict, who found otherwise on a number of the counts, but that's the jury's decision as to what happened and we respect it. That doesn't mean that's the truth, and that doesn't mean that's what he believes."

That statement was hard for me to swallow, since I was in the courtroom and saw the same photos of the babies, all with the wounds on the backs of their necks. I could only conclude that Gosnell did not live in reality with the rest of us, but allowed his mind to dwell in a fantasy world of his own making. That was the only way to explain his defiant and unrepentant attitude. After the misery and death that characterized Gosnell's medical career, it was clear that he didn't feel sorry even one bit.

CHAPTER 41

CO-DEFENDANTS SENTENCED

Once Gosnell was sentenced, it was time for his co-defendants to meet their fates. Those who testified against their former employer hoped for leniency and the best deal they could get. It seemed that there were endless delays and that sentencing hearings were postponed over and over. Eventually, each of Gosnell's co-defendants appeared before Philadelphia Common Pleas Court Judge Benjamin Lerner for sentencing.

The first to be sentenced was Elizabeth Hampton, who had been charged with perjury for fabricating a story she told to the FBI and the grand jury to cover up the truth behind the death of Karnamaya Mongar, who was drugged to death by Hampton's unqualified, untrained co-workers.

During her sentencing, Hampton tearfully pleaded for mercy from the court, something she did not grant to the women and innocent babies murdered at Gosnell's squalid West Philadelphia abortion clinic. Judge Lerner indicated that he appreciated Hampton pleading guilty and testifying against Gosnell, who he described accurately as a "charismatic sociopath." Hampton tearfully told the judge she still feared Gosnell.

Hampton was sentenced to one year of probation, an extremely light sentence considering the gravity of the case and her initial lies meant to cover up Gosnell's crimes.

One by one, the rest of those charged with Gosnell were sentenced. Below is a summary of each one.

Adrienne Moton
Plea Bargain: Pled guilty to third-degree murder in the death of Baby D, and agreed to cooperate with the prosecution in exchange for leniency. She testified against Gosnell at his trial.
Sentence: Time served (28 months) and 3 years of probation.

Lynda Williams

Plea Bargain: Pled guilty to 2 counts of third degree murder, distribution of a controlled substance, and conspiracy. She agreed to cooperate with the prosecution in exchange for sentencing leniency. She testified against Gosnell at his trial but did so less than enthusiastically.

Sentence: 2 1/2 years in prison, which was less than prosecutors had wanted.

Steven Massof

Plea Bargain: Pled guilty to two counts of third-degree murder and agreed to cooperate with the prosecution in exchange for sentencing leniency. He testified against Gosnell at his trial.

Sentence: six to twelve years in prison.

At Massof's sentencing, Prosecutor Ed Cameron asked for a prison term of ten to twenty years, even though Massof cooperated with the prosecution and testified against Gosnell. Massof's attorneys argued for leniency because of "the price he paid." Massof choked back sobs as he admitted culpability for his crimes. While he could not explain why he continued to work for Gosnell, Massof described his employment at the Women's Medical Society as "a horrific part of my life."[1]

Sentencing Judge Benjamin Lerner responded, "As evil as Dr. Gosnell was, as charismatic as he may have been, he didn't do this alone. He couldn't do this without the assistance of someone like you."[2]

Sherry West

Plea Bargain: Pled guilty to third-degree murder and other charges, admitting that she administered some of the overdose of Demerol that killed abortion patient Karnamaya Mongar. She also admitted to participating in a cover-up by lying about what happened and destroying files. During her court testimony for the prosecution, West denied ever having done anything wrong.

Sentence: five to ten years in prison.

Pearl Gosnell

Pled Guilty: Illegal late-term abortions, racketeering, and conspiracy. She turned against her husband to save herself, but did not testify against him at his trial.

Sentenced: Seven to twenty-three months in prison.

Tina Baldwin

Plea Bargain: Pled guilty to sustaining a corrupt organization and other offenses.

Sentence: Thirty months of probation.

Maddaline Joe

Charges Dropped: Joe's single charge of conspiracy was dropped. She never testified at Gosnell's trial.

Eileen O'Neill

Found Guilty at Trial: O'Neill was the only one of Gosnell's co-defendants that did not accept a plea bargain. She stood trial with Gosnell. She was found guilty of numerous crimes, including conspiracy, participation in a corrupt organization, and two counts of theft by deception.

Initial Sentence: six to twenty-three months of house arrest, two years of probation, and 100 hours of community service.

O'Neill filed a motion for and was granted a new trial based on her allegation that her case was prejudiced by having to stand trial alongside Gosnell. But instead of a new trial, O'Neill reached a negotiated guilty plea agreement and was resentenced.

Negotiated Plea Agreement: Pled guilty to one count of theft by deception (level 1 misdemeanor) and one count of theft by deception (level 3 misdemeanor).

Final Sentence: Time-in 51 days to 12 months with immediate parole.

Kermit Gosnell

Gosnell faced both state charges that resulted in the trial and federal charges that were handled without a trial in federal court.

Found Guilty at Trial: Jury found him guilty of three counts of first degree murder, twenty-one felony counts of illegal abortions beyond the twenty-four-week limit, 211 counts of misdemeanor counts of violating the twenty-four-hour informed consent law, numerous conspiracy and corrupt organization charges. In addition, he was found guilty of involuntary manslaughter in the death of abortion patient Karnamaya Mongar.

Sentence: Three consecutive life terms in state prison without the possibility of parole. Gosnell gave up his right to appeal the verdicts in exchange for not receiving the death penalty.

Federal Plea Bargain: Gosnell pled guilty to federal charges of conspiracy to distribute controlled substances, including oxycodone, alprazolam, and codeine; distribution and aiding and abetting the distribution of oxycodone; and maintaining a place for the illegal distribution of controlled substances.

Federal Sentence: Gosnell was sentenced to an additional thirty years in prison on the Federal drug charges.

CHAPTER 42

THE TEXAS GOSNELL

I was well aware that Gosnell was not an outlier, as so many in the media had been saying. During breaks in the trial, I remembered showing certain reporters photographs of equally squalid conditions that had been recently documented by the Fire Marshall at Robert Alexander's appalling abortion mill in Muskegon, Michigan. So horrific were the conditions there that the facility was shut down immediately and Alexander's medical license was indefinitely suspended.[1]

However, there was another abortionist in Texas that surpassed even Alexander, not in the condition of his clinic, but in his gruesome practices. Deborah Edge worked for Douglas Karpen at his abortion facility, Aaron Women's Surgical Center, located at 2505 North Shepherd in Houston. She had been employed as a surgical assistant for Karpen for about fifteen years until leaving for good in March, 2011. She was concerned about what she believed was Karpen's mistreatment of women and his female staff.

One day in 2010, a postcard arrived in the mail at the clinic during her work shift. It was from Operation Rescue. We routinely mail out postcards to abortion facilities informing the employees of our Abortion Whistleblower Program that offers a reward of $25,000 for information leading to the arrest and conviction of abortionists that are breaking the law. The cards urge clinic workers to contact us and share what they know. In order to keep from tainting the witnesses, no money is paid until after the offending abortionist is convicted. We patterned this program after law enforcement reward programs, such as Crime Stoppers.

On the day she saw the post card, Deborah had undergone a particularly rough shift and was frustrated with Karpen's behavior. She was upset about what she considered to be sexual harassment of her co-workers and mistreatment of patients. She slipped the postcard into her purse. When she got home, she dialed the number and offered the beginning bits of information that would soon expose Karpen as the "Texas Gosnell."

When Deborah called our office, she was put in contact with me. I was responsible for understanding her complaints and determining whether those complaints violated any state or federal laws. It was my job to maintain a relationship with her. If the information she supplied warranted further action, I planned to get her notarized witness statement, along with any evidence she might have in her possession, so I could file the appropriate complaints.

Deciding where to send a particular complaint was not always a simple task. Each state has its own unique way of handling complaints. In general, if the complaint was related to physician misconduct, I would file with the state medical board. If it was a facility deficiency complaint, I would file with the state's department of health. Some states require abortion facilities to be licensed. When that is the case, I forward complaints to the licensing oversight agency, which can differ from state to state. If information we receive from informants is criminal in nature, I notify, usually in writing, police, the local district attorney's office, and/or the state attorney general's office.

In the event that the main complaint is a facility issue or allegations of criminal misconduct by abortion facility staff, I usually will also file a complaint against the abortionist(s) with the medical board in addition to the other complaints. The reason for this is two-fold.

First, I never like to put all my eggs in one basket. If a complaint is rejected by one agency, it might still make traction with another. I try to cover all bases and neglect no opportunity. Secondly, it is worth trying to obtain discipline against the abortionist. The best-case scenario is license revocation, which is very difficult to get, but is well worth the sometimes exhausting effort. This removes an abortionist from the business and can result in the closure of one or more abortion facilities. As Troy Newman is fond of saying, "When abortion clinics close, lives are saved." It is a documented fact that when abortion facilities shut down in a particular state, health statistics maintained by the majority of states show that abortion numbers drop more dramatically.

In Karpen's case, there was an opportunity for not only license revocation, but also two Karpen-owned clinic closures, and perhaps criminal charges. He had a long and sordid history of disregard for the safety of his patients that created a pattern of bad behavior of which I wanted regulatory agencies to be aware dating back over two decades.

***

I had some experience with Karpen prior to Deborah Edge contacting our office. Over several months near the end of 2009 and the beginning of 2010, Operation Rescue had conducted an investigation of randomly chosen Texas abortion facilities. During that investigation, we found evidence that Karpen was not observing the state's twenty-four-hour waiting period prior to abortions. We filed a complaint against him with the Texas Medical Board (TMB) and asked them to also consider his documented pattern of disregard for his patients and the law. I submitted documentation of the following incidents.

January 21, 1988: Diana A. went to Aaron Family Planning Clinic in Houston on January 21, 1988, where she was examined and treated by Karpen. Karpen suggested several possible diagnoses for Diana's symptoms including a cyst associated with pregnancy, infection in her right tube-ovary, and ectopic pregnancy. Without utilizing available ultrasound equipment to determine the location of fetus, Karpen performed an abortion on January 28. On February 7, Diana suffered a ruptured ectopic pregnancy that had not been diagnosed at Aaron due to improper reading and interpreting lab results which had arrived February 2.[2]

May 13, 1988: Denise Montoya was fifteen years old when she went to Karpen for an abortion in her twenty-sixth week of pregnancy. Denise suffered severe bleeding, and was admitted to Ben Taub hospital. Her condition deteriorated, and she died on May 29, 1988. Her parents filed suit against Karpen and the Houston clinic where he worked, saying that they had failed to adequately explain the risks of the procedure, and had not provided consent forms, or had the parents sign any informed consent document, prior to the fatal abortion.[3]

December, 1989: Chad Traywick, a newly active pro-life activist, went to Karpen's Houston abortion clinic for the first time to check out the best place for a protest he was planning. According to an article that appeared on WorldNetDaily.com on January 21, 2003, Traywick indicated that when he got to the clinic the place was empty but the door was inexplicably open. He walked inside and discovered a room containing several buckets. Suspecting the nature of the contents, Traywick grabbed one of the buckets and left. Once at home, Traywick and his wife removed the remains of a twenty-eight-week-old aborted baby boy and photographed them. Horrifically, the baby's head and arm had been removed during the abortion process. Traywick named him Baby David and gave him a proper burial with over 100 people in attendance. Baby David's image has been used on pro-life signs and literature to reveal the horrors of abortion to the nation.[4]

August 28, 1990: Ruth Ann S. went to Dallas Medical Ladies Clinic, co-owned by Karpen, for an abortion that was done by Norman Tompkins. After the abortion, Ruth Ann complained of hemorrhaging, but was told that this was normal and that there was no need to return to the clinic. On November 7, Ruth Ann collapsed at work. She was taken to Richardson Medical Center, where a second procedure was performed to remove necrotic tissue that had been left in her uterus. Ruth Ann later sued Karpen and Tompkins. [5]

August 22, 1991: Nicolette C. was sixteen years old when she drove from her home in Louisiana without her parent's knowledge or consent for a second-trimester abortion at Karpen's Women's Pavilion. Karpen took the $1,800 dollars she had scraped together by pawning personal items and inserted laminaria. Nicolette was told to return the following day.

After leaving the facility, Nicolette felt fetal movements. Since she had not been informed of the nature of the procedure or the development of her preborn baby, she began to have misgivings. Nicolette changed her mind about wanting her baby dead. Karpen refused and told her to continue with abortion. He wrongly told her that the procedure was irreversible and that any attempt to allow the pregnancy to continue would seriously threaten her health, which of course is not true. Many women have had laminaria removed and continued on to deliver healthy babies, although the risk of miscarriage remains high.

Nicolette's mother eventually tracked her down and joined her in Houston. Together they attempted to persuade Karpen to stop the abortion. He falsely told them that that reversal of the procedure could cause her to bleed to death, that it had never been done, and that Nicolette would not be accepted in any hospital due to having the laminaria in place. Nicolette's mother requested a referral to another doctor or hospital but was refused such and told to report to the facility the next day.

When they got to Women's Pavilion, mother and daughter were met by another clinic physician, Richard Cunningham, rather than by Karpen. They were informed that Cunningham and Karpen had consulted and did not wish to remove the laminaria and release Nicolette to other care. After thirty minutes of "high pressure scare tactics," mother and daughter still wished to have the procedure stopped. Cunningham instructed them "to look in the yellow pages for an anti-abortion group," insisted that they sign a release form, and had them leave the facility.

Mother and daughter sought emergency care at a hospital, where Nicolette delivered a 1 lb. 13 oz. infant girl, whom Nicolette named Ashley. The hospital staff did what they could for the tiny premie, but Ashley died six months later as a result of persistent complications.[6]

August, 2000: Cherise Mosley, 17, obtained an obviously fake ID from a local grocery store and used it to convince Karpen to give her an abortion in violation of the 1999 Texas forty-eight-hour parental notification law. Mosley and her father later sued Karpen, saying that he should have known that the ID was an obvious fake because it was stated on the ID, "This is not a government document," and "Not to be used for check-cashing purposes." Karpen lost the lawsuit, but because he was found only 10 percent culpable for violating the law, he was not ordered to pay any monetary damages.[7]

February 6, 2005: A sewer broke at Karpen's Texas Ambulatory Surgical Center, located at 2421 N. Shepherd in Houston, causing sewage to spill into the parking lot of a neighboring car dealership. Maribeth Smith, an employee of the car dealership said she is convinced she saw human body parts mixed in with the sewage. She took photographs, believing the human tissue came from the clinic.

"Whether it's legal or not, it's not right," Smith said. "This whole area is nothing but raw sewage and bloody pieces. There were little legs coming out from one side."

A Health Department worker called 911 to report a second spill at the same abortion clinic. When asked who she was with she told the dispatcher, "Health Department . . . and we handle *normal* medical waste, but this is beyond us. He says he can see fetuses and fingers and everything." (Emphasis in transcript.)[8]

At first, it looked like there would be some kind of discipline against Karpen and several other Texas abortionists. Karpen was among ten abortionists ordered by the TMB to attend an informal review. The first two to attend such hearings were actually fined thousands of dollars.[9]

That's when Karpen lawyered up, and the case against him was suddenly dismissed.[10]

***

Karpen's well-established pattern of ignoring the law and disregarding a woman's right to information about medical procedures lent credibility to Deborah Edge's allegations. I believed her. Deborah was great to work with. She was friendly and outgoing, and eager to follow through. At the time, she was a single mother who was solely responsible for a family that included five children. She wanted to do the right thing, but also understood that her cooperation might cause a temporary hardship on her family, but if she was ever able to help convict Karpen of any crimes, her family would eventually benefit.

When she quit her job, Karpen aggressively opposed her unemployment benefits. Despite the financial strain, she courageously pressed on and never hesitated to provide me with the information I needed to file a complaint against Karpen.

At first, her information seemed routine and of the type we hear frequently about abortion facilities. Deborah seemed most upset by incidents of what she viewed as sexual harassment, when Karpen would create discomfort among the staff by engaging in inappropriate sexual "horseplay."

For example, according to Deborah, one of her co-workers once bent over to pick up a piece of trash from the floor. Karpen was said to have come up behind her and began to bump her bottom with his groin area in a simulated sex act. That kind of treatment was humiliating, of course, but he would also embarrass employees by harshly berating them in public if they make even the smallest mistake. Deborah told of more than one of her co-workers who quit because of their mistreatment by Karpen. Those who quit often found applications for unemployment blocked. This created nightmare scenarios for his former employees, most of which had families and could not afford to miss a paycheck.

But the staff weren't the only ones that were subjected to mistreatment. Deborah explained that when Karpen found a patient attractive, he would sometimes touch her inappropriately while she was under sedation. Women he found to be fat or unattractive were called "cows" or "whales" even though they were lightly sedated and could hear his insulting remarks.

Karpen used a wheelchair to transport women from the surgical area to the recovery room. While still sedated, those he found unattractive were dropped hard into the chairs and otherwise physically mishandled. The patients would wake up sore, but did not understand why.

Deborah also detailed a laundry list of patient care infractions and dishonest conduct on Karpen's part. She never saw him wash his hands except at the end of the day. She once observed that he went into the rest room with surgical gloves on, never washed his hands and emerged with the same gloves. He then went straight to the surgical room to conduct an abortion without changing those contaminated gloves.

Karpen was supposed to have a licensed practical nurse on duty every day, but often she would be off or working at his other location. The other workers were told to stack the medical charts so the LPN could sign them later, at her convenience. Sometimes, Deborah said, the charts were taken home and returned at a later date, signed as if the LPN had been present during the abortions when she had not.

Deborah alleged that women who deserved refunds for certain services never got them, and abortion funds that helped cover the cost of abortions were intentionally overbilled.

There were allegations of improperly stored drugs. The sterilization room was a "mess." Surgical instruments were not properly sanitized. Workers were asked to reuse disposable items.

Deborah worked to get her co-workers to come forward. Three other former Karpen employees, some still working for him when I first talked to them, provided corroborating statements of Karpen's misconduct. As I worked with them to prepare a complaint with the Texas Medical Board, the ladies began to open up. Slowly, new details began to emerge. We began to work with a pro-life legal advocacy group, Alliance Defending Freedom, to make sure the women had the legal representation they needed.

Soon after I filed the complaint with the Texas Medical Board, I began to learn that there may have been serious crimes committed by Karpen. It took several months for our informants to open up completely. I got the impression that they honestly didn't understand that some of the things that took place at Karpen's abortion facilities were not standard medical practices. It was only after I began to discuss the Gosnell case with them that they realized that similar things had happened at Karpen's abortion business.

The women began to explain how ultrasound images were falsified in order to make some abortions appear to be under the Texas legal abortion limit of twenty-four weeks when they were actually over the limit. They began to describe how they saw babies born alive during these late abortions only to be killed by Karpen slashing their necks or twisting their heads nearly off.

To back up those accusations, I was provided with images of an Excel file that contained four months of abortion billing information for 2011. The abortions listed all indicated that several abortion funds, including the

National Abortion Federation Fund, the Hersey Fund, the Lilith Fund, and others had been billed for part of the abortion fee. The allegation made by the informant was that Karpen was bilking the funds out of money by over-billing them. While that allegation could not be substantiated by Operation Rescue, the list was revealing as to the price of the late-term abortions that the women all said were done beyond the legal limit and the amount of cash taken in to the clinic.[11]

March, 2011 listed thirty-three abortions that were partially paid for with abortion funds or other sources. Over $38,000 in cash was paid by patients. The file showed five abortions that cost under $1,000, seven that were between $1,000–$2,000, twelve that cost between $2,000–$3,000, and three that were over $3,000.[12]

The greater the gestational age, the higher the abortion fee. How old were the two babies whose abortions cost $3,700? The file didn't say, but the high figure seemed to confirm the allegations that abortions were being done very late—much later than twenty-four weeks.

But the case took on a new sense of urgency and importance when one worker, Gigi Aguilar, told me she had pictures on her cell phone that she had taken at Karpen's clinic of some of the larger babies aborted by Karpen. She had initially used her co-worker Krystal Rodriguez's cell phone to take the photos while Krystal held the baby, then forwarded them to her own phone. I asked her to send them to me.

When I opened up Gigi's email message, it was as if I had been punched in the gut. The first photo was of a baby, fully formed, with dark hair and pink skin. The poor little boy was being held up by the neck over a sink for the photo.[13]

His head had clearly been compressed to the point that his left eye bulged from its socket. His neck bore evidence of a huge jagged gash from ear to ear that appeared to me may have been accomplished by the violent twisting of the head, just as the ladies had claimed. I believed it was very likely that I was looking at the body of a murder victim.

I sent the photos to one of the ADF attorneys, Catherine Foster. Soon, I received a call back. Catherine was stunned by what she saw, and called that email a "day-stopper." She had the same impression as I that a crime had been committed, and told me that she thought that photo could be the "Emmett Till" moment for the pro-life movement.

Catherine was referencing the brutal murder of Emmett Till, a fourteen-year-old African American who was brutally beaten, shot, lynched, and mutilated by two white men after the teen allegedly "flirted" with a twenty-one-year-old married white woman. His body was dumped in the Tallahatchie River and was retrieved three days later.

Emmett's body was shipped back to his mother, Mamie Cathan Till Bradley of Chicago, who insisted on an open casket funeral. Images of Emmett's mutilated body lying in his coffin appeared in *The Chicago Defender* and *Jet Magazine*. These horrific images helped draw attention to segregation and bigotry in America and served as a rallying point for what later became the Civil Rights Movement of the 1960s.

Once Catherine contacted Gigi about the pictures, Gigi sent the attorney two more photos that were also shared with me of another baby who had suffered similar injuries.

I immediately filed amendments to my initial complaint to include the information about what Deborah and Gigi believed were illegal late-term abortions and the killing of babies born alive. I submitted the photos as well as other evidence. I had frequent conversations with the TMB investigator assigned to the case, Leslie Coe, who interviewed the women. As the other Karpen whistleblowers came forward with similar stories, their affidavits were also submitted to Coe.

Everything seemed to be progressing through the investigative process. Coe seemed cooperative and willing to take more information as it came in. Settlement conference hearings were scheduled and hopes rose, but the hearings were repeatedly delayed and reset over the course of months until finally they were simply not rescheduled.

I thought perhaps the additional information had sent the case back to the investigative phase and that the Board just needed more time to process everything. Medical boards take a very long time to work through things. After being involved in numerous board actions against abortionists, I understood that delays were normal.

But then something changed. It was like someone turned the spigot off. Ms. Coe stopped returning my calls and did not acknowledge my emails. I could not account for the change in attitude. Then, in a classic blindside, I received a letter he TMB completely dismissing the case. No one even bothered to sign the letter.

The TMB letter, dated February 8, 2013, stated:

The investigation referenced above has been dismissed because the Board determined there was insufficient evidence to prove that a violation of the

Medical Practices Act occurred. Specifically, this investigation determined that Dr. Karpen did not violate the laws connected with the practice of medicine and there is no evidence of inappropriate behavior, therefore no further action will be taken.[14]

I couldn't believe what I was reading. How could anyone look at those pictures of the two babies and still say "there is no evidence of inappropriate behavior"?

Troy and I consulted with attorneys about what should be done next. The Gosnell trial had just begun and I headed off to Philadelphia. I decided that when I returned I would fly to Houston to meet with my informants and record their statements on video. However, the trial drug on for several weeks, and Troy Newman decided to contact our friend in Texas, Mark Crutcher, director of Life Dynamics, Inc. He agreed to record interviews with my informants. When I finally returned to Wichita after Gosnell's trial, I was told Crutcher had already conducted the interviews and was editing them for release.

At first, I was a bit miffed at having my work parceled out to another organization, but once I saw the video, I realized that my amateur movie skills could never have produced such a professional product.

Crutcher had interviewed three women, Deborah Edge, Gigi Aguilar, and Krystal Rodriguez, all of whom had worked recently for Karpen's abortion business. The content of the interview exceeded even my expectations.

"When [Karpen] did an abortion, especially one over twenty weeks, most of the time the fetus would come completely out before he cut the spinal cord or he introduced one of the instruments into the soft spot of the fetus, in order to kill the fetus," said Edge.[15]

"I thought, well, it's an abortion you know, that's what he does, but I wasn't aware that it was illegal . . . Most of the time we would see him where the fetus would come completely out, and of course, the fetus would still be alive," Edge continued.

How often did this happen?

"I think every morning I saw several, on several occasions," she said. "If we had twenty-something patients, of course ten, or twelve, or fifteen patients would be large procedures, and out of those large procedures, I'm pretty sure that I was seeing at least three or four fetuses that were completely delivered in some way or another," said Edge, acknowledging that these babies would be alive.

She described how some babies would emerge too soon and would be alive, moving, and breathing. She also told of how Karpen would sometimes deliver the babies feet first with the toes wiggling until he stabbed them with a surgical implement. At the moment the toes would suddenly splay out before going limp. Sometimes he would kill the babies by "twisting the head off the neck," according to Edge.

Women would be given doses of Cytotec, also known as misoprostol, a drug that causes strong and unpredictable uterine contractions. This could sometimes cause the women to deliver while they were waiting in line to see Karpen, sometimes in the toilets and at least once in the hallway.

"[Karpen] just picked it up with one of those [blue chux] pads and put it in the trash bag," said Krystal Rodriguez of the baby born in the hallway.

"As long as the patient had the cash, he was going to do it past twenty-five weeks," she said.

But not all the babies came out intact. When there was difficulty, Karpen would dismember them, a process which, according to surgical assistant Deborah Edge, was a bloody mess.

"Sometimes he couldn't get the fetus out" she explained. "He would yank pieces, piece by piece, when they were oversize. And I'm talking about the whole floor dirty. I'm talking about me drenched in blood."[16]

***

The day after Gosnell was convicted in Philadelphia of murdering babies born alive during illegal late-term abortions, Life Dynamics released their video of the witness interviews, followed immediately by my release of Operation Rescue's full investigative report along with the color photos of disfigured and bruised bodies of the aborted babies photographed by Gigi Aguilar on Krystal Rodriguez' cell phone.[17] That investigative report also included the fact that the TMB had access to all the evidence and witnesses, but had decided to sweep it under the rug.

Immediately, the release of the former Karpen employees' interviews, photos, and my report caused a firestorm of reaction, especially in Texas. Texas Lt. Governor David Dewhurst issued a statement responding to my investigative report and the interview video demanding a full-scale investigation into Karpen's practices that were akin to those used by now-convicted murderer Kermit Gosnell.

In addition, the *Houston Chronicle* reported that the Texas Department of State Health Services had launched an investigation into Karpen's abortion business. Carrie Williams, spokeswoman for the DSHS told the paper in an email that it was "aware of the allegations, and we are investigating . . . This is a very high priority for us."[18]

Also looking into the allegations against Karpen was the Harris County District Attorney's office.

"We have several people looking into the allegations," Sara Marie Kinney, a spokeswoman for the Harris County District Attorney confirmed.[19]

I suddenly realized that a formal complaint had never been filed with the Harris County prosecutor. I prepared such a complaint, sending it directly to District Attorney Mike Anderson.

Meanwhile, Leigh Hopper of the Texas Medical Board began telling reporters that the information released by Operation Rescue concerning abortion abuses alleged to have been committed by Karpen "raises concerns, for certain."

But as far as I was concerned, the Texas Medical Board had a lot of explaining to do. I publicly stated that the TMB should have taken my fully documented complaint more seriously, since it was backed up by hard evidence and courageous eye witnesses. It was a regulatory failure akin to that uncovered and sternly denounced by the grand jury that indicted Gosnell in Pennsylvania.

***

In June 2013, a special legislative session convened at the request of Texas Gov. Rick Perry, a pro-life Republican who was shocked by the Gosnell trial and appalled that similar abuses might be occurring in his state. The purpose was to pass a bill, known then as Senate Bill 5, which would require Texas abortion facilities to be licensed, meet basic safety requirements, and employ abortionists who maintained hospital privileges within thirty miles of the facility where they conducted abortions. There were a number of other provisions also included, such as a ban on abortions at twenty weeks or later, and the requirement that the abortion pill, RU-486, be administered only in the presence of a licensed physician. It was the kind of legislation that pro-lifers like me dreamed about. It gave the state the tools to shut down abortion facilities that were violating the law.

The special session drew a raucous band of abortion supporters who filled the gallery at the Texas statehouse on June 25, 2013, while Democratic Rep. Wendy Davis famously filibustered the bill for over ten hours. Davis's filibuster was halted when she violated the rules and began to discuss an ultrasound law unrelated to the bill at hand. With the session rapidly approaching the midnight deadline when the session was to expire, Lt. Gov. David Dewhurst rushed to record a vote as chaos broke out.

Instigated by a group of leftist socialists and hold-ons from the anarchy-driven Occupy movement, those in the gallery began to disrupt the session by with jeers and chants, making so much noise that the proceedings on the floor could not be heard. A lack of security personnel made attempts to clear the unruly gallery futile. A vote was hastily taken and Dewhurst proclaimed that SB 5 had passed with a vote of 19–11.

But the confusion was far from over. Democrats claimed that the vote was recorded after the midnight expiration of the special session. A time stamp on the vote seemed to support their claims, and Dewhurst was forced to admit the vote was invalid. The bill had failed.

Not to be deterred, the following day Gov. Perry called a second special thirty-day session to consider the same pro-life legislation, now known as House Bill 2, or HB2 for short. This time, extra state troopers were called in to ensure order was maintained.

Empowered by Davis' filibuster and the first's session's victory, abortion supporters flooded the Texas Capitol. They wore orange T-shirts that identified their opposition to the proposed law. But this time, pro-life supporters rallied, jamming the statehouse with throngs in blue shirts that signaled support for HB2.

I drove to Austin to observe the session for myself, and arrived in time for a huge pro-life rally that was held on the capital grounds. Thousands of pro-life supporters jammed together on the capital steps and lawn on a hot, muggy evening to hear notable speakers such as Lt. Gov. David Dewhurst, Attorney General Greg Abbott, and Fox News personality former Gov. Mike Huckabee speak in support of a Texas abortion law that had been thwarted by an angry pro-abortion mob two weeks earlier.

The rally had a street-fair quality, with a sea of blue-shirted pro-lifers cheering and chanting, "Pass the bill" while orange-clad abortion supporters who were woefully outnumbered, occasionally recited mantras such as, "Separate Church and State." The pro-abortion chants were generally ignored and drowned out by the enthusiastic multitude comprised mostly of pro-life families, which took every opportunity punctuate the speakers' messages with hoots and cheers.

There was a palpable sense of history in the making.

The next day, I decided to try to get a seat in the gallery. By the time I arrived, the line of people with similar ambitions snaked down a flight of stairs and around the capital rotunda, then down another flight and down a very long hallway.

I waited patiently while the line slowly moved. From time to time, the pro-life Christians would break out in song with a favorite hymn or patriotic anthem. Finally, I arrived at the front of the line. The gallery was full, and if I were to get a seat, I would have to wait for someone to leave. After hours in line, I finally abandoned my quest for a gallery seat and looked for other opportunities.

I was allowed by State Troopers to join the staffers from the Texas Alliance for Life in Gov. Perry's conference room where we all watched the floor debate on my iPad. Realizing that I could do that from my office in Wichita, I left for home the next day, still proud to have witnessed such an amazing moment, inspired at least in part, by my work from the Gosnell trial and the Karpen investigation.

Within days, once again I watched on my iPad (this time from the comforts of my living room) as HB2 was passed. It was signed into law on July 18, 2013 by Gov. Perry in the presence of several pro-life leaders.

Almost immediately, abortion facilities began to close as their owners realized that their shoddy businesses could not meet the minimum requirements of the law. Before the passage of HB2, forty-one abortion facilities operated in Texas. By the time the law went into effect in October, over half of them had closed.

A study published a year later in July 2014, by the Texas Policy Evaluation Project showed that abortion numbers dramatically declined by 13 percent, ten percentage points higher than the average national decrease in abortions that year. That decline represented approximately 9,200 lives spared due to the new law in just one year. The decrease in abortions in Texas was a direct result of abortion facilities that closed due to HB2.

**

Meanwhile, I continued to monitor the Karpen investigations. I had hoped for a quick prosecution from Republican Harris County District Attorney Mike Anderson, who was considered a solid pro-life conservative. However, the day after our Karpen report was released, Anderson announced that he had been diagnosed with cancer.

Because of Anderson's illness, a decision on the Karpen case had been delayed. Tragically, Mike Anderson lost is battle with cancer and died on August 31, 2013. What would happen to any hope of a criminal prosecution now?

I learned that Anderson's wife, Devon, was also an attorney and had served in the Harris County District Attorney's office for twelve years before becoming a State District Judge. On September 26, 2013, Gov. Rick Perry appointed her to fill the remainder of her husband's term.[20]

As the new District Attorney, Devon Anderson launched a grand jury investigation of Karpen. Hopes rose again that Karpen would face criminal charges for allegations made by his former employees, who said they saw him murder late-term babies who were born alive during abortions. Grand jury proceedings are supposed to be secret, but we heard rumors and tidbits of information. We knew witnesses were being called to testify before the grand jury panel.

During that time, I was represented by Mike Norton was at that time with the Alliance Defending Freedom. He called me one day in the fall and told me to preserve the computer files that showed the photos of the aborted baby we believed was illegally aborted by Karpen then killed after birth, came directly from Gigi Aguilar's cell phone. He said that the Houston police would want to get the metadata from my laptop to corroborate the authenticity of the photos. There was a real possibility that I may be called to testify before the grand jury.

"Get ready to go to Houston," Mike told me.

I was more than willing to assist the police and even testify before the grand jury. I waited anxiously for the call. December rolled around, and still no call. The call never came.

On December 20, 2013, Devon Anderson announced that the grand jury had failed to issue a "true bill" against Karpen, meaning he would not be indicted or charged.[21]

Karpen had gotten away with murder.

**

I was, frankly, shocked at the grand jury's decision to "no-bill" Karpen. How could the grand jury have concluded their investigation without the photos, which were the most damaging evidence against Karpen? The wounds on those babies could not have all been done inside the womb. If an expert in fetal development could have inspected the pictures, it would have been possible to determine that the babies were older than the legal limit in Texas of twenty-four weeks. I was certain that the grand jury was never shown the photos and may not have had access to all the evidence that was in my possession. It was a miscarriage of justice.

After Karpen was "no-billed," his attorney, Chip Lewis, went public with threatening statements against Operation Rescue. Lewis falsely accused Operation Rescue of paying three former Karpen employees to testify against him and of "doctoring" grisly photographs of babies Karpen had allegedly murdered.

"Those responsible for bringing these wholly unfounded allegations against Dr. Karpen will be held responsible for their crimes," Lewis told the *Houston Chronicle*. He threatened a criminal investigation of Operation Rescue and raised the possibility of suing us, neither of which ever materialized.[22]

We later learned that Lewis had tight connections to District Attorney Devon Anderson. He was a longtime personal friend of the Anderson family, and was the largest political donor to Devon Anderson's political campaigns. There was something fishy here, but for me, it looked like all the doors had closed on any possible investigations of Douglas Karpen. It was time to move on.

***

The following year, a seemingly unrelated series of events took place that helped Troy Newman and I understand exactly what went wrong with the "Texas Gosnell" grand jury. Troy was paid a visit at our office by a young California man who had a plan to investigate Planned Parenthood's practice of selling aborted baby organs and tissue. His name was David Daleiden.

Troy and David hit it off and seemed to be on the same page when it came to the strategy of documenting and exposing abortion abuses for the purpose of seeking criminal prosecutions for violations. I knew nothing of their plans at the time, except that something very secret was happening. I paid it little attention at the time.

David had created an organization called the Center for Medical Progress (CMP). Troy was one of three founding board members of the CMP, along with David and an older California pro-life activist, Albin Rhomberg.

Over several months, David had been conducting an undercover investigation the likes of which had never been attempted by any pro-life organization. He set up a "dummy" business and posed as a representative of an organ procurement company. He was invited to attend Planned

Parenthood and NAF meetings and even visited several Planned Parenthood abortion facilities for the purpose of negotiating deals for the sale of aborted baby remains by Planned Parenthood to his company. One of those facilities was the Planned Parenthood Gulf Coast "mega-center" in Houston, Texas. During this undercover investigation, David wore a hidden camera. He taped everything.

In July 2015, David was ready to release a series of videos that showed Planned Parenthood's involvement in selling aborted baby parts for profit. My job was to prepare press releases for Troy when each new video dropped. The impact of David's investigation was meteoric. The bombshell story tore a path into the mainstream media that rarely covered abortion stories, especially if the story reflected badly on the business of abortion.

At first, Planned Parenthood was stunned and struggled to come up with a response that didn't make things worse. Later they went on the offense with a vengeance. David, Troy, and the CMP were sued in Federal Court by the National Abortion Federation and Planned Parenthood, which accused them of racketeering and sought to block the release of any yet unpublished video.

Meanwhile, Harris County District Attorney Devon Anderson launched a grand jury investigation into evidence that Planned Parenthood was breaking the law by profiting from the sale of aborted baby remains. I was skeptical of Anderson's supposed investigation because of what transpired during the Karpen grand jury that protected the late-term abortionist from prosecution. It was hard for me to believe that Anderson would ever indict Planned Parenthood. But what actually happened was much worse than just letting Planned Parenthood off the hook.

On January 26, 2016 Anderson announced that the grand jury that was created to investigate Planned Parenthood had issued indictments against David Daleiden and Sandra Merritt, Daleiden's undercover partner who appeared in the CMP videos as a representative of Daleiden's shadow procurement company.[23]

Not only had Anderson flipped the grand jury, but a report by the Associated Press the following day indicated it was Daleiden and Merritt who were the subjects of the grand jury from the onset. The focus was never on Planned Parenthood.

Josh Schaffer, attorney for Planned Parenthood, informed the news organization that "the grand jury never even voted on possible criminal charges" against Planned Parenthood.[24]

No vote meant no investigation. Planned Parenthood appeared to have escaped justice just as Karpen had.

The AP story also revealed that Karpen's attorney and Anderson family friend, Chip Lewis, had been on a vendetta against Operation Rescue since the 2013 Karpen grand jury. After the Karpen grand jury, Lewis helped "soften the fallout" for Anderson in "Republican circles" by telling them falsehoods about Operation Rescue.[25]

"I told them, 'Don't hitch your wagon to this. They're crooks, and it's going to be exposed,'" Lewis told the AP.[26]

It was apparent to me that Lewis saw the new grand jury investigation as an opportunity to finally get his revenge on Operation Rescue.

The AP article also noted that Sunni Mitchell, the same female Assistant District Attorney that handled the Karpen investigation, also directed the grand jury that indicted Daleiden and Merritt. Of Mitchell, Lewis said, "I don't think she forgot what she uncovered," referring to the Karpen grand jury, which now appeared to also have been influenced by Lewis. Her bias, based at least in part on Lewis' falsehoods, likely tainted the grand jury process, turning it against Daleiden because of his association with Troy Newman. The only reason Troy wasn't charged was because he did not accompany David to the Houston Planned Parenthood abortion facility during the CMP undercover investigation.

Both Lewis and Planned Parenthood's attorney Josh Schaffer had inside information about the grand jury investigation that they never should have had due to the secrecy of the grand jury process. He had improperly obtained unedited recording made by David Daleiden from Assistant District Attorney Sunni Mitchell. It was later learned that Anderson's office had been consulting with Schaffer throughout the entire so-called investigation.

It was now clear that both of the Harris County grand juries were contaminated by Lewis's hatred of Operation Rescue, Anderson's loyalty to Lewis. The latter grand jury was also compromised by Planned Parenthood's improper participation.

"Anderson said that she would let the evidence take her where it would, and we say the evidence reveals an agenda in the District Attorney's office, under the influence of Chip Lewis, to get even with pro-life whistleblowers who have reported evidence against abortion providers of serious crimes, including murder," I stated an Operation Rescue's press release. "In order for there to be justice, we need to stop dipping from a poisoned well and seek unbiased people to push forward with investigations against the real culprits."[27]

Of course, the mainstream media had always been in Planned Parenthood's corner and parroted all their talking points without question. When news of David and Sandra's criminal charges broke, they crowed that this was final exoneration of Planned Parenthood and proof that the pro-life activists were the real criminals.

Rev. Patrick Mahoney, Director of the Christian Defense Coalition, offered to help expose the injustice of David and Sandra's charges. He volunteered to hand-deliver to Devon Anderson a petition circulated by LifeSiteNews.com that gathered 100,000 signatures in support of David and Sandra that demanded their bogus charges be dismissed.

Since I was traveling that week anyway, it was simple to redirect one of my flights to Houston to help Pat with what looked like would be a small event. However, as plans to deliver the petitions progressed, more and more organizations joined in. It looked like we were going to have a large crowd. Then we received word that on the day we planned to be in Houston to deliver the petitions, David planned to surrender to the authorities. Pat's planned a press conference in advance of the delivery of the petition took on much more importance.

As we planned our event, Operation Rescue's Texas attorney, Briscoe Cain, released another bombshell on Planned Parenthood and Devon Anderson. He had obtained invoices through a Freedom of Information Act request that showed Planned Parenthood Gulf Coast had billed the publicly funded University of Texas Medical Branch in Galveston, Texas, thousands of dollars for aborted baby organs and tissue. This evidence was never seen by the grand jury that was supposed to have investigated Planned Parenthood. Instead of being "cleared," Planned Parenthood was again under suspicion of breaking the law.

Cain was in the cadre of attorneys that escorted David to court to enter his "not guilty" pleas. Pat and I met the group was they entered the courthouse, then ran up to the courtroom to witness David's appearance. Thankfully, David was never jailed and was released to his attorneys after his court appearance.

The entire event was a media circus. Outside the courtroom, reporters and cameramen jockeyed for the best position. David and his attorneys, including Peter Breen from the pro-life Thomas More Society of Chicago, Illinois, briefly addressed the media in the hallway outside the courtroom. I broadcast the comments on Periscope with my cell phone raised high behind the throng of cameras.

Outside the court, several hundred people gathered to show support for David. There must have been a dozen pro-life leaders and pastors who addressed the media in turn while Pat directed the event. My own comments that called for new, untainted investigations into Planned Parenthood's conduct and accusations against Karpen's received scant notice from the news media, while fact that David was charged with crimes was well covered.

After our press conference, Pat and I, along with Lisa Bourne of LifeSiteNews.com, walked up to Devon Anderson's office and presented the petitions to one of her representatives. For the moment, we had wrested control of the narrative away from Planned Parenthood and successfully turned the heat up on the Harris County District Attorney.

It was later discovered that Anderson had improperly extended the grand jury into the new year and failed to properly notify David and Sandra that they were the subjects of the grand jury, as required by law. In essence, Anderson was forced to admit that she had broken the law.

All charges against the pro-life journalists were dropped.

The failed attempt to make criminals out of citizen journalists that had exposed criminal conduct on the part of Planned Parenthood took its toll on Anderson's conservative support. On November 8, 2016, Anderson was defeated in her re-election bid, ridding the Harris County District Attorney's office of what we viewed as a major source of corruption and bias.

A few days after Anderson's defeat, the Congressional Select Panel on Infant Lives, which investigated allegations related to the illegal trafficking of aborted baby organs, made public their criminal referral of Planned Parenthood Gulf Coast to the Texas Attorney General's office for illegally selling aborted baby remains to the University of Texas, as discovered by our own Briscoe Caine.[28,29]

To cap off the ironies, Cain was handily elected to the Texas House of Representatives during the same election that handed Anderson her hat and showed her the door out.

***

The Center for Medical Progress's explosive videos prompted Congressional investigations by the House Select Investigative Panel on Infant Lives and the Senate Judiciary Committee. Both investigative panels concluded that Planned Parenthood and several other businesses violated the law regarding the sale of aborted baby remains. Included in the House Select Panel's referrals were the two related to Douglas Karpen. We had cooperated with House investigators and supplied them with our evidence on Karpen. They determined that Karpen's case was so serious, that they referred him to the Texas Attorney General's office and the US Department of Justice for further investigation and prosecution.

Under the Obama Administration, we could expect no action from the DOJ. But on November 2, 2016 the voters of America elected Donald J. Trump to serve as the forty-fifth President of the United States. With the DOJ headed by a Trump appointee, we expect that the Karpen case will be treated very seriously.

My work was vindicated to some extent by the Select Panel's referrals, but a guilty verdict would be the ultimate vindication. Now, with the pro-abortion Obama administration out of the way and corruption purged from the Harris county District Attorney's office, Karpen, like Gosnell, may still get his day in court.

***

As for Deborah Edge, Karpen's former employee who first had the courage to blow the whistle on him, she was subjected to harsh attacks after Crutcher's video of her interview was released. I was so proud to see her stand courageously in the midst of sometimes vicious assaults on her character by the biased media and bitter abortion supporters. We remain friends to this day and continue to converse from time to time via social media. Deborah later married and moved her family out of Texas. She now enjoys a happy life free from the horrors she witnessed from within the abortion cartel.

CHAPTER 43

LAID TO REST

Once the Gosnell trial was over, Rev. Pat Mahoney began efforts to secure the remains for burial of forty-seven infants recovered from the Women's Medical Society. Since their discovery, the remains of those babies had languished in storage in the City of Philadelphia's Medical Examiner's office.

Each request to bury the babies was denied.

In August 2013, Mahoney gathered together a coalition of pro-life groups that gathered at Drexel University and marched with police escort to Gosnell's shuttered and deteriorating abortion clinic. There, they held a moving candlelight prayer vigil where they prayed for closure and a decent Christian burial for the murdered babies.

The group gathered again the following day outside the Medical Examiner's office for a press conference where Mahoney released the following statement:

The official guidelines and regulations set forth by the Medical Examiner make it clear that any "interested" party can put in a request asking for any unidentified person to be released into their care.

Numerous national and local faith and community organizations have put in written formal requests for these children.

The conviction of Kermit Gosnell on murder charges makes it clear that these babies are "persons" and must be afforded the same equal rights as anyone else under the law.

It is tragic and barbaric that government officials are playing 'abortion politics' with these innocent babies. These children were brutalized once by Kermit Gosnell. We are now demanding that they are not brutalized again by the City of Philadelphia.[1]

Mahoney continued to petition for the release of the babies' remains for burial, holding events from time to time with the hope that the Medical Examiner would relent. It just seemed so wrong for them to be stuck in what seemed to be endless limbo. They deserved the dignity of a proper burial. In June 2015, Mahoney again sought the release of the remains for burial when he inadvertently discovered that the babies' bodies had been unceremoniously cremated and buried in an unmarked grave at Laurel Hill Cemetery by the City of Philadelphia on September 12, 2013.

It might have been nice if the Medical Examiner's office had informed him of that months ago!

On June 15, 2015, Mahoney gathered with Fr. Frank Pavone of Priests for Life and about forty pro-life supporters to place flowers, a temporary marker, and forty-seven white crosses at the grave site. The group then briefly memorialized the babies that were at the heart of the sensational murder trial that revealed shocking details of shoddy abortions done by incompetent staff in squalid conditions at a run-down brick office building located at 3801 Lancaster.

City officials told reporters they were simply following protocol when they cremated and buried the "unclaimed" remains without notice. However, Mahoney refuted that notion. "We came for months after months, seeking these children in love. They were not unclaimed. They were wanted, they were desired, they had meaning and purpose. And so even though we are thankful they are not still in the morgue, it is deeply troubling . . . not making this a more public affair," Mahoney told the *Philadelphia Inquirer.*[2]

The gravesite remains without a marker, something Operation Rescue hopes to someday remedy, so the lessons learned from Gosnell's case will not be forgotten.

CHAPTER 44

IMPACT

Soon after Philadelphia District Attorney Seth Williams released the epic grand jury report that castigated Pennsylvania's regulatory failure and corrupt political climate that encouraged regulators to turn a blind eye, several states began to institute abortion reforms. Conditions were ripe for this kind of legislation with pro-life Republicans dominating state houses beginning with the mid-term elections of 2010. With favorable legislatures that were willing to keep their campaign promises, it is estimated that over 300 pro-life state laws have been enacted that have closed abortion facilities and saved lives.

That wave of pro-life legislation has been a dominant contributing factor to the abortion clinic closures. In 2013, the year Gosnell was convicted, ninety-two abortion facilities closed, according to a meticulous survey conducted by Operation Rescue. This represented an impressive 12 percent net decrease in surgical abortion clinics in the US that year alone.[1]

During the following two years, 125 more abortion facilities would shut down with just two or three new facilities opening nationwide. While all closures cannot be directly linked what we at Operation Rescue call the "Gosnell Effect," it is fair to say that Gosnell's trial initiated a domino effect that continues to reverberate throughout the nation.

Soon after Gosnell's horrors broke into the news in 2011, Pennsylvania passed a new abortion clinic licensing law that required abortion clinics to submit to health inspections and meet minimum safety standards. One abortion clinic, Allegheny Women's Center, voluntary closed on June 15, 2012, rather than comply with the law. The fact that just months earlier two of that business' abortionists had been arrested for illegally prescribing drugs many have contributed to the owner's desire to avoid deeper scrutiny.

Five other abortion facilities soon stopped surgical abortions or closed rather than make the effort to bring their facilities into compliance. Out of Pennsylvania's twenty-two abortion clinics in operation at the time the law was passed, only one actually met all requirements and received a full license. This failure of the twenty-one other facilities speaks volumes about the condition of abortion facilities in Pennsylvania prior to Gosnell, including the every Planned Parenthood abortion facilities in the state. In an act of unmerited grace bestowed by Pennsylvania regulators, Planned Parenthood clinics received provisional licenses until they were able to correct the deficiencies found during initial licensing inspections.

In Delaware, regulators shut down two more abortion facilities that were linked to Gosnell. All over the country, oversight agencies were viewing abortion clinics with new scrutiny.

Most notable of the state regulations passed in the post-Gosnell era was Texas' HB2, a clinic licensing law that shuttered half the state's previously unaccountable abortion facilities. That law was challenged and appealed all the way to the Supreme Court in a case captioned *Whole Women's Health v. Hellerstedt*. Most pro-life leaders believed that the Supreme Court would never strike down HB2, but nevertheless flooded the Court with amicus briefs, including one filed by the Liberty Counsel on behalf of Operation Rescue that highlighted abortion abuses and injuries documented during our many investigations.

But then, Justice Antonin Scalia was found dead on February 13, 2016, just four months before the Supreme Court was scheduled to release on opinion on *Hellerstedt*. It changed everything.

A firebrand for the right and steadfastly pro-life, Scalia's loss was deeply felt. Without his wise influence, an eight-member Supreme Court ruled 5–4 that certain provisions of HB2 were unconstitutional, including the requirements that abortion facilities maintain high safety standards and that abortionists maintain hospital privileges within thirty miles of the clinics where they do abortions.

While this was a blow to pro-life efforts to rein in shoddy and unaccountable abortion businesses, it certainly was not the end of the matter. While other leaders were discouraged, I simply shrugged it off and carried on trying to think of other ways to save lives. If there is one thing I have learned in over three decades of pro-life activism, it is that conditions always change, especially when least expected. I have learned that I need to be ready adapt to the ever-swinging pendulum of life, whether it swings against me or in my favor.

While the pendulum swung against us in the *Hellerstedt* decision, it took only five months for it to swing radically toward the pro-life side like never before due to the presidential election of 2016. With the unexpected election of Donald J. Trump as president and pro-life warrior Mike Pence as vice president, we can expect that their campaign promises to appoint conservative, prolife constitutionalists to the Supreme Court will be kept. The pro-life movement is full of hope that real progress can be made to push child-killing though abortion onto the junk pile of history's worst ideas. We found we were no longer stroking upstream against a system that was stacked against us. It was time to throw out the old play book and write a new one!

President Trump has worked hard to halt the flow of public funds to abortion facilities like Planned Parenthood through executive orders and legislation. Within less than six months after his inauguration, Planned Parenthood announced the closure of over a dozen of its facilities nationwide. That is a trend that will likely intensify as Planned Parenthood struggles to survive without the benefit of our tax money.

CHAPTER 45

AFTERMATH

Journalist Steve Volk published an e-book, *Gosnell Babies: Inside the Mind of America's Most Notorious Abortionist*, based on his jailhouse communications with Gosnell after his conviction that explored his thinking and mental state. I found Volk's essay to be an honest account written by a man who was struggling in his own mind over the moral implications of the grisly testimony that those of us in the courtroom endured day after day during Kermit Gosnell's murder trial in the spring of 2013.

I remember Steve Volk well from my own time in the courtroom and the conversations we had during breaks concerning the morality of abortion in general and the question of whether Gosnell was unique in his field. His quest for truth and personal struggle with the matter of abortion was evident in his fifty-two-page book that revealed insights into Gosnell's personality gleaned through his interviews with Gosnell over a span of several weeks after his convictions on three counts of first degree murder and hundreds of other crimes.

Volk's account is troubling, yet answers the question posed most in horrific cases such as this involving the infliction of unspeakable acts of barbarity by one human being upon another: Why?

For Gosnell, he embraced "situational ethics." The boundaries of right and wrong were relative and dependent upon his own needs. His claims of innocence were based not on the laws that he felt justified in ignoring, but on his own comfort level with his behavior as part of some esoteric "war on poverty."

But for me, Gosnell's bizarre justifications and even his poetic ramblings are more convincing evidence that Gosnell suffers from some sort of mental illness. Certainly, I'm no expert, but Gosnell displays behaviors that are more reflective of those of a serial killer than those one would expect to find in a stable, mentally healthy human being. Kermit Gosnell appears to live in a fantasy world of his own making where he is the lone determiner and controller of the rules of life. Perhaps Gosnell cocooned himself in his fantasy world as a mechanism whereby he could maintain his heroic self-image while avoiding the reality and repercussions of his sick behavior.

Gosnell believed that pro-life forces had conspired to use his conviction to deprive poor women, whom he often referred to as the "throwed," of abortions that he thought were necessary to reduced crime and poverty. "Catholics" that he believed pervaded the police department and District Attorney's office were religious bigots that had prejudged him through the filter of their Catholic teachings. He was in a "righteous" war and "they" had won.

Gosnell appears only thinly tethered to reality, if he is even tethered at all. He always believed that he would be completely exonerated, and even now fantasizes about the improbable possibility of withdrawing an agreement he made to drop all appeals in exchange for avoiding the death penalty. He maintains his innocence even though he admits to actions that were violations of the law. In his own mind, he was innocent because those laws simply did not apply to him.

He wonders why he never heard from the Bill and Melinda Gates Foundation or Bill Clinton's Global Initiative, to which he sent proposals and job applications. He believes even now that he is a "fitting person" to teach young people before they embark on medical careers.

Gosnell maintained a disturbingly serene veneer that made him appear relaxed and cordial even under the stress of a murder investigation and trial. His winsome smile throughout the trial and efforts to make eye contact in order to connect with those of us in the gallery every day could seem manipulative, but may have just been a result of his inability to grasp the gravity of the moment.

There were macabre accounts of his bizarre behavior during the police raid at his ramshackle, squalid abortion clinic and the police search of his home. Volk referred to Gosnell as "unflappable." During the initial raid on his clinic, Gosnell asked permission to feed his turtles, then proceeded to attend to a woman in the delivery of a stillborn baby after which he "calmly" sat down to eat his lunch still wearing torn and bloody surgical gloves.

At his home, Gosnell sat down at the piano to entertain the investigators with a Chopin selection while they searched his home for additional bodies, stopping to warn police that his basement, which they were about to search, was infested with fleas.

In fact, Gosnell's living conditions at his two homes were as bad, if not worse, than his "House of Horrors" clinic. Photos of his bedroom shown during the trial revealed a "hoarder house" appearance with junk and rotten, partially eaten food piled and strewn everywhere. Volk notes that even high-end belongings, such as designer purses and Viking appliances, were filthy and neglected. The disorder and squalor seemed indicative of the inner working of Gosnell's mind, according to Volk.

Then there were the feet. Gosnell kept the severed feet of some of the larger babies he aborted floating in liquid in specimen jars. Kareema Cross photographed shelves that she testified held as many as fifty jars of such grisly remains. Gosnell was never able to fully explain why he kept the feet. His excuses that they were to document fetal age were ridiculous and completely unbelievable. The behavior was more likely the keeping of victim trophies, something that is well documented as the sick behavior of serial killers.

Gosnell seemed to seek out those for employment whose lives were in even worse disarray than his own. He targeted the undereducated and the mentally ill to work in his clinic, where they became dependent on him and under his control. He eased any concerned they might have had with bold-faced lies about "grandfather clauses" that made it okay for the unqualified to practice medicine. He convinced these workers that the movements of live babies as merely the "reflexes" of "dead" babies that were to be halted with the "snipping" of their spinal cords.

The lies were justified in the same way as he justified the murders; they were for the greater good. After all, those of us fortunate enough to have avoided poverty simply cannot understand the "throwed." In Gosnell's perverted world, the difficult circumstances faced by poor urban women warranted, even justified, the squalid conditions, the venereal diseases transmitted by dirty and reused disposable tools, drug overdoses, and the murder of their live infants. That, in his mind, was somehow compassionate treatment and work that was beneficial to society in general.

The mental illness theory is supported by a poem written by Gosnell and reprinted by Volk describing the vulnerabilities of abortionists that he believes society misunderstands.

Abortion Providers

Are Labeled Killers!

Horrendous, Exploitive

Barbaric, Inhumane

Not Physicians, Oathed To Heal

Lest We Forget,

What Chance Have Those?

Those Without The Support

Of Their Parents

Their Families

Their Communities

Their Societies . . .

So Many

Without Sufficient Support

Stumble Into Drugs

Into Crime

Into Mental Illness

Into Institutions . . . And . . .

Languish In Jails . . .[1]

While Gosnell considered himself somewhat of a misunderstood intellectual "Renaissance Man," perhaps "Monster" is a more fitting designation. He remains without remorse, justifying in his mind the squalor and murder as heroic acts that those who are not "throwed" simply cannot comprehend. He continues to justify cold-blooded murder and neglect done without a shred conscience.

What is troubling is that Gosnell isn't simply describing himself in his self-indulgent poem. He is describing his colleagues as well. I have long suspected mental illness might be rampant within the abortion cartel. Gosnell's poem is somewhat of a confession as well as a verification of my suspicions.

Gosnell laced his justifications to Volk with ample doses of pro-abortion rhetoric. It's frightening to think that those "pro-choice" platitudes justify bad behavior on the part of abortionists everywhere. This reveals a crisis in the abortion industry where criminals, drug addicts, mentally ill men and women subject pregnant women to shockingly low standards hidden behind the inherent respectability that the title of "doctor" evokes.

On January 23, 2017, The *Daily Mail* printed an interview with two movie-makers who recently visited Gosnell in prison which further emphasized the fantasy world that Gosnell has created for himself, where he chooses to live in delusional denial rather than face reality. The movie-makers claim that he told them that he is so convinced he will be completely exonerated in his lifetime that he is training to participate in a triathlon when he is released from incarceration, even though there is no possibility he could ever be released.[2]

Gosnell reportedly replied to a question about how he was coping with the following comment:

> *It helps that I very strongly believe myself to be innocent of the heinous crimes of which I am accused . . . . I continue to feel optimistic of the eventual outcome…the vindication of what I've done, why I've done it and how [it] will become accepted within my lifetime.*[3]

Apparently, Gosnell has begun to study the Bible since his incarceration, and I pray that his callous heart and twisted mind will somehow be softened by the gospel and he will experience true repentance and spiritual regeneration. We wish that for all abortionists. But until that time, the world would be a better place if they all joined Gosnell behind bars for the rest of their lives.

***

Another journalist wrote of the impact of Gosnell's case on the former abortionist's own neighborhood two years after his conviction. Ronnie Polaneczky, a columnist for the *Daily News*, visited Gosnell's old house and interviewed his neighbors in an article published by the *Philadelphia Inquirer* on April 15, 2015.

When she visited his home at the corner of 32nd Street and Mantua Avenue in Mantua, less than a mile from his abortion facility, she found that time had not been kind to what she described as a "once majestic property." She described the beautiful Victorian architecture that featured round turrets and a wrap-around veranda where she imagined Gosnell sitting, enjoying a cup of coffee.

This was the same house where Gosnell serenaded law enforcement with a piano recital of Chopin as they searched for human remains. Polaneczy described Gosnell's home his "other house of horror."

The yard was shin-deep in trash. The second floor's bay window was gone, opening a huge hole to the elements. An extension cord ran from the house to an alley light, dangerously affixed there by God-knows-who.

As I picked my way past another missing window, the spring breeze caught the stench of feces (Animal? Human? Does it matter?), jolting me to my senses. I hadn't told anyone that I'd be eyeballing the property that morning. If I came to harm in this abandoned hellhole, no one would think to look for me here.[4]

The property had become much more than an eye sore. It had become dangerous.

"It's scaring the hell out of neighbors," Polaneczy wrote.

Virginia Booker, 73, and her partner Howard Williams, 89, lived just two doors down. They told Polaneczy that it hadn't taken long for squatters to move in and destroy the place.

"They've stripped the plumbing. They store their clothes and bags on the porch. They come and go like it's their own home," Booker told the writer. Williams feared that the whole house would soon come crashing down and kill someone.

Polaneczy found that property taxes were delinquent to the tune of $7,479.42 in 2015. She tried to find out why the property wasn't sold. Gosnell's attorney Jack McMahon wouldn't return her calls, and when she visited Gosnell's wife, Pearl, who still lives in the neighborhood, the only response she got was, "There's nothing I can tell you," before Pearl closed the door on her.

Licenses & Inspections Commissioner Carlton Williams was more willing to discuss the property with the journalist. He told her the building was "classified unsafe in November 2013 and was cleaned and sealed in October 2014." But later there were complaints of "unsafe conditions" and even reports of a break-in. When Polaneczy shared the neighbors' concerns, Williams took them seriously, according to her report.

Yesterday, as workers were cleaning up the site, they came across a pile of tiny bones. All work stopped as the Police Department's Crime Scene

Unit and homicide detectives swarmed the scene. Given Gosnell's history - many aborted, late-term fetuses from his clinic have never been accounted for - police wondered whether the bones were human.

They were quickly determined to be animal remains. A sad and fitting find, given the animal who once called the place home.[5]

***

Meanwhile, pro-life activists continue to hold an occasional prayer vigil outside Gosnell's Women's Medical Society. It looks much as it did during the trial, only maybe a bit more run-down. Disheveled vertical blinds only partially covering the windows affording passersby glimpses of the chaotic interior with its dead potted plants and strewn papers lying haphazardly about.

During the trial, the building posed such a hazard that the jury was not allowed to inspect the crime scene for their own safety. Even then the roof leaked and CSI Officer Taggart worried the roof would soon fall in.

The properly remains the center of a dispute between the family of Karnamaya Mongar and the Gosnell estate. Mongar's family sued Gosnell for the wrongful death of their loved one in 2009 during a grossly negligent second-trimester abortion. In September, 2015, the family's case finally went to trial. Gosnell's attorneys did not contest their client's guilt. How could they? Two years before Gosnell stood convicted of Involuntary manslaughter in Mongar's death. No argument could change that fact.

Common Pleas Judge Jacqueline Allen awarded Mongar's daughter, Yashoda Devi Gurung $650,000 in compensatory damages, and $3.25 million in punitive damages, for a total of $3.9 million.[6]

But the family would have a hard time collecting. Gosnell held no insurance on his abortion business, and despite owning up to twenty properties and having made millions, Gosnell's attorneys claim he has no assets. Meanwhile, Gosnell's property holdings, including his deteriorating Mantua home and his ramshackle abortion office, could be sold to pay a portion of the judgment, but so far, they remain in legal limbo.

After causing so much misery for Mongar's family he continues to put them in pain.

***

Gosnell's family has fared little better after his conviction. The shame of Gosnell's heinous acts will never be relegated completely to the past.

In 2012, Gosnell's twenty-year-old son, Barron Alexander Gosnell officially dropped his family name and became Barron Alexander. In early June 2014, Alexander was involved in what news reports referred to as a "bizarre" robbery. He broke into a house occupied by three men near his family's Mantua property, stealing an Xbox console and other electronics along with some cash. Later, he returned to rob the house again. Alexander slipped into a bedroom where one of the residents lay sleeping and attempted to steal his cell phone. But the man woke up and confronted Alexander, who attacked the man and stabbed him with a bayonet. Another resident of the robbed home came to his friend's aid and shot Alexander four times in self-defense.

Alexander survived his wounds and remained in custody for seventeen months, until he was finally sentenced in November 2015 after pleading guilty to burglary, aggravated assault, possession of an instrument of crime and other offenses. Common Pleas Judge Rayford Means gave Alexander, now twenty-three years old, 11 1/2 to 23 months in jail, which amounted to time served. He was placed on parole, to be followed by eight years of probation.

Alexander's attorney, Mary Maran, told Judge Means of her client's behavior, "This was someone acting out, perhaps having a breakdown."[7]

The apple doesn't fall far from the tree, apparently.

"You can't look at [Alexander's] background and say [his father's criminal case] didn't affect him, with the national press calling your father a monster," Maran had said in an attempt to mitigate Alexander's crimes.[8]

It is unfair to anyone for Alexander to shift the blame for his own bad behavior onto his troubled father. He alone made his choices and must bear the responsibility for them. But there is something to say for Maran's argument that Gosnell's trial and conviction affected his son and sent his life on a trajectory that may have been much different had Gosnell's criminal conduct not been found out.

***

Such are the consequences of life-dominating sin. Gosnell's actions didn't just affect himself. They affected his family, including his son. They affected his employees, many of which paid with jail time and mental torment. They affected his patients, who developed sexually transmitted diseases from his filthy instruments and bear the scars, some emotional and some physical, of his criminal incompetence. They affected the families of Karnamaya Mongar and Semika Shaw, who must live forever without their loved ones killed by Gosnell's unspeakable practices. And Gosnell's actions cut short the lives of hundreds of babies, forty-seven of which lie today in an unmarked grave.

Today, some are calling for the repeal of abortion facility oversight laws, claiming they are too "harsh" and pose an undue burden to women, when they really mean they inconvenience abortion providers. They want us to forget about Kermit Gosnell and the women and babies he killed. They want us to act like none of it ever happened.

But it did. I saw the evidence of his crimes with my own two eyes, and yes, what Gosnell did had an effect on me as well. It has made me more determined than ever to expose his crimes and those committed by others like him. And there are far too many of those.

We must hold fast to the abortion regulations we have and press harder for more. We must change the political climate until there can be no more Gosnells, no more Karnamaya Mongars, and no more dead babies.

The often-quoted words of novelist George Santayana are appropriate and instructive.

"Those who cannot remember the past are condemned to repeat it."

May we never forget the lessons we learned from Gosnell and his victims, for if we do, may God help us all.

ENDNOTES

CHAPTER 1

1. James Taranto, "Back Alley Abortion Never Ended," *Wall Street Journal*, April 18, 2013.

CHAPTER 2

1. R. Seth Williams, "Report of the Grand Jury," Misc. Case No. 0009901-2008, pp. 20-21.
2. Commonwealth of Pennsylvania Bureau of Professional and Occupational Affairs v. Kermit B. Gosnell, MD, Petition for Immediate Temporary Suspension, File No. 10-49-01572, February 22, 2010.
3. Ibid.
4. Cheryl Sullenger, "Shop of Horrors: Abortion Death Prompts Raid, Grisly Discovery," February 23, 2010, Operation Rescue.

CHAPTER 3

1. "Kermit Gosnell Lived in 'Squalor,' Had Fleas in Home: CSI," by Vince Lattanzio and David Chang, May 15, 2013, NBC10 Philadelphia.
2. Ibid.
3. Ibid.
4. Commonwealth of Pennsylvania Bureau of Professional and Occupational Affairs v. Kermit B. Gosnell, MD, Petition for Immediate Temporary Suspension, File No. 10-49-01572, February 22, 2010.

5. Vince Lattanzio and David Chang, "Kermit Gosnell Lived in 'Squalor,' Had Fleas in Home: CSI," May 15, 2013, NBC10 Philadelphia.
6. Ibid.
7. Ibid.
8. Ibid.

CHAPTER 4

1. Commonwealth of Pennsylvania Bureau of Professional and Occupational Affairs v. Kermit B. Gosnell, MD, Petition for Immediate Temporary Suspension, File No. 10-49-01572, February 22, 2010.
2. http://AbortionDocs.org.
3. https://cemeteryofchoice.wikispaces.com/Sheila%C2%A0Hebert.
4. https://cemeteryofchoice.wikispaces.com/Ingar+Weber.
5. Complaint Affidavit in the case of Mary Frances Gardner, April 20, 2011.
6. http://www.newarkpostonline.com/news/local/article_a2291710-382c-5ab6-b465-4497dd2e78d6.html.

CHAPTER 5

1. CNN Wire Staff, "With doctor in jail, brother of dead woman vows, 'We want justice'" January 25, 2011.
2. http://cemeteryofchoice.wikispaces.com/Semika+Shaw.
3. Amy Worden, "The personal stake behind abortion vote," *Philadelphia Inquirer,* December 16, 2011.
4. "Ex-patient: 'I think he should get life in prison," by David Gambacorta, February 4, 2011, *Philadelphia Inquirer* http://www.philly.com/philly/news/year-in-review/20110120_Ex-patient___I_think_he_should_get_life_in_prison_.html.
5. David Altrogge, *3801 Lancaster* video, January 14, 2013.
6. Ibid.
7. David Gambacorta, "A child herself, she awoke after abortion to a sight of horror," *Philadelphia Inquirer,* February 25, 2010.
8. Thomas Drayton, "Interview of Kermit Gosnell," Fox 29 News, February 28, 2010.

9. Ibid.

CHAPTER 6

1. R. Seth Williams, "Report of the Grand Jury," Misc. Case No. 0009901-2008.
2. Marie McCullough, "Gruesome details in report on Philadelphia abortion doctor," *Philadelphia Inquirer,* January 19, 2011.

CHAPTER 7

1. *CBS Evening News* with Katie Couric, January 19, 2013.
2. Tiffany Gabbay, "A Haunting Look Into Abortion Doctor Kermit Gosnell's 'House of Horrors' (Warning: Very Graphic)", *The Blaze*, April 15, 2013.
3. R. Seth Williams, "Report of the Grand Jury," Misc. Case No. 0009901-2008.
4. Ibid.
5. Ibid.
6. Ibid.
7. Ibid.
8. Ibid.

CHAPTER 8

1. Ibid.
2. Ibid.
3. Ibid.
4. Ibid.
5. Ibid.
6. Ibid.
7. Cheryl Sullenger, "Pro-life Groups Ask For Federal Inspections, Congressional Hearings In Wake of Gosnell, Brigham Abortion Scandals," OperationRescue.org, January 27, 2011.
8. Cheryl Sullenger, "Botched Abortion Nightmare: 'I wish I never heard of them,'" OperationRescue.org, September 13, 2010.

9. Cheryl Sullenger, "Brigham Abortionist Riley Did Federal Prison Time, Records Show," OperationRescue.org, September 24, 2010.

10. Eileen Smith, as told by Kim Nichols, "Blowing the Whistle: How one abortion worker allowed the truth to set her free—and put an abortionist behind bars," OperationRescue.org, January 20, 2011.

11. Cheryl Sullenger, "California Abortionist Rutland, Who Killed Woman, Will Surrender His License," OperationRescue.org, January 26, 2011.

12. Cheryl Sullenger, ''Hellish Abortion Operation:' KY Abortionist's License Suspended, Clinic Closed," OperationRescue.org, June 20, 2008.

13. Cheryl Sullenger, "NE Attorney General Takes Custody Of Affidavits," OperationRescue.org, September 4, 2009.

14. Cheryl Sullenger, "Carhart Dinged with Admonishment from Maryland Board of Physicians," Operation Rescue.org, November 29, 2011.

CHAPTER 10

1. Associated Press, "Kermit Gosnell abortion trial: Defense team for doctor set to begin case," April 22, 2013.

CHAPTER 11

1. F. H. Rubino, "Judge Jeffrey Minehart Hammers Down," *Philadelphia Weekly*, January 19, 2010.

2. Martha Neil, "Convicted Teen Spits in Lawyer's Face; Pa. Judge Orders Him Bound & Gagged," *ABA Journal*, April 1, 2009.

3. Associated Press, "Lawyer for Philadelphia abortion doctor Kermit Gosnell accused of killing live babies plays the race card, says client victim of 'prosecutorial lynching,'" March 13, 2013.

4. Ronnie Polaneczky, "'No Cat Urine' Equals Mayo Clinic Standards?" *Philadelphia Daily News*, March 19, 2013.

5. R. Seth Williams, "Report of the Grand Jury," Misc. No. 0009901-2008.

CHAPTER 12

1. Associated Press, "Kermit Gosnell abortion trial: Defense team for doctor set to begin case," April 22, 2013.
2. Joseph A. Slobodzian, "Gosnell trial mystery: Why were fetus feet in specimen jars?" *Philadelphia Inquirer*, March 20, 2013.
3. NBCPhiladelphia.com, March 20, 2013.

CHAPTER 13

1. Vince Lattanzio and Emad Khalil, "Gosnell Abortion Clinic Inspection Reveals 'Filthy' Conditions," NBCPhiladelphia.com, March 25, 2013.
2. Commonwealth of Pennsylvania Bureau of Professional and Occupational Affairs v. Kermit B. Gosnell, MD, Petition for Immediate Temporary Suspension, File No. 10-49-01572, February 22, 2010.

CHAPTER 14

1. Autopsy Report of Christin A. Gilbert, 05-MV-374, August 24, 2005.
2. Vince Lattanzio and Emad Khalil, "Shouting Match Breaks Out at Gosnell Trial," NBCPhiladelphia.com, March 18, 2013.

CHAPTER 15

1. Maryclaire Dale, "Med. examiner, lawyer clash at doc's murder trial," Associated Press, March 28, 2013.

CHAPTER 17

1. Cheryl Sullenger, "911 for 35-Wk Abortion with Ruptured Uterus by Sella- May 12, 2011," YouTube.com, November 11, 2012.
2. Cheryl Sullenger, "New Docs Reveal Horrific Details of Botched 35-Week Abortion, Gross Negligence in NM Disciplinary Case," OperationRescue.org, January 31, 2013.
3. Ibid.
4. Ibid.

5.   Ibid.

CHAPTER 18
1.   "Operation Rescue Buys Abortion Clinic," WND.com, June 30, 2006.

CHAPTER 21
1.   Cheryl Sullenger, "Illegal Fetal Age/Viability Deception Scheme Uncovered by Operation Rescue at Tiller's Abortion Clinic," OperationRescue.org, January 11, 2009.
2.   Cheryl Sullenger, "Forced Abortion, Rape Victim Comes Forward After Abortionist Given Probation," OperationRescue.org, February 11, 2009.
3.   Cheryl Sullenger, "Notorious Abortionist Hodari Denied License, Lacks 'Good Moral Character,'" OperationRescue. org, September 24, 2014.

CHAPTER 22
1.   Cheryl Sullenger, "Shocking Michigan Abortion Clinic Photos Show Conditions that 'Pose a Danger to Human Life,'" OperationRescue.org, January 8, 2013.
2.   Muskegon Fire Department letter to Robert Alexander, December 27, 2012.
3.   Press Release, "Two Women Removed from Birmingham Abortion Clinic by Paramedics," ChristianNewswire.com, January 21, 2012.
4.   Alabama Department of Public Health Press Release, "Action taken against license of New Woman All Women Health Care," April 6, 2012.
5.   Thomas Larson, "Bertha Bugarin Heads to Jail," *The San Diego Reader*, February 18, 2009.
6.   Josh Kleinbaum, "Osteopath surrenders license, avoids hearing," *The Los Angeles Daily News*, February 16, 2006.
7.   Leia Baez-Mendoza, "Ex-employees aid abortion foes," *Omaha World Herald*, August 28, 2009.
8.   Det. William Howard, Statement before the Kansas House Committee on Health and Human Services, March 15, 2005.

9. "History of Our Headquarters," OperationRescue.org, February 12, 2011.

10. "Board revokes license of Fla. Abortion doctor," by Associated Press, February 6, 2009.

11. Ron Strom, "Abortion staff ignores baby boy born alive?" WND.com, April 25, 2005.

12. Angel Manuel Soto, Director, *22 Weeks* (2009).

13. David Daleiden, video "Human Capital - Episode 3: Planned Parenthood's Custom Abortions for Superior Product," the Center for Medical Progress, August 19, 2015.

14. Ibid.

CHAPTER 23

1. R. Seth Williams, "Report of the Grand Jury," Misc. No. 0009901-2008.

2. Ibid.

3. Sean O'Sullivan, "Staffer recalls horrors at Pennsylvania abortion clinic," *The News Journal*, April 9, 2013.

4. Ibid.

5. Ibid.

CHAPTER 24

1. Cheryl Sullenger, "Michigan Abortionist Exhibits Bizarre Behavior, Admits Mental Illness, at Revocation Hearing," OperationRescue.org, September 5, 2014.

2. Accusation by the California Medical Board against Gary T. Prohaska, Case no. 8002013002177, August 12, 2014.

3. Recovery Room Log, Elkton, August 4, 2010.

4. Transcript, "In the Matter of Board of Physicians Interview with Kimberly Walker, MD," August 23, 2010.

5. "Post Mortem Examination Report, Kimberly Marion Walker," January 15, 2014.

CHAPTER 25

1. R. Seth Williams, "Report of the Grand Jury," Misc. No. 0009901-2008.

2. Deborah Nucatola, N. Roth, and M. Gatter, "A randomized pilot study on the effectiveness and side-effect profiles of two doses of digoxin as fetocide when administered intraamniotically or intrafetally prior to second-trimester surgical abortion," National Institutes of Health, August 14, 2009.
3. Society of Family Planning Clinical Guideline, "Induction of fetal demise before abortion," January 2010.
4. Sullenger, "Former Tiller Patient Drops Bombshell Testimony of Illegal, Coerced Abortion on Legislative Committee," OperationRescue.org, September 7, 2007.
5. Ron Strom, "Abortion staff ignores baby boy born alive?" WND.com, April 25, 2005.
6. Cheryl Sullenger, "Dead or Alive: Gosnell Defense Floats Theory That Babies were Dead When Necks Were Snipped," OperationRescue.org, April 11, 2013. http://www.operationrescue.org/archives/dead-or-alive-gosnell-defense-floats-theory-that-babies-were-dead-when-necks-were-snipped/
7. "Laminaria Insertion and Induction of Fetal Demise" form for patient D. B., August 12, 2010.

CHAPTER 26

1. Cheryl Sullenger, "#Gosnell 'Tweet-Up' Grabs Attention as Grisly Murder Trial Continues," OperationRescue.org, April 14, 2013.
2. Kristin Powers, "Philadelphia abortion clinic horror: Column," *USA Today*, April 11, 2013.
3. Anderson Cooper, video, "Doctor's 'House of Horrors'" *Anderson Cooper 360*, CNN, April 12, 2013.
4. Bret Baier, Host, *See No Evil: The Kermit Gosnell Case*, Fox News, aired May 3, 2013.
5. Joseph A. Slobodzian "Gosnell Witness: I assisted in abortions while in high school," the *Philadelphia Inquirer*, April 11, 2013.
6. Ibid.
7. Ibid.
8. Ibid.

CHAPTER 32

1. Cheryl Sullenger, "Hodari Forced Abortion Suit Alleges Woman's Mouth Covered to Muffle Her Screams," OperationRescue.org, November 18, 2009.
2. Ibid.
3. Cheryl Sullenger, "Special Report: Why Virginia's Appallingly Substandard Abortion Facilities Must Not Be Excepted from the Law," OperationRescue.org, September 16, 2014.

CHAPTER 38

1. Bret Baier, host, *See No Evil: The Kermit Gosnell Case*, Fox News, aired May 3, 2013.
2. Priests for Life, "Naming the Gosnell Babies," PriestsForLife. org, June 3, 2013.
3. Press Release, "Press Conference and Legislative Briefing," May 14, 2013.

CHAPTER 39

1. Sarah Hoye and Sunny Hostin, "Doctor found guilty of first-degree murder in Philadelphia abortion case," CNN, May 14, 2013.
2. Ibid.
3. Press Release, "GUILTY! Gosnell Found Guilty of 3 Counts of First Degree Murder," OperationRescue.org, May 13, 2013.

CHAPTER 40

1. NBC10 News video, March 15, 2013.
2. Ibid.
3. Ibid.
4. Ibid.
5. Ibid.

CHAPTER 41

1. *Philadelphia Inquirer,* February 13, 2014.
2. Ibid.

CHAPTER 42

1. Final Order, In the Matter of Robert Louis Alexander, MD, File no. 43-12-125776, November 19, 2014
2. Harris County District Court Case No. 89-003719.
3. Harris County District Court Case No. 89-16747.
4. http://www.wnd.com/index.php?pageId=16826.
5. Dallas County District Court Case No. 18282.
6. Harris County District Court Case No. 93-33063.
7. Ron Nissimov, *Houston Chronicle* April 13 and 15, 2004.
8. 911 transcript dated Feb. 16, 2005; City of Houston Complaint Report Feb. 16, 2005; LifeSiteNews.com, Feb. 17, 2005.
9. Cheryl Sullenger, "Two Texas Abortionists Ordered to Pay Thousands in Fines," OperationRescue.org, March 1, 2012.
10. Texas Medical Board letter to Sullenger, February 8, 2013.
11. Sullenger, "Special Report: New Stunning Photos, Testimony Show Texas Abortionist Kills Babies Born Alive," OperationRescue.org, May 15, 2013.
12. Ibid.
13. Ibid.
14. Texas Medical Board letter to Sullenger, February 8, 2013.
15. Video, *Abortion Clinic Employees – 'Babies born alive daily,'* Life Dynamics, Inc., May 14, 2013.
16. Ibid.
17. Cheryl Sullenger, "Special Report: New Stunning Photos, Testimony Show Texas Abortionist Kills Babies Born Alive," OperationRescue.org, May 15, 2013.
18. Brian Rogers and Becca Aaronson, "Houston doctor accused of illegal abortions," *Houston Chronicle*, May 17, 2013.
19. Ibid.
20. "Gov. Perry appoints widow Devon Anderson to succeed her late husband as Harris County DA," *Houston Chronicle*, September 24, 2013.
21. Press Release from Harris County District Attorney's Office, "Grand jury no bills Dr. Douglas Karpen," December 20, 2013.

22. Brian Rogers, "Houston doctor cleared of late-term abortion claims," *Houston Chronicle*, December 20, 2013.

23. Brian M. Rosenthal, "Planned Parenthood cleared, but 2 indicted over videos," *Houston Chronicle*, February 2, 2016.

24. Paul J. Weber, "Houston prosecutor has angered anti-abortion groups before," Associated Press, January 27, 2016.

25. Ibid.

26. Ibid.

27. Cheryl Sullenger, "Operation Rescue's Statement on Daleiden's Grand Jury Indictments in Texas," OperationRescue.org, January 26, 2016.

28. Blackburn letter to Paxton, EnergyCommerce.House.gov, December 7, 2016.

29. Blackburn letter to US Attorney General, EnergyCommerce. House.gov, December 7, 2016.

CHAPTER 43

1. Rev. Patrick J. Mahoney, Press Release, "Philadelphia Medical Examiner's Office May Take 10 Years to Release Babies Murdered by Abortionist Kermit Gosnell," ChristianNewsWire.com, August 25, 2013.

2. *The Philadelphia Inquirer*, June 15, 2015.

3. Cheryl Sullenger, "Death Throes of the Death Industry: A Record 87 Surgical Abortion Clinics Close in 2013," OperationRescue.org, December 23, 2013.

CHAPTER 45

1. Steve Volk, *Gosnell's Babies: Inside the Mind of America's Most Notorious Abortion Doctor*, *Philadelphia Magazine*, 2013.

2. Martin Gould, "Baby-Killer Says Release is Imminent," *The Daily Mail*, January 23, 2017.

3. Ibid.

4. Ronnie Polaneczy, "Gosnell's other House of Horrors," *Philadelphia Inquirer*, April 15, 2015.

5. Ibid.

6. Larry Miller, "Family of abortion doctor victim wins $3.9 million court decision," *Philadelphia Tribune*, September 22, 2015.
7. Julie Shaw, "Gosnell's son sentenced in bizarre burglary," *Philadelphia Inquirer*, November 30, 2015.
8. Ibid.

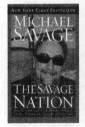    

CPSIA information can be obtained
at www.ICGtesting.com
Printed in the USA
LVOW03s0712270717
542404LV00001B/4/P